WIDENING THE HORIZON

Dedicated to Amelia, who made her own wonderfully 'exotic' sounds while 'assisting' me in the editing of this book.

WIDENING THE HORIZON

Exoticism in Post-War Popular
Music

Edited by
Philip Hayward

John Libbey
JL
LONDON · PARIS · ROME · SYDNEY

perfect
beat
publications

Cataloguing in Publication Data

Widening the horizon: exoticism in post-war popular music.

    Bibliography.
    Includes index.

1. Popular music – History and criticism. 2. Music – Effect of multiculturalism on.
3. Exoticism in music. I. Hayward, Philip.

781.63

ISBN: 1 86462 047 1 (Paperback)

Published by

John Libbey & Company Pty Ltd, Level 10, 15–17 Young Street, Sydney, NSW 2000, Australia. Telephone: +61 (0)2 9251 4099 Fax: +61 (0)2 9251 4428
e-mail: jlsydney@mpx.com.au

John Libbey & Company Ltd, 13 Smiths Yard, Summerley Street, London SW18 4HR, England; John Libbey Eurotext Ltd, 127 avenue de la République, 92120 Montrouge, France. John Libbey at C.I.C. Edizioni s.r.l., via Lazzaro Spallanzani 11, 00161 Rome, Italy.

Printed in Malaysia by Kum-Vivar Printing Sdn. Bhd., 48000 Rawang, Selangor Darul Ehsan.

Contents

Acknowledgements

Thanks firstly to Shuhei Hosokawa, for encouraging me to edit this anthology. Further thanks are due to Rob Bowman, Claire Butkus, Brent Clough, Jackey Coyle, Mark Evans, Jon Fitzgerald, Nicholas Kent, Tony Langford, Ralph Locke, David Mitchell, Tony Mitchell, Toru Mitsui, Stuart Rogers, Aline Scott-Maxwell, Yngar Steinholt, Amy Stillman, Will Straw, Van Dyke Parks, Karen Ward, John Whiteoak and Mark Worth for their various assistances. Bruce Johnson also contributed a valuable critique of the first version of my Introduction to the volume.

Rebecca Coyle, as ever, provided all-round help, guidance and assistance; and Rosa Coyle-Hayward kept me sane and well-cuddled.

Van Dyke Parks and Stony Browder Jr. also merit acknowledgement for widening my own musical horizons during formative teenage years.

I should also note the contribution of three cities, Honolulu, Montreal and Sydney, whose clubs, bars, universities and second-hand record shops helped me to triangulate the phenomena analysed in these pages.

Research for this book was assisted, in various ways, by the departments of Media and Communication Studies and Music Studies at Macquarie University, Sydney – for which many thanks.

Editor's Note

Bibliography – the bibliographical references for individual chapters are collated on pages 192-198.

Discography – all original recordings are referred to in the body of text of individual chapters by dates. Details of relevant CD reissues/compilations of this material are included at the end of each chapter.

Internet Sources – individual articles published on world wide web sites are included (together with their web site addresses), in the book's end bibliography; general web site references are included at the end of each chapter (where relevant).

Cover photograph: Philip Hayward.

Widening the Horizon is co-published in Sydney by John Libbey and Co and Perfect Beat Publications.

Perfect Beat Publications also publish *Perfect Beat – the Pacific Journal of Contemporary Music and Popular Culture*.

General information about the journal can be obtained from:

The Music Office, Division of Humanities, Macquarie University, NSW 2109, Australia
http://www.ccms.mq.edu.au/pbeat
phayward@humanities.mq.edu.au

Subscription information for the journal *Perfect Beat* is available from John Libbey and Company Pty Ltd, Level 10, 15–17 Young Street, Sydney NSW 2000, Australia
jlsydney@mpx.com.au
Tel: +61 2 9251 4099; Fax: +61 2 9251 4428

THE COCKTAIL SHIFT

Aligning Musical Exotica

PHILIP HAYWARD

F or anyone interested in exploring beyond the boundaries of the contemporary popular music scene, the past is a strange and wonderful place. Much of it is also a realm of amnesia. While the histories of forms such as the blues and jazz have been studiously recovered, recorded and analysed, other styles and genres remain obscure. Taste (and its politics) are the key factors here. The histories of blues and jazz have been explored by a loose association of enthusiasts, collectors and scholars. The motivation for such initiatives has been a curiosity which derives from particular combinations of personal, class and/or cultural/sub-cultural tastes[1]. Due to its reliance on such taste agendas the archaeology of popular music – both popular and academic – has been essentially arbitrary and *ad hoc*. While Popular Music Studies has established itself as an academic discipline in the West over the last 10–15 years, it has not identified any methodical excavation and characterisation of its historical object of study as essential to its project. Even in its most accomplished and insightful forms, it is still largely premised on the curiosity of the individual researcher/writer and the fortuities of funding, institutional enablement etc. It has therefore allowed itself to settle within a frame inherited from (traditional forms of) Art History and Literary Studies, where the gourmet aesthetic of leading practitioners creates explicit and implicit canons[2] which act as focal points for the construction of critical and/or historical discourse.

There are two principal ways of addressing this weakness in the field. One involves the external revision of the whole project. The other, a revision and displacement of the central canon and the specific analytical models which led to its establishment. Noble as the former option is, such a meta-analytical enterprise has never been attempted, nor accomplished, by a Humanities discipline – old or New – and remains

1

a task unlikely to be undertaken by the disparate, fragmented community of scholars who constitute the global intellectual resource of Popular Music Studies. The latter is, therefore, a more realistic option, and it is within such a revisionist project that this anthology locates itself.

Given the relatively arbitrary, taste-derived model I have characterised above, it is un-surprising that the impetus to revise and/or expand the canonical grid of Popular Music Studies (or any other cultural studies field for that matter) often derives from similar impulses. One recurrent factor is synchronicity – the simultaneous re-dis-covery and re-emergence of interest in particular historical phenomena in various cultural and geographical locations[3]. I write (and edit) from experience here. During the early 1990s I spent considerable time researching aspects of inter-cultural musical collaborations in the Australia/Western Pacific region since the end of World War Two. The historical trail proved rich and complex and I often veered off to follow tantalising, seductive paths into adjacent cultural and geographical areas. During this period I first became aware of the broad genre of musical exotica popularised by musicians such as Les Baxter, Martin Denny, Arthur Lyman, Korla Pandit, Yma Sumac and others[4] (to which the opening chapters of this book are addressed). If I *had* ever been aware of this music as a child, I had not recalled it; nor did subsequent encounters trigger any such memories. This made it all the more enticing, a shadowy history, only thinly covered by the sands of time, still retriev-able.

Two particular accounts, which arose from research interviews I conducted in 1992, whetted my appetite to explore further:

> *It was completely wild ! Growing up in Turramurra* [a northern suburb of Sydney, Australia]*, in the 1960s, having family dinner together, and my father would put on Arthur Lyman's* Taboo *– or similar records – and while you'd be eating you'd have these birds and rhythms and odd noises... bells and whatever ... and you would be carrying on a regular, everyday conver-sation like it was all normal ! It sounds pretty odd now but it was one of those things at the time.*[5]

> *I thought it was wild, really 'out there', when I first heard it. It was like they* [Martin Denny and Arthur Lyman] *were trying all these crazy, crazy things (all at once). I don't know whether it reminded me of growing up* [in Papua New Guinea]*, and whether that's why I liked it ... I don't know ... but you'd have to say it sounded pretty weird, even for Melbourne!*[6]

Together with such comments, a particular silence attracted my attention – the silence which represents the academic disdain for musical exotica which prevailed from the 1950s to the near-present.

In 1994 I visited Hawai'i on a brief research visit. While there, I met with several leading Hawaiian-based ethnomusicologists, all of whom extended me considerable hospitality. Late one afternoon, drinking a beer in a Waikiki hotel cocktail bar, I looked over my companion's shoulder and was immediately transfixed. A small, unassuming sign stated 'Tuesday Night – Arthur Lyman'. I had thought that he was dead. Why else would such a stylistically remarkable, prolific and (once) so-popular musician have vanished from the critical map ? I immediately began questioning my companion about Lyman. How often and where did Lyman perform ? Where had he been, all the long years since his heyday ? Was he in good health ? etc. etc. While studiously polite, my companion was obviously both bemused by the intensity of my inquiries and far less interested in Lyman, who he appeared to perceive as an ever-present and largely unremarkable figure operating within Honolulu's hotel culture[7]. Despite this relative indifference I pursued this academic, and a more senior colleague of his, by e-mail and airmail for the best part of eighteen months, attempting to get them to record an interview with Lyman for *Perfect Beat*, the Pacific music research journal I edit, but to no avail.

In my enthusiasm – and clearly, in retrospect, extreme naivety – what I had not taken into account was the very awkwardness of figures such as Lyman to (even more contemporarily-orientated) ethnomusicologists, and, in particular, to Hawaiian-based ethnomusicologists principally preoccupied with studying facets of traditional Hawaiian music and/or its post- 1970s 'Renaissance'. I had not taken into account the element of embarrassment at examining styles which current tastes (until recently) deemed so irredeemably kitsch as to be one of the final frontiers of pop music study. Nor had I realised that, whatever my own academic curiosity, local cultural-political issues (both within academia and more broadly) prioritised traditional-orientated Hawaiian music as a credible area of analysis. Without any precedent for serious study, the territory remained too *outré* for (academic) words. Despite my best editorial endeavours, the Lyman interview remained an unfulfilled commission.

Two years later, I became aware that the critical-cultural moment had shifted significantly. Visiting the apartment of a learned Popular Music Studies academic in Montreal, I was confronted by a mass of (mostly) vinyl recordings of classic musical exotica. I soon learnt that the academic in question – Will Straw from Montreal's McGill University – was an exotica aficionado and had even flown down to Mexico to interview seminal 'space age bachelor pad' music practitioner Juan Esquivel. Enthused by my similar interests, in both exotica and the earlier, and partly related, internationalisation of Hawaiian musics[8]; he presented me with a vinyl curio which he (rightly) perceived would appeal to me. The album was entitled *Aloha... Michel Louvain* and was a recording of mixed musical exotica – some Hawaiian-influenced, some not discernibly so. The record was produced for the Quebeçois vocalist Michel Louvain by Pierre Noles, apparently as a one-off foray into the genre, and recorded in Montreal for the Disques Apex label. (Though undated, the album was probably released in 1961–62).

3

The cover features a photo of Louvain relaxing in a high, curve-backed cane chair, with a lei draped round his neck, holding a hollowed-out pineapple. Sitting opposite him is a young, blonde female, complete with bee-hive hairdo, holding a cocktail glass adorned with an ornamental paper umbrella. In the background, to their right, a carved tiki pole is present. The sleeve credits inform the reader that the cover shot was taken at Montreal's Kon-Tiki bar (which opened in 1959 as the first of Stephen Crane's lucrative chain of North American Tiki bars). The liner notes begin with the claim (in translation) that:

> It is said that there are two types of people. Those who know Hawai'i well and those who have not tasted the romantic ecstasy which emanates from these enchanted/enchantress islands [îles enchanteresses].

And conclude with the instruction:

> Relax, let Michel Louvain transport you by the magic of sound towards these mysterious islands. Let yourself be soothed by the undulating waves of the deep blue sea and the murmurs of the tropical breeze. Dream on!

The material featured on the album comprises a selection of French language versions of Hawaiian standards together with new and/or less well-known compositions[9]. The arrangements feature steel guitar on some tracks, alongside more archetypical francophone instrumentation such as the piano-accordion, with occasional surf and seagull noises. Louvain's own vocal style is firmly within the contemporary ballad idiom, with smooth melodic contours and few, if any, concessions to Hawaiian vocal techniques such as falsetto[10].

I carried this album with me, like a precious artefact, to my next port-of-call, Memorial University in St Johns, Newfoundland. One Sunday lunchtime, the musical-folklorist Peter Narváez invited me to meet two of his colleagues, Bluegrass specialist Neil Rosen and Kati Szego, an academic involved in researching traditional Hawaiian hula schools, at his home. During our conversation I briefly mentioned acquiring the album in Montreal. Much to my surprise, all present expressed considerable curiosity about it. Once retrieved from my luggage, the album cover was pored over and the French language sleeve notes translated, while we sat around and listened to the music emerging from the worn, scratched grooves – punctuated by amused and/or delighted comments and snap analyses of aspects of songs, their arrangements and instrumentation.

On my return from Canada I received a letter from the Japanese academic Shuhei Hosokawa. Unaware of my own interest in Lyman and the broad genre of exotica, he was inquiring as to whether *Perfect Beat* would be interested in a pair of substantial articles, one exploring the musical oeuvre and cultural significance of the work of Martin Denny, and the other, his influence on the Japanese composer-performer Haruomi Hosono. Emphasising both continued perceptions of the *outré* nature of the musical styles concerned, and the conservatism of much contemporary music studies; Shuhei's letter, almost apologetically, emphasised that *Perfect Beat* – with its Pacific focus and broad historical address – was one of the few places that might countenance publishing such work.

In parallel with the academic narrative I have sketched above, another factor facilitated and encouraged the production of this volume. After several years of scouring second-hand emporia for precious vinyl artefacts, I, and fellow enthusiasts, found exotica increasingly available on CD in the early-mid 1990s, re-released by labels such as EMI-Capitol and Rykodisc, making study of the area substantially easier. This, in turn, was a response to a revival of interest in the form amongst a fashionable metropolitan youth subculture. Prompted by such stimuli as the publication of the Re/Search Publications anthologies *Incredibly Strange Music* (Juno and Vale [eds], 1993 and 1994) and Joseph Lanza's *Elevator Music* (1994) and the (re)discovery and championing of exotica by metropolitan radio DJs (such as Brent Clough in Australia, whose exotica-centred show *Other Worlds* began broadcasting in 1994[11]); an aficionado movement arose, focused on theme parties, associated fanzines (such as the U.S.-produced *Lounge* and *Tiki News*) and the establishment of a series of aficionado web sites.

The revival of interest in musical exotica was also manifest in North American cinema. Two notable films released in 1994 included musical exotica in both their musical scores and aspects of their narratives. The first of these was Atom Egoyan's *Exotica*, a film about an exotic dancer working in a nightclub, which featured a (stylistically appropriate) score by Mychael Danna, performed on a variety of Middle-Eastern instruments[12]. Tim Burton's *Ed Wood* went one further, by not only including vintage post-War exotica on its soundtrack – in the form of Korla Pandit's *Nautch Dance* and Perez Prado's *Kuba Mambo* – but also featuring an on-screen performance of *Nautch Dance* by Pandit himself[13]. Confirming 1994 as a focal moment in the cultural history I am sketching, I found myself being invited along to exotica and lounge club nights in Sydney, somewhat shyly at first, by students who were unaware that there was any interest in such styles from academics. Their perceptions in this regard were entirely understandable. Such work was entirely un-referenced, off-syllabus and out of sight within university popular music teaching and academic publishing at that time. These various contacts confirmed for me that the cultural-critical and academic moment had changed decisively in the mid-1990s; and such synchronous expressions of interest – combined with my own interests in the reasons for this synchronicity itself – prompted the production of this anthology[14].

The second factor informing the production of this book was the manner in which the analysis of seminal post-War exotica created a vantage point from which to view subsequent musical 'eccentricities' which had previously remained off-the-map of the popular musical mainstream and its principal tributaries. In particular, the archaeology of vintage post-war exotica allowed aspects of the work of composer-

5

performers such as Haruomi Hosono and Van Dyke Parks to come into focus. Consequently, Chapters Five and Six of this anthology extend the address of the opening chapters to analyse Hosono's and Van Dyke Parks' work and to demonstrate the manner in which their use of musical tropicalism and orientalism represent an applied, self-reflexive use of such musical approaches. Similarly, the conceptual frame of exotica also allows for the consideration of commercially successful recording artists whose contemporary work exists outside the mainstream of (critically-sanctioned) rock/pop/world/avant garde music and is unheard, unmentioned and thereby unattended to by scholars. The career of New Age composer-performer Yanni, analysed by Karl Neuenfeldt in Chapter Seven, is a notable example; and one which, by dint of Yanni's staging of live concerts in spectacular exotic locales, has added another dimension to the history of 20th Century exotica.

Unbeknownst to me, and to the authors who contributed to this anthology, a parallel scholarly enterprise was under way during the writing and editing of this volume[15]. One outcome of this was Jonathan Bellman's anthology *The Exotic In Western Music* (1998), which appeared in print as this book was at the proofing stage. Emphasising the parallelism of its address, the rear-cover notes for Bellman's volume could have been written specifically for *this* anthology:

> *Exoticism has flourished in Western music since the seventeenth century. A blend of familiar and unfamiliar gestures, this vibrant musical language takes the listener beyond the ordinary by evoking foreign cultures and forbidden desires ... this pioneering collection ... explore[s] the ways in which Western composers have used exotic elements for dramatic and striking effect. Interweaving historical, musical and cultural perspectives, the contributors examine the compositional use of exotic styles and traditions in the work of [diverse] artists ... The volume sheds new light on a significant yet largely neglected art form.*

The elisions in the above quotation remove reference to the specific focus which differentiates Bellman's anthology from this volume, namely that Bellman's authors are predominantly academics from the mainstream classical music establishment (such as Ralph Locke and Miriam Wharples, distinguished professors, respectively, at the University of Rochester's Eastman School of Music and the University of Massachusetts, Amhurst). The subject of Bellman's anthology, its accomplishment and the inclusion of contributions from such scholars, more than justifies the rear cover's contention that the volume "makes a valuable contribution to music history *and* cultural studies" (my emphasis). This claim also suggests a gratifying convergence of two academic areas which have too often remained estranged and uncomfortable with each other (and each other's claims for validity). The subject material of the first ten chapters of Bellman's volume provides a pre-history to the forms of post-War exotica discussed in this volume, ranging from exoticism in 15th and 16th century music, through the various work of composers such as Debussy, de Falla, Rachmaninoff and McPhee, to the use of musical 'Indianisms' in 1960s pop music.

Despite this admirable historical spread, the "realm of amnesia" and/or critical perceptions of the minimal aesthetic adequacy/interest of the form of post-War exotica I posited earlier also intrudes into Bellman's anthology, in that it lacks even a single passing acknowledgement of the range of musical exoticisms and exoticists to which this volume is devoted. While this produces a convenient complementarity (and lack of overlap) between the anthology and this volume; the exclusion of such a broad area from such a ground-breaking anthology principally serves to underline the timeliness of the focus of *this* anthology – re-illuminating an implausibly neglected area of (once) popular cultural and musical practice[16].

Aspects of exotica

The term exotica – referring to an object or quality which embodies the exotic – derives from the adjective 'exotic', first used in the English Language in the early 1600s, at a time of Western European maritime exploration of the Americas, the African Coast and the Indian Ocean. The term derives from the Greek *exo* (outside), and was applied to that which was outside the Old World of the West. In its original usage, the adjective denoted foreign and/or alien locales, products, fauna or flora, and the characterisation of these as "barbarous" and/or "outlandish" (SOED, 1973: 704)[17]. It evoked combined associations of difference and danger, and the appeal of exotic forms and products was premised on these aspects[18]. By the 19th and 20th centuries, with the spread of European empires across the globe and the increasing exploration and colonisation of the planet, the *frisson* of danger had faded from the term and it came to either simply signify "non-native" (as in its popular botanical usage) or else conveyed a softer *frisson*, that of having "glamour" in the form of "the attraction of the strange or foreign" (*SOED*, 1973: 2625).

The noun 'exotica' is more recent in origin and, in its specific musical application, can be defined in terms of a music which features aspects of melodic and rhythmic structure, instrumentation and/or musical colour which mark a composition as different from established (western) musical genres (while still retaining substantial, recognisable affinities to these). The fuzziness of this definition reflects the range of articulations of musical exoticism, from mild 'flavourings' through to more full-blown, musically-integrated projects.

With regard to the musical practices addressed in this anthology, it is possible to identify three major sub-sets of musical exotica – often used in various combinations with each other: Orientalism, the Hawaiianesque and Afro-tropicalism.

Orientalism is an established musical term (and, of course, a broader concept extensively excavated by Said [1978]) referring to the borrowing of particular stylistic elements of Asian culture (ie Chinese, Japanese, Indian etc.) for use in western art practices. The term also has more specific national sub-sets, such as chinoiserie, japonaiserie, Indianism etc. (which are also used at various points in the anthology). In addition to the use of distinctive instruments, such as the koto, sitar and various gongs; one of the principal characteristics of the (varieties of) musical orientalism discussed in this anthology is its frequent use of stock devices such as pentatonic scales, melodic ostinatos and parallel fourth and fifth intervals.

By the *Hawaiianesque*, I refer to the use of a combination of Hawaiian-associ-ated/derived string instruments, namely the ukulele, slack-key and steel guitars; Hawaiianesque chanting and vocal melodies; various indigenous Hawaiian percus-sion and wind instruments; and the frequent use of Hawaiian standards (ie well-known compositions), particularly in the repertoires of Lyman and Denny. (For a detailed study of the rise of Hawaiian music in the 20th Century, see Kannahele [ed] [1978] and Buck [1993].)

I use the term *Afro-tropicalism* to refer to both the geo-cultural origin (and/or assumed origin) of particular rhythmic styles, instruments and musical applications and the connotation of the tropics as "hot, ardent, or luxuriant" (SOED, 1973: 2369). Prominent rhythm patterns, often produced by/complemented with identifiably 'exotic' percussion instruments (such as congas, bongo drums, maracas etc) repre-sent the most obvious feature of this sub-set[19]. The rhythms it uses are predominantly African, Latin American or Caribbean in origin, and repeated patterns are often used to underpin dramatic twists in arrangements. The use of imitation bird noises, vocal chanting etc. also conforms to this category. (By a somewhat secondary association, unorthodox western instruments such as the marimba and vibraphone also evince this quality.)

Although it did not use the specific designation, the notion of Afro-tropicalism which developed in the early 1800s represented a re-mapping of notions of the European primitive (imagination) onto a geographically displaced 'other'. As Barkan and Bush have identified :

> [o]rgiastic dancing and drumming ... had been a constant in representations
> of peasantry and non-Western culture from the seventeenth to the twentieth
> century. When the late nineteenth and early twentieth centuries reimagined
> a "primitive" world, this long standing trope, with its overtones of lascivi-
> ousness, became a highly charged signal of otherness. (1995: 3)

As Barkan and Bush also emphasise, a paradoxical aspect of this trope was that it "came to signify modernity" (ibid) and inspired such seminal modernist artists as T.S. Eliot[20], Picasso[21] and Debussy, to name but three prominent examples.

Reference to Debussy is appropriate at this point since, as various contributors to Bellman (ed) (1998) and Rebecca Leydon (in Chapter Two of this anthology) discuss, there was a significant body of earlier musical exotica, produced within the contemporary western fine music tradition, from the 1500s on. As Scott-Maxwell (1997) has detailed, over the last century this work has ranged from relatively superficial musical 'flavourings' in 'light classical' music, such as Ketèlbey's highly popular composition *In A Persian Market*, to the more sophisticated introduction of aspects of exotic elements into western compositions. As Cooke (1998) discusses, composers such as Debussy and McPhee are usually regarded as exemplifying the latter tendency. Yet Neil Sorrell's discussion of western appropriations of aspects of gamelan music from the Indonesian archipelago (1990) includes an illuminating aside in this regard. Discussing the specific nature of the influence of gamelan music on Debussy's compositions (such as *La Mer*, and others[22]), Sorrell relates that Joko Purwanto, a Javanese gamelan player, commented to him that (for those conversant with East Asian musics) such compositions primarily possessed a "vaguely south-east Asian" feel, "from Cambodia for example" (ibid: 6). This evaluation is signifi-cant. To western ears, some western originated styles appear to resemble and/or evoke the music of specific cultures and/or geographical points of origin (particu-larly if those places are exotic and largely unreachable). Yet to people from such places, they sound less specifically referential and even, as in the example discussed above, suggest somewhere else entirely. For recognised modernist composers who were not, in the early 20th Century at least, motivated by any scientist ethnomu-sicological impulse, this was insignificant. The example offered by musical differ-ence, the transgression of western cultural norms, was what was deemed most significant in Modernism's connection with otherness and/or (assumed) primitiv-ism.

Post-war exotica: historical contexts

The retro fashionability of exotica, which has tended to freeze on a moment at the cusp of the 1950s/early 1960s, has tended to suggest that the form was both discrete and short-lived. The picture is, however, more complex. The creative and commer-cial heydays of Baxter, Denny, Lyman, Pandit and Sumac, for instance, spanned a period from the early 1950s through to the mid-1960s. While their careers declined at this point, both Baxter and Sumac continued, and attempted to connect with the rock generation, adding prominent electric guitars to their instrumental line-ups (on *Que Mango!* [1970] and *Miracles* [1972] respectively)[23]; while Denny and Lyman simply played on in their existing styles, sustained – albeit in relative obscurity – by the Hawaiian tourist industry. There is therefore a historical overlap between these performers and the work of Van Dyke Parks (whose Caribbean-tropicalist album *Discover America* was released in 1972) and Hosono (whose 'Soy Sauce Music' trilogy commenced in 1973).

But while the chronologies may overlap, there are clear differences between the moment of exotica's broad-based, popular first wave (in the early 1950s-mid 1960s); the period in the 1970s and 1980s when several composer-performers (at the esoteric fringe of the mainstream) applied exoticism in particular projects[24]; and the moment of exotica's revival in the early-mid 1990s. Indeed, it is possible to identify a significant disjuncture between the first and second of these phases which foreshadows the conditions of emergence of the third. Put simply, the disjuncture is between the naive, popular spontaneity of first wave exotica; the more self-conscious applied exoticism of the second phase; and the camp-revivalism of the third phase (enabled by and predicated upon the style's historicity). The work of Yanni, and other contemporary exoticists, can be seen to comprise a fourth phase. This is one parallel, but clearly distinct from, camp-revivalism; informed and enabled by a New Age spiritualism with significant affinities to that associated with Pandit in the late 1940s–50s, creating another historical loop (which also intersects with Hosono's work in certain regards[25]).

As several contributors to this anthology suggest, exotica's slide into obscurity can be seen to have been directly triggered by those shifts in popular taste which installed pop/rock as the dominant genre(s) of western popular music, shuffling its predecessors off into niche and/or particular age-demographic markets. Pop/rock's ascendancy was also associated with a set of values – youthful difference, rebellion, emotion, intensity (etc.) – which were perceived to have a degree of homologous inscription in the music's sound. This factor, above all, explains the distance pop/rock perceived between itself and previous styles of popular music, which were, implicitly or explicitly, read as indexical of a (rejected) cultural mainstream, as emblematic of a stylistic generation gap. But while the disjuncture between the first and second phases of exotica posited above can be readily explained in these terms, the period of the mid-1960s–1970s is not simply marked by exotica's abrupt wane in popularity, followed by a cluster of fringe re-engagements a decade later; it is also a period of stylistic turbulence and eddies. The best known of these comprises pop/rock's awkward attempts to complement its 'progressive' development of musical style – and interrelated psychedelic mysticism – by variously embracing and incorporating elements of non-western music.

As Bellman (1998) details, the best known of these initiatives remains The Beatles' involvement with Indian, and particularly sitar, music. This arose from the band's (short-lived) fascination with the Mahareeshi Yoga and George Harrison's longer term interests in Indian culture and, later, the Hari Kishna cult[26]. The Beatles' track *Norwegian Wood* (1965), on which Harrison played sitar, remains the most enduring musical example of such incorporation[27]. More widespread however was the playing of recordings of sitar music, particularly those produced by the virtuoso musician Ravi Shankar, in various socio-cultural contexts[28]. In such environments, this music functioned as 'pure' exotica, neither 'filtered' nor adapted by western interpreters or by foreign musicians consciously targeting the western market (in the manner of the previous exponents of exotica). Free from such musical adaptations and recontextualisations the music undoubtedly had an authenticity-effect (at the very least) which exotica lacked. However, its 'otherness' proved significant in another manner. Despite its complex musicality, it was largely the affective attributes of the music as an exotic non-western *noise* with which western audiences, uneducated in Indian musical traditions and unable to distinguish the intricacies of non-western scales, identified with. Shankar himself recognised this aspect and inscribed it in the vinyl history of the form during the recording of the George Harrison co-ordinated Concert for Bangladesh (1971). The most telling part of the project is the exchange between Shankar and the audience, captured on disk, when after minutes of twanging, unstructured musical meandering, the audience bursts into applause. Shankar politely thanks them for having enjoyed listening to the musicians tuning-up and begins his concert.

I relate this exchange not simply to stress the western audience's lack of sophistication – after all, how *would* they be expected to know the subtleties of Indian music given its almost total exclusion from education and public culture in the West ? – but rather to indicate the manner in which exotic *sounds* (and the perception of their exoticism) are key to the exotic imaginary and the satisfactions such products offer. In this manner, despite Shankar and his music's formal and expressive achievement, its reception by western audiences is usually on a far more simplistic level. Shankar as exotic Indian, and his music as exotic noise, symbolise, for western audiences, a wide variety of cultural othernesses.

Within the frame of inquiry established in this anthology there is another facet of western popular music which merits closer attention – the cultural *fakery* of a series of avant-garde rock projects produced in the late 1960s to late 1970s[29]. The German group Can appear to have been pioneers of the form, recording a series of compositions, over a number of years, which reworked elements of previous musical styles and genres. The band referred to these as their 'Ethnological Forgery Series' and individual tracks were given the title 'E.F.S.' followed by a number[30]. The majority of these tracks incorporated blues, jazz and/or other Afro-American elements (relatively unproblematically) into the band's experimental rock style. Can's approach was subsequently expanded upon by other 'progressive' rock artists, most notably U.S. avant gardists The Residents.

In 1979, The Residents released an album entitled *Eskimo* which, in contrast to its current critical obscurity, received considerable – and often hyperbolic – acclaim from the music press[31]. The album comprised a series of tracks which attempted to "recreate" the (purely fictional) music of a nomadic Eskimo tribe living "North of Greenland, well within the Arctic Circle" (liner notes). Its sleeve notes recall those of vintage exotica albums by referring to the use of (supposedly) authentic exotic instruments on the recording – in this case, the *kooa*, *pooeye*, *sedrak* and various drums[32] – and by the use of "the Eskimo scale", specified as the five note set "Approx. F, G, B flat, D flat, E flat" (ibid) on the recording. The sleeve notes also specify a recommended mode of listening, which – in all but its repeated emphasis of the project's (spurious) authenticity – closely resembles the instructions for listeners to immerse themselves in sound, in order to transport themselves to exotic locales, included on early albums by Denny, Lyman and other exoticists:

[f]or maximum enjoyment, this record should be listened to with headphones

11

> *while reading the enclosed verbal accounts of what you hear. The disc*
> *should be played in its entirety and in the proper sequence of sides. A relaxed*
> *state of mind is essential.*

As Jon Hassell has recounted, the origins of Brian Eno and David Byrne's seminal album *My Life in The Bush of Ghosts* (recorded in 1979, released in 1981) arose from a similar conceptual project:

> *[a]fter* Remain in Light *David and Brian came up with this idea that we*
> *should go off into the desert someplace ... and make a record that, at that*
> *time, we were thinking would be somewhat like the Residents'* Eskimo *- that*
> *is a* faux *tribe, invented, that doesn't exist ...* (cited in Toop, 1995: 123)

While Eno and Byrne subsequently discarded the fictionalisation, in favour of a bricolage of found exotic sounds married to a rock-funk base[33]; both The Residents' approach on their *Eskimo* album and the original inspiration for *My Life in The Bush of Ghosts* involved the fabrication of a cultural identity in order to allow for musical experimentation. One of the notable aspects of this is that the artists concerned felt that they *needed* such a frame to justify/explain musical experimentation – the manifest *in*authenticity of almost all post-war exotica needed no such legitimising excuse[34]. This, in itself, indicates just how *outré* and unconscionable exotica was as a practice in the late 1970s and early 1980s. Another notable aspect of the 'fauxist' tendency discussed here is the manner in which it reflected a historical moment (immediately) prior to the arrival of world music in the early-mid 1980s, a period when such projects were neither formulated, nor subsequently criticised, with an address to the politics of indigenous cultural assertion and appropriation of such identities. Indeed, it is some indication of the shift in sensibilities that no music act not actively seeking blanket critical condemnation and notoriety would attempt to put out an album in the 1990s which include reference to a specific indigenous group – albeit a fictionalised clan – indulging in routine ritual child murder, bathing in their own urine and relishing putrefied animal flesh (as the Residents did in the sleeve notes to their *Eskimo* album)[35].

Re-engagement

While industrial 'mavericks' such as Hosono and Van Dyke Parks produced a series of musical works which employed a number of tropicalist and/or orientalist techniques on albums recorded in the 1970s and 1980s, their work remains essentially isolated, and hence – until now, at least – critically neglected. The popular 're-imagination' and re-engagement with post-War exotica in the 1990s has proceeded independently of their earlier initiatives and has not been premised on such major shifts in aesthetics and/or formal complexity. Rather the engagement has been superficial, an appreciation premised on a play of musical surfaces which might best be described as infra-stylistic. While it is often 'too soon to speak' in popular culture, it looks unlikely that the current moment will throw up its own Dennys or Lymans, or, at least, figures with any comparable success. Their most obvious contemporary equivalent, in terms of popularity, is Yanni, whose sales have eclipsed even those of exotica's most renown exponents. However, as elaborated in Chapter Seven, his style and public image is so substantially different from that of the original exoticists (or their self-conscious revivalists) that he occupies a distinctly different cultural niche.

The group of retro-exoticist ensembles which have established themselves on metropolitan club circuits in North America and Western Europe over the last five years (such as Combustible Edison and Karla Pundit in the U.S.A., and Arling and Cameron in the Netherlands), usually confine themselves to the self-conscious imitation of previous styles, not so much parody – since, after all, who could out-parody exotica itself ? – as gleeful homage, a contemporary, and largely 'cool' camp. A double page spread in the fanzine *Lounge* (v2 n1 – unattributed, 1995: 20–21) provides a playfully succinct summary of the pleasures of exotica as identified and promoted by the metropolitan club culture which has nurtured its recent revival. The fanzine provides the layout of a board game called 'Olivelandia'. The playing circuit is a map of the world. At the north pole is a bottle of vermouth, at the south pole, Olivelandia, the homeland of a global cocktail culture which imagines the world as its playground and source of vital ingredients. On their quest to collect the "necessary ingredients to concoct the elixir of life" – ie the Olivelandia Martini – the players slide round the five continents, finally arriving at the 'end of the Earth', Australasia, where, equipped with the perfect cocktail, they get a chance to flip a quarter and enter cocktail nirvana[36]. The game represents the planet through a prism of commodified western pleasure and requires players to cross geo-political borders with impunity, bent on pursuit of a (necessarily unattainable – but nevertheless keenly anticipated) pinnacle of sensory bliss.

In one sense, the revival in popularity of exotica can be linked to the broader nostalgia for imagined 1950sness (of the sort so perfectly crystallised in Francis Ford Coppola's film *Peggy Sue Got Married* [1987]) and various other forms of kitsch culture. In this, the re-engagement with exotica parallels and amplifies its original context of tiki bars, back yard luaus and unashamed hedonism. But in this invocation of an original context of consumption, the 1990s' re-engagement triggers a double displacement, once, historically, from the 1950s, and then again, geo-cul-turally, from mainland U.S.A. to the (largely fabricated) tropical and oriental points of origin of the music itself. In this way, both nostalgia and exoticism become doubled. It is precisely this doubling which allows us a cool distance. As Rebecca Leydon has identified:

> *...as we smile at the uncritical processing of primitivist codes by exotica's practitioners, we implicitly attribute a set of characteristics to the enlight-ened present, such as "global awareness" or multicultural sensitivity.*[37]

The recent western vogue for world music[38] and world beat[39], which began in the mid 1980s, and its associated validation of previously subordinate and/or submerged cultures, can be seen to represent a manifest – if vaguely defined – sense of loss in western culture[40]. In this way, world music and world beat can be seen to service a desire for difference(s), for cultural diversity (as for bio-diversity). By virtue of their associated values – ethnic authenticity (real or imagined) in the case of world music; and/or collaborative integrity, in the case of world beat projects – these musics come (heavily) value laden. By contrast, vintage (and/or revivalist) exotica, with its historical distance and manifestly fabricated *exoticness*, appears a simpler, more immediately accessible commodity. Due to its carefully emphasised and exploited datedness[41] and its lack of any (necessary) connection to any *actual* foreign culture, it is open for guilt-free consumption and complex refraction within western subcultural communities (ie without any worries over 'political correctness' and/or troublesome issues of cultural appropriation, copyright etc.)

Despite the clear antecedence of post-War musical exotica in the previous history of western classical and popular music (and in Hosono's case, localised Japanese forms[42]); the more concentrated, variegated eclecticism of post-War exotica embodies another, arguably more complex aesthetic. In his 1995 book *Ocean of Sound*, David Toop drew on James Clifford's discussion of the work of the early 20th Century surrealist and anthropologist Michel Learis (1988) to coin a definition of a musical aesthetic of "ethno-surrealism" (1995: 162). In Toop's formation, the 'ethno' component of this involved the employment of elements of non-western musics. Drawing on Clifford's discussion, Toop used 'surrealism':

> *... in an obviously expanded sense to circumscribe an aesthetic that values fragments, curious collections, unexpected juxtapositions –* [one] *that works to provoke the manifestations of extraordinary realities drawn from the domains of the erotic, the exotic and the unconscious.* (ibid: 182)

While Toop specifically coined this aesthetic category to describe Jon Hassell's studiously respectful musical syncretism – which Hassell has described in terms of a 'Fourth World' approach[43] – Toop's aesthetic definition might also be seen to express the *ideal* of musical exotica manifest in the sleeve notes of Baxter, Denny, Lyman, Pandit and Sumac's albums (as discussed in Chapters 1–4); various public statements by the form's proponents; and the analyses offered in this anthology. I stress the *ideal* of exotica since Toop's definition also embodies its problem. While the majority of practices and practitioners discussed in this book could be understood to adhere to the aesthetic values that Toop identifies, the second half of his definition switches frames of reference and characterises how the aesthetic *works*. This is obviously a more complex area, one which would require a detailed historical-ethnographic study to evaluate. Practitioners, critics, liner-note authors and/or individual listeners may attest to how the perceived aesthetic works *for them* – and suggest it may work in such a manner for others – but claims for such an innate radical affectivity for the form are, to say the least, tendentious. It may therefore be more appropriate to state that the contemporary re-engagement with various combinations of musical tropicalism and orientalism *perceives* the ambition and potential of the form to achieve a distinct aesthetic aspect and thereby values it for its difference from other contemporary musics.

Along with its analyses of various examples of musical practice, this anthology offers case studies of the musical *imagination* of a group of composer/performers and, more broadly, of western (and predominantly U.S.) culture at particular post-War moments. More precisely, this volume considers various uses of music to create identity narratives constructed by edging, however tentatively, into zones of cultural otherness; by departures on sonic voyages, guaranteed to return, but intended to broaden the sensibilities and imagination of the traveller along the way. In this manner, the anthology attempts to provide insights into both post-war cultural imagination *and* production. Therefore, this anthology's attempt to broaden the horizons of Popular Music Studies does not confine itself to arguing for adjustments to the canonical matrix; it also involves a broader consideration of the nature and horizons of post-War musical imagination and its association with issues of cultural identity and pluralism. In this regard, the practices it analyses are far from incidental curiosities – colourful blips on a historical map – but rather vivid and undiminished points of cultural efflorescence whose serious consideration has been long overdue.

Notes

1. Of the sort that Bourdieu attempted to identify in operation in his major study *Distinction* (1979).

2. The linguistic derivation of the word is significant in emphasising the power of inscription within a canon. The original meaning of the term, formulated some 500 years ago, was the "list of books of the Bible accepted by the Christian Church as genuine and inspired" and – later – "a list of the saints canonised by the church" (*The Shorter Oxford English Dictionary – on Historical Principles* [1975]: 277).

3. This phenomenon merits sustained analysis in its own right, comparing various examples and constructing models of operation – such an enterprise is however, beyond the scope of this introductory essay.

4. Other notable exponents who merit individual study include Ethel Azama, Juan Esquivel, Russ Garcia, Tak Shindo, Sondi Sodsai and Si Zentner.

5. David Mitchell, audio-visual production manager at Macquarie University, Sydney, interviewed in 1992.

6. Mark Worth, (currently) a Sydney-based documentary film maker and journalist, interviewed in 1992.

7. Unfortunately, I was due to fly out the next day and was denied the opportunity of seeing Lyman perform live and of speaking to him in person – a chance I still regret having passed up.

8. See Kannahele (1979), Coyle and Coyle (1994), Hosokawa (1995), Scott-Maxwell (1997) and Whiteoak (1995) for further accounts of this.

9. Such as *Aloha Oe* (re-titled *C'Est Un Secret*, and credited as composed by the album's producer Noles), *The Hawaiian Wedding Song* (re-titled *Noces de Soleil*) and *Sweet Leilani* (*Douce Leilani*).

10. And a somewhat variable pitch.

15

11.   The show originally ran as a summer-season special and followed an earlier documentary item on post-war musical exotica Clough had produced for the Australian Broadcasting Corporation program *In The Mix* in 1991.

12.   Which won the composer a Genie award.

13.   Howard Shore's score was also given added exotica appeal through its prominent use of theremin and ondes martenot parts (performed by Lydia Kavina and Cynthia Miller respectively). (See Hayward, 1997 and 1999 for further discussion of the theremin in film soundtracks.)

14.   The extent of renewed interest in the form was further underlined by the response to an informally circulated call for expressions of interest in contributing to this anthology. The response was notable. Not only were several of the chapters included here elicited by this means; there were also sufficient further proposals to fill a volume twice this size.

15.   As Bellman's 'Introduction' (ix-xiii) details, his anthology reflects a growing interest in exoticism amongst mainstream – classical-orientated – musicologists during the 1990s, of which only McClary (1992) has come to the notice of more popular music orientated scholars. As Rebecca Leydon's chapter in this volume establishes, Dahlhaus (1989) also provides valuable perspectives on exoticism in 19th Century music. (Also see Wharples, 1998: 3–5, for a discussion of pre-1990s research on this topic and reference to her own pioneering work in this field.)

16.   I should emphasise that I stress this lack in order to emphasise the pervasive nature of the associated amnesia effect/*outré* perception of post-war exotica (and its effect of stifling critical analysis) rather than intending any specific critique of the editor and his project. I should also add that Jonathan Bellman has subsequently welcomed the project of *this* anthology (e-mail to the author 6.8.98); as has Ralph Locke (whose discussions with Bellman are credited in the Acknowledgements section to Bellman's book as inspiring the production of his anthology) (e-mail to the author 12.7.98).

17.   As defined in the *Shorter Oxford English Dictionary*, 1978: 704.

18.   Such as, for instance, tobacco or the now-humble potato.

19.   Indeed, whole albums were specifically addressed to this aspect of the music. One notable example is George Cates' album *Polynesian Percussion* (1962?) which has cover notes which boast that the "foundation for [its] exciting performances is provided by nearly a score of percussion instruments, some familiar, such as the tympani, marimbas and xylophones; some exotic, including the Uli Uli, the Pu Ili and the Boo-Bams"; and goes on to include a full list of these in a separate note.

20.   Who became fascinated by 'primitive' cultures and, subsequently, anthropology after attending the 1904 St Louis World's Fair – see Bush (1995: 25–32). (Also see Hosokawa, 1994: fn2, for further discussion of the significance of international expositions for western cultural producers.)

21.   Whose move to Cubism was, as is well documented, inspired, at least in part, by the exhibition of African masks at the Musée d'Ethnographique at the Palais du Trocadero in 1906 – see North (1995) for further discussion.

22.   Cooke (1998) also provides an insightful discussion of this topic.

23.   Their popularity may have waned, but the genre, and their careers, persisted; they have all continued to perform and record, albeit less frequently, to the present.

24.   Along with Van Dyke Parks and Hosono, the work of other musicians, such as Stony Browder Jnr, August Darnell and Andy Hernandez, who worked together in Dr Buzzard's Original Savannah Band in the mid-1970s, also merits detailed attention and analysis in this regard.

25.   See Chapter Five: 114–144 (this anthology).

26.   Harrison produced two hit singles for the London-based Radha Krishna Temple, released on the Beatles' Apple label, *Hare Krishna Mantra* (1969) and *Govinda* (1970).

27. Although, as Bellman (1998) argues, the track is neither the most strongly 'Indianist' Beatles' recording (*Love To You* [1966], *Within You Without You* [1967] and *Inner Light* [1968] all featuring more prominent Indian-influenced aspects) nor even the first 1960s British pop track to show such influences (The Kinks' *See My Friends* [1965] appearing to have set the precedent).

28. Such as cafes, restaurants, parties and meditation sessions.

29. See Hayward (1998: 28–45) for a discussion of the term 'avant garde rock' and the musical styles it is usually taken to include.

30. A selection of these are included on the album *Limited Edition* (1974 – United Artists).

31. Somewhat curiously perhaps, *Eskimo* was the most critically acclaimed of all The Residents' albums. Critics such as Andy Gill, reviewing the album in the British weekly *New Musical Express*, for instance, was inspired to a dizzy height of hyperbole, stating that:

    I'm not sure quite how to convey the magnitude of the Residents' accomplishment with Eskimo. What I am sure of is that it's without doubt one of the most important albums ever made, if not the most important, and that its implications are of such an unprecedentedly revolutionary nature that the weak-minded polemical posturing of purportedly 'political' bands are positively bourgeois by comparison. (cited in Ginsburg, 1997: 10)

    Despite such claims, the album has slipped into a semi-obscurity and now appears more of a curiosity than an historical turning-point.)

32. The sleeve notes describe these in the following terms:

    Kooa – a plucked string instrument made out of seal gut stretched over a dog skull sounding board.
    Pooeye – a three to five note flute made from hollowed whale or walrus bone.
    Sedrak – a tuned percussive instrument made of walrus and whale ribs which are struck with frozen fish.
    Segook, Annorak, Ooluksak, Atseak, others – drums of various types, all made by stretching skins over skulls, rib cages, etc.

33. For a more detailed discussion of *My Life In the Bush of Ghosts*, see Hayward (1998: 30–43).

34. It should be noted that aspects of Sumac's work, as described by Rebecca Leydon in Chapter Two, made some partial appeal to authenticity.

35. In the 1990s such claims are the near-exclusive province of the rabidly racist political right, such as the Australian One Nation party, led by Pauline Hanson, which has promulgated spurious claims of Aboriginal cannibalism and infanticide in order to boost its profile.

36. Ingredients: 2 parts dry gin, 1 part sweet vermouth, a jigger of dark rum, a splash of hot saké, a dash of cayenne pepper and 1 teaspoon full of juice of kiwi fruit (unattributed: 21).

37. In an earlier draft of Chapter Two of this anthology.

38. Understood here as the recording and/or packaging of non-western musics for the western music market.

39. Understood here as a syncretic/fusion practice involving musicians and/or musical styles from the West and 'non-West'.

40. An excavation of the history and ideologies informing world music/world beat is beyond the scope of this Introduction, for more detailed discussion see Feld (1994), Hayward (1998) and Taylor (1998).

41. Most obvious in its packaging and marketing.

42. See Hosokawa (1995) for discussion of these.

43. Hassell has outlined the concept as premised on:

    ... the range of possible relations between individual, tribe and nation in the mass electronic age. Imagine a grid of national boundaries, and on to those project a new, non-physical communications-derived geography – tribes of like-minded thinkers. Since a situation like this has never

17

before existed, it follows that old, narrow-band approaches can't work and that new approaches must be creative. This means intuitive and improvisational. I would like the message of the Fourth World to be that things shouldn't be diluted. This balance between the native identity and the global identity via various electronic extensions is not one which can be dictated or necessarily predicted. One should be very humble and respectful of our lack of knowledge about how those things combine, and be informed by knowledge of the way things used to be in smaller numbers – that's where it becomes very useful to look at other cultures, small cultures, and try to develop a modus operandi for the new age, not New Age. (cited in Toop, 1995: 168)

Chapter One

KORLA PANDIT

Music, Exoticism and Mysticism

TIMOTHY D. TAYLOR

In 1947, Klaus Landsberg, a German emigré, begin a stint as the head of station KTLA in Los Angeles. In this period there was no network support that far west, so Landsberg had to rely on his own ingenuity in devising programming for this new station. His partiality for "bright, ethnic music" (quoted by Stan Chambers, one-time KTLA employee, in Kisseloff, 1995: 174) resulted in, amongst other things, an off-beat program called *Musical Adventure with Korla Pandit*, which was broadcast three times per week from 1949 to 1951. Pandit was the son of an Indian Brahman, "a member of one of India's first families", he has stated, and his mother was a French singer (1966: np). He played every one of his programs wearing a turban bejewelled with a ruby, and never spoke. In this chapter I want to try to situate Pandit in the cultural moment of his greatest popularity, the late 1940s-early 1950s, focusing on a few key issues: the kinds of representations of India and Indians, both visual and musical, offered in his TV show; representations by and of Pandit; and the ways that Pandit slipped in and out of these representations, finally becoming a New Age guru/musician[1].

The 1950s, suburbia, nostalgia, and difference

Several national trends occurred in the same historical moment as Pandit's popularity; the most important of these was the growth of suburbs after World War II; this has been widely discussed and so my own discussion will be fairly brief, and concentrate on the ways that suburbanisation as a cultural phenomenon relates to Pandit[2]. In areas such as Orange County, California (where Pandit first lived when he moved to California in 1949), the movement out of the cities into suburbs in the 1950s resulted in a near doubling in population between 1940 and 1950, rising from

130,760 to 216,224 (Jezer, 1982: 188). Nationally, as a result of the GI Bill of Rights, passed in 1944, and the tax benefits to home owners that were increased during the 1940s, housing starts rose from 114,000 in 1944 to 937,000 in 1946, 1,118,000 in 1948, to an all-time high of 1,692,000 in 1950 (Halberstam, 1993: 134). Even before this, in 1946, "for the first time a majority of the nation's families lived in homes they owned" (May, 1988: 170). The housing industry contributed to this growth with millions of 'cookie-cutter' homes, made to look the same no matter in which part of the country they were intended to be built[3]. "Even flora varied little from place to place", writes Marty Jezer, with the ubiquitous Colorado blue spruce becoming the conifer of choice (Jezer, 1982: 191)[4].

During the 1940s, suburbs became centres of the erasure of racial and ethnic difference. Until the early 1960s they were occupied almost wholly by whites. Some residents of the whitewashed suburbs suffered a kind of nostalgia for the web of family and other social connections in the cities, as well as, seemingly contradictorily, nostalgia for the kind of ethnic diversity that cities provide. Before the early 1950s, radio and television programs had often featured a variety of ethnic groups[5]. But by the mid-1950s television and radio had moved toward a *Father Knows Best* model, in which people were white, mom stayed at home, kids were obedient, and dad was an organisation man who "had no politics, no opinions, and no connection with the world about him" (Jezer, 1982: 198)[6].

These radio and then television programs (many of which made the transition from one medium to the other) mirrored the lives of their listeners (so Mama's family in *I Remember Mama* moves to the suburbs, as did Lucy and Ricky in *I Love Lucy*). Even having moved, though, many of these characters were still caught up in the network of family and social relations that was damaged when people moved out of the cities. Many early television programs featured a wide variety of ethnic and/or age groups, and were generally diverse. Horace Newcomb describes an episode of *The Texaco Star Theater* (which later become *The Milton Berle Show*) from 2/4/51 that features a sketch in which a singer performs a number called *Tenement City* that lasts ten minutes, and includes the characters "Mrs. Cohen", who makes a wonderful Irish stew, and "Mrs. Kelly", who makes the best gefilte fish; these and other characters later listen appreciatively as a young black man sings *Somewhere over the Rainbow* (Newcomb, 1997: 114).

Representations of race and ethnicity found their way into suburban homes in other ways. Mark Burns and Louis DiBonis, serious collectors of 1950s objects, have written of the kinds and nature of all manner of 1950s household items, arguing that "[d]epiction of other races – generally with contented, nubile or exotic, but not threatening, overtones – was a general common feature of the ornament" (1988: 42). They also observe that:

> Chinamen and Mexicans were represented as childlike, innocent, fun loving
> – and lazy. White folk were serious adults, brown and yellow people were

engaging, the Korean war notwithstanding. These objects were born out of ignorance, reinforced by TV and the developing tourist trade and its propaganda. (Burns and DiBonis, 1988: 20).

At the same time, veterans who had returned from World War II, after having served in the South Pacific, continued their interest in Hawaiian and other Pacific cultures and their musics[7]. It was in this historical moment that the fad for things Hawaiian was born, a fad so potent that most popular musicians learned some of this music, although the national popularity of lounge and exotica musics – discussed at length in this volume – occurs after its heyday.

India ?

Even though various 'exotic' peoples and cultures made their way into mainstream North American representations, most North Americans in the 1950s knew little of India, which, when represented at all, seemed to provide a little dash of colour or exoticism. In 1952, *House & Garden* advertised a new living room decor, designed by Lord & Taylor, whose centrepiece was colourful fabrics that "bring you the magnificent patterns and colors of India under the name of 'Indra', the Hindu deity who rules the bright firmament" (*House & Garden*, 1952: 141). The drawing of this living room was captioned "Hot colors of the sleepy sun in a modern living room." This ad was accompanied by a story by Rumer Godden entitled 'Diwali Lights', about the festival marking the Hindu New Year; Godden would have fairly been well known to her readers as a British novelist who authored many books of fiction and non-fiction that were set in India.

But most U.S. citizens knew little of India, due mainly to restrictive immigration laws. While Congress declared South Asians eligible for citizenship in 1910, in 1917 it enacted a law barring them and other Asians from becoming citizens. This changed in 1926 when an Indian lawyer successfully argued that South Asians should be considered Aryans (that is, white) and be accorded citizenship. In 1946, Congress enacted a law allowing South Asians citizenship, but the annual quota was only one hundred people[8]. Between the years 1923, when official immigration by South Asians ceased, and 1946, when it began again, only a few hundred South Asians came legally to the U.S.A.; most of these were students. There were also around three thousand illegals (Gibson, 1988: 41). According to Joan Jensen, "in 1942, only forty percent of Americans could locate India on a map" (1988: 278). A poll taken in Iowa in 1945 revealed that, while the majority of those asked had a rough idea of how many people lived in India and had heard of Gandhi, most hadn't heard of Pakistan (Chandrasekhar, 1945). Even though there were some 250,000 American soldiers stationed in India during World War Two, most brought home no more knowledge than "a tale of a sordid, illiterate, depressed country" (Kiell, 1946: 204)[9].

In addition to the acquisition of colour for living rooms, North America's conceptions of India and Indians in the 1950s tended to be concerned with a clash of the mystical with the 'real' or scientific. For example, a 1949 photograph of an Indian landscape in *House & Garden* is introduced with the statement, "India, vast, imponderable and infinitely diverse, is a country where mysticism co-exists with science, where shimmering saris sing against the ash-gray hides of elephants and a whole city is colored pink"[10]. Likewise, the opening to the film of Rudyard Kipling's *Kim* (1950) begins with an 'Indian' narrator (played by an uncredited actor, almost certainly not South Asian as none of the named actors in this production were) stating:

> *India. Gateway to the East. Empire of magnificent pageantry and exotic colour – the jewel of the Orient. Land of mysticism and reality, whose history is filled with the romance and intrigue of the nineteenth century, which already belongs to a legendary past.*

Another example comes from the *New Yorker*, in which a doctor, Victor Barnouw, address these issues head-on. Barnouw is working with an U.S.-trained Brahman doctor, Narayan Ghodme, in a lab in India:

> *Sometimes, when he and I sat drinking tea in the lab, I tried to find out what his own religious views were. Once I asked him if he believed in reincarnation. For answer, he waved a thin brown hand toward the lab equipment and said, "I believe in that."*
> *"The plethysmograph?"*
> *"No. Science."*
> *I liked to badger him. "But at home you take part in the family rituals," I said.*
> *"Of course." Narayan shrugged. "Family is one thing, science another."*
> *"But by taking part you give assent, don't you? Let's face it, Narayan – do you* want *people to go on worshipping elephant-headed gods?"*
> *Narayan raised his eyebrows. "What's wrong with elephant-headed gods?"*
> *I couldn't think of any sensible answer, so I dropped this line of argument.*
> (Barnouw, 1956: 69)

Things go downhill from there when it comes time to worship tools. Barnouw is shocked that so much time and energy are spent offering *puja* to the automobile, and then the tools in the laboratory, that he once again accosts his friend. Ghodme again insists that he participates willingly in religious rituals in order to preserve family harmony, but the two men clearly diverge: Barnouw cannot conceive of what he views as a premodern religion coexisting with modern science.

Mysticism

North Americans seem to have been interested in India's so-called mysticism in this period[11]. Perceptions of the mystical Indian were fuelled in 1942 with the publication of *The Wisdom of China and India*, compiled and edited by the well-known public authority on eastern religions Lin Yutang. He writes in the introduction that:

> *[n]ot until we see the richness of the Hindu mind and its essential spirituality can we understand India or hope to share with it the freedom and equality of peoples which we in some lame and halting fashion are trying to create out of this morally and politically chaotic world.* (Lin, 1942: 3)

His introductory chapter to Indian writings is entitled 'Indian Piety', and begins:

> *India is a land and a people intoxicated with God. This is the impression of anyone who reads through the Hymns from the* Rigveda, *and follows through the* Upanishads *to the arrival of Buddha in 563 B.C. The Hindu preoccupation with questions of the world soul and the individual soul is so intense that at times it must seem oppressive to a less spiritual people. I doubt there is a nation on earth that equals the Hindus in religious emotional intensity except the Jews.* (Lin, 1942: 11)

North Americans' conceptions of India as spiritual were also fortified by the publication of *Autobiography of a Yogi* in 1946 by Paramhansa Yogananda (1893–1952), who had emigrated to the U.S.A. in 1920 and eventually settled in southern California, where he established a centre in Encinitas (on the coast between Los Angeles and San Diego) in 1937. Yogananda and his book, which has sold over a million copies and has been translated into nineteen languages, were widely reported in the popular press, including *Time* and *Newsweek*, and both publications didn't quite know what to make of it. The anonymous reviewer for *Newsweek* was the most sanguine in his/her description, writing that "it is a fascinating and clearly annotated study of a religious way of life, ingenuously described in the lush style of the Orient" (unattributed, 1947a: 76). But *Time*'s anonymous reviewer could hardly contain him-/herself. Entitling the review 'Here comes the Yogiman', this person wrote the entire review in a ridiculing tone:

> *"Sometimes – usually when the bills rolled in," muses Anchorite Yogananda (who is now a rather stout, smiling gentleman), "I thought longingly of the simple peace of India." But he looks forward with unruffled demeanour to the "enigmatic Atomic Age." Yogananda is thought by other swamis to be too successful, but, seated before the sweet-toned organ of his San Diego church, he himself believes that in California he has effected not merely a meeting between East and West, but also an "Eternal Anchorage."* (unattributed, 1947b: 112)

Textbooks

Other glimpses into American attitudes toward India during this period can be had from some of the 'History of World Civilizations' textbooks used at the time. Many of these consider India only with regard to the British Empire, but some take it seriously as a place and complex of cultures in its own right. Most offer fairly straightforward histories, but when the discussions turn to religion their biases show pretty strongly. Some authors emphasise the "otherworldly" aspects of Hinduism in particular and India in general, which prevented people from becoming citizens as in the West, ie productive members of a society and polity[12]. One author wrote in a book published in 1941:

> *... such a feeling* [of "a profound world weariness"] *moved men to pursue as the ideal a life of inaction. By accepting misery as the basis for the quest for spiritual release, Indian culture became anchored in social conserva- tism. If, on the one hand, the problem set by the disintegration of primitive custom under the influence of urban culture was solved socially by a rigidity – caste – justified in religious terms, on the other hand, it was solved emotionally and intellectually by a compensation for rigidity – for such indeed was the release set as the goal of life by Indian religious teachers and philosophers. To seek release by meditation did not disturb the social order; to enjoy its achievement by loss of identity was to conform to the basic social principle of Indian culture, namely, the individual standing alone in nothing.* (Turner, 1941: 404) [emphasis in original]

The final portion in this quotation – concerning Indians as individuals all alone – is rather ironic from this author writing from the vantage point of a bourgeois capitalist culture. For this writer, Hinduism stultifies.

For other authors, Hinduism prevented India from modernising (in a western manner), as in this excerpt from *Civilization Past and Present*, published in 1954:

> *It has been natural for the Hindu to regard our physical world and its pains and limitations as evils from which to escape – a view certainly strengthened by the unhappy political and economic features of so much of India's history. Again, because the Hindus believe in the social and religious necessity of a caste system, their unique theory of society has endured for three thousand years and has kept India's social life fixed ...* (Wallbank and Taylor, 1954: 321)

Perhaps the most revealing discussion comes from *A History of Civilization* (1955), in which the authors focus on their perception of Hinduism as "other-worldly". Their longest consideration of India occurs in the first volume of the two-volume text and concludes thus:

> *The religious thought of India has left a residue of greater other-worldliness, of greater emphasis on a mystical subduing of the flesh, on a revulsion from struggle for wealth, satisfaction of the common human appetites, worldly place and power, than has Christianity or Islam. In the practice of Indian*

life even before the Europeans came to India, there was plenty of violence, plenty of greed, cruelty, and self-indulgence. Except as superstition and tabu and ritual, little of the higher religions of India had seeped down to the masses. To certain types of western minds, indeed, the educated classes of India have seemed to take refuge in other-worldly doctrines as a psychological defense against the worldly superiority of the West and the poverty and superstition of their own masses. But the fact remains that for three hundred years educated Indians have insisted that they feel differently about the universe and man's place in it than do we, that theirs is a higher spirituality. (Brinton, Christopher, and Wolff, 1955: 586)

This passage comes from Volume 1, *Prehistory to 1715*, but the authors' evident passion for disputing what they construe as some Indians' views of India as superior allows them to leap over the date strictures of their volumes.

Music

If most North Americans had little idea of India in the late 1940s and 1950s, they had even less of an idea of Indian music. Very few South Asian musicians travelled to the United States before World War II, although Uday Shankar, Ravi Shankar's older brother, a dancer, appeared twice in this period. Reviews of his 1933 appearances tended to be baffled, or respectful, rarely discussing much about the performances themselves[13]. Even reviews that tried to be well meaning and diligent sometimes backfired, as in this account from *News-Week* :

Contrary to expectations, instead of being assailed by a barbaric bedlam of sound, the audience hears a comparatively faint symphony of tinkling and thumping sounds. This is because Hindu music, besides using a different tonal system from ours, has little harmony as we know it, and requires that the various instruments merely join in for descriptive and rhythmic effect. (unattributed, 1933: 31)[14]

But it was not until 1955, when sarod player Ali Akbar Khan first toured the United States, that the average listener had the opportunity to hear first-rate Indian classical musicians. This, however, didn't mean the music was easily understood. The eminent classical music critic Winthrop Sargeant wrote in the *New Yorker* in 1955 of a concert by Khan and Chatur Lal warning that:

... one's first impression is apt to be that it [ie the music] *is mere exoticism. One is struck by its great differences from our own; one is lulled by its distinctive "Oriental" flavor; and one conjures up all sorts of tropical and picturesque associations, which, I am sure, never occur to those who make it or who understand it thoroughly.* (Sargeant, 1955: 113).

But the indefatigable Sargeant, unlike most critics, maintained that the listener who

25

studies the music could move beyond these impressions of the music as exotic and pass to a "second stage – an interest in abstract form" (ibid). (Sargeant means that it is possible for a westerner to learn to listen to Indian classical music as s/he listens to western European classical music; to assume that Hindustani classical music would hold up to such scrutiny was meant as a very high compliment from Sergeant's perspective). By the time Ravi Shankar made his first visit to the U.S.A. in 1956, the ground was set for the 1960s (rock music) fascination for sitars.

Recordings of classical Indian music were similarly few and far between in this period; there were occasional 78 rpm recordings available in the U.S.A., but the first LP recording was by Khan in 1955, recently re-released as part of a 2-CD set entitled *Ali Akbar Khan: Then and Now* (1995). Not long after this there were a few introductory anthologies, most prominently *Music of India* (1956), a project curated by classical violinist Yehudi Menuhin, famous for his support of Indian classical music, who also wrote the liner notes, and featuring performances by Shirish Gor, Khan, Lal, and Shankar; and *The Sounds of India: Exotic Improvisations on Indian Classical Instruments* (1958), with performances by Shankar and Lal.

Korla Pandit

Into this cultural landscape comes Korla Pandit, every bit as engaging as the brown people in the figurines described by Burns and DiBonis above: he smiles into the camera, he wears a coat and tie. He doesn't play any traditional South Asian instrument, but, rather, a Hammond organ and a piano. And he does this on television. He seems to be an ideal personification of 1950s' North American views of India and Indians, a perfect but seemingly impossible blend of the mystical and the modern, the enigmatic Hindu on a program in the most technologically advanced communications medium the world had ever known – television – playing a modern, electric instrument, the Hammond organ, along with an older instrument, the piano. Of course, Pandit helps this impression, particularly with the use of his ruby-bejewelled turban. If he is a Brahman (a Hindu caste) -as all of his biographical information claims – the turban is thus an affectation, since Hindus do not traditionally wear turbans, and the South Asians who do tend not to put jewels in them. But, historically, the vast majority of South Asian immigrants to California before 1965 were Sikhs, who do wear turbans as part of their religious beliefs, and it is probably the case that, for most Californians in the 1950s, 'Indians' wore turbans.

In keeping with his mysterious public persona, little is known about Pandit's life. I will recount, with a few extrapolations, the standard story he tells, although this is largely unverifiable. Pandit was born in New Delhi, India sometime in the 1920s. At age twelve his family emigrated to the U.S.A., and he attended the University of Chicago, beginning at the age of thirteen[15]. In 1949 he moved west to Los Angeles where he played for a time with various Latin musical groups, going by the name Juan Orlando. Later he played the organ for radio programs, including *Hollywood Holiday*, broadcast from a restaurant at Hollywood and Vine, and *Chandu, the*

26

Magician; and the early television program for children produced at KTLA in Los Angeles, *Time for Beany*. In the 1950s he also cut fourteen albums for Fantasy Records. After his television show ended and his popularity began to wane, he began his own record company, India Records, and made a few more records in the 1960s. He still performed concerts in this decade, and seemed to sell most of these albums at these concerts[16]. He died in October 1998 after enjoying a minor professional revival.

Pandit had the opportunity to master the western codes of musical exoticism while serving as the organist for *Chandu, the Magician* (beginning in 1948), an adventure program based on the eponymous 1932 film, featuring Edmund Lowe in the title role and Bela Lugosi as the villain[17]. It may be that Pandit (or, more likely, the producers and directors at KTLA) conceived the idea of the turban and jewel from the original *Chandu* movie, since a promotional poster features Lugosi wearing a turban quite like Pandit's, jewel and all, as does an advert for the *Chandu, the Magician* radio program.

Chandu, the Magician featured Chandu , the 'native' persona of the American secret agent, Frank Chandler, who had learned the ancient arts of the occult from a Hindu yogi and used the supernatural powers to combat evil-doers. The program opened each week with a loud gong heralding an announcer saying, mysteriously, "Chandu ... the Magician!" followed by, according to radio historians Buxton and Owen: "Oriental music up full" (cited in Buxton and Owen [eds], 1997).

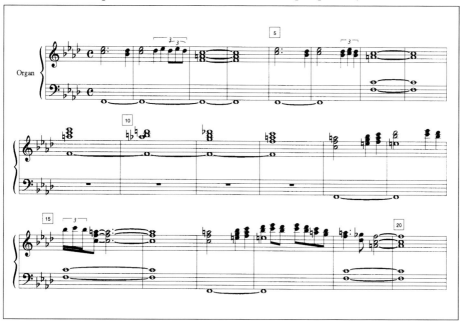

Example 1. Pandit: *Trance Dance, internal excerpt – theme from Chandu, the Magician*[18].

27

This theme music, at least in the programs I have heard (on which musicians other than Pandit were credited), is derived from Pandit's own composition, *Trance Dance*, which, like most 1950s 'eastern' exotica music, makes use of the augmented second in measure 19 (above), the sound that, more than any other musical device, signifies the Orient to western listeners.

Musical Adventure with Korla Pandit

Very few videos of Pandit's television program for KTLA, *Musical Adventure with Korla Pandit*, are available, so it is difficult to get a sense of what the show was like over the span of its nine hundred episodes. But those episodes that are extant would probably strike most contemporary viewers as the height of camp. In the few I have seen, Pandit would sometimes be alone on a set, without any furniture or props of any kind, staring into the camera, with flowing clouds in the background. Other programs featured less severe settings; many programs seem to have been filmed in a room like a living room, through which an occasional dancer or pair of dancers would flit.

Some programs would occasionally feature dancers, or little tableaux. One scene shows three Indian classical musicians – a tabla player, a sitar player, and a flute player. They are obviously playing, but the sound is Pandit's organ. The announcer says "[h]ere are the mystic strains of ancient Eastern melodies. Music as old as time … Listen … as Korla Pandit renders *Kumar*." *Kumar* is, however, an original Pandit composition which makes use of entirely familiar western musical exoticisms, and the South Asian musicians we see are actually never heard. Another excerpt depicts a very stagey Middle Eastern market scene that looks as though it could have been left over from a Hollywood movie. A woman walks through this; the camera zooms out and we're in a living room where Pandit's instruments are set up. He plays Ketèlby's *In a Persian Market*[19] while the woman does a belly-dance.

Even more interesting, though, is Pandit's presentation of self in these programs. *Musical Adventure with Korla Pandit* opened with a brief introduction by an announcer:

> … *come with us through melody to the four corners of the earth. Hear music exotic and familiar spring from the amazing hands of Korla Pandit, on a musical adventure …*

- followed by a shot of something far out of focus; it turns out to be the jewel on Pandit's turban. The camera then zooms out, and we see Pandit looking directly into it, staring, never blinking or wavering. Clouds move by in the background, then Pandit's image fades into them. This opening is about thirty seconds long. In some of these programs, which I think were recorded rather later than the one just described, Pandit's self-presentation is a little more varied; he appears more relaxed on camera, less shy. He doesn't always wear a coat and tie, but occasionally a satiny Nehru jacket.

Pandit, as is often reported about him, never spoke on any of these programs. He was an archetypal mysterious, mystical Indian on his program, communicating at the same time a kind of vulnerability. In the very brief time allotted to him in the documentary marking the 45th anniversary of KTLA, it was this point he addressed, after a discussion of the use of the clouds, which helped contribute to the construction of Pandit as a mystical Indian. As he has stated:

> ... and we used clouds, mystic clouds, and that kept the transition from the show to the commercials, and that kept the thread as you would in a concert. And that was my original concept. And of course once it started ... everyone said, 'Can he talk?" and Klaus [Landsberg, the founding station manager] said, "Never talk!" And it went on. And each day or each year it got more mysterious so they never would let me talk. In nine hundred live shows we never spoke.[20]

He now says that this silence helped transmit the universal language of music:

> I was speaking the universal language of music and that goes beyond all borders and languages. I never spoke, yet I received letters from around the world that communicated as if people knew exactly what was on my mind. I once asked a parapsychologist if it were possible that the technology that transmitted my image and music could also transmit my brain waves and he said yes, it was possible. (cited by McKenna, 1988: 8)

It wasn't just that Pandit stared into the camera; the direction of the program seemed to encourage this. Most pianists or organists are shot from the side, so that we never see them head on; they are off in their private world, communing with the Great Composers; it is not *their* genius that is supposed to be on display (though of course this is a fiction – one that performers and audiences are happy to indulge in). Even other low- or middle-brow pianists such as Liberace were filmed this way. But on *Musical Adventure with Korla Pandit*, the camera is pointed straight at him; he looks at it and looks at it. More than that, he keeps his mouth open, and it's sometimes possible to see his tongue moving a bit, almost as though he's talking to himself. The camera is aimed at him at least half the time; the other time it's on his hands. That's all– no live studio audience, no beautiful pastoral scenes accompanying the beautiful meditative music, just the occasional dancer or tableau in some programs.

Musical Adventure with Korla Pandit was a popular program. According to KTLA's retrospective, *TV Guide* named his program the 'Best Show'in Los Angeles in the early 1950s, and Pandit was also named 'Top Male Personality'. The program was also syndicated in selected markets around the country[21] and, to this day, some cities where the program aired are meccas of used Pandit LPs.

Pandit has never said why his television program ended in 1951, although he is full of vituperation about the workings of the entertainment industry in the early 1950s and the ways that it excluded him for not going along with its practices. He believes that by refusing to allow himself to be owned by a particular studio, he was drummed out of the business:

> In the early days of television, syndication companies were completely unregulated. They often refused to pay performers, but what was worse, they basically owned many performers – and that's what I balked at. They insisted on controlling my mail – everything sent to me would be theirs – and I refused to allow them to use me to rob people. We see many religious groups doing that today and I could see where things were headed then.

> I refused to do business with them so they hired Liberace instead. They approached me a second time, I again refused, and they told me I'd never work again. After that, whenever someone approached me about performing, they'd receive a phone call and suddenly lose interest. (cited in McKenna, 1988: 8)

With the end of his program, which was cancelled for unknown reasons, he was thrust into relative obscurity.

The music

In 1951, at the peak of his popularity, Pandit appeared live in Pasadena in front of an audience of some 1,950 people. The concert grossed $3,000 for one concert, which was a huge amount for the time, and indicates the degree of Pandit's following in Southern California (unattributed, 1951). This report of a live concert, the only one I have found from Pandit's heyday, describes the program as divided into six parts, "*Grand Moghul Suite*, religious music, instrumental folk songs and clasics [*sic*], orchestral sounds and interpretations, Hindustani folk songs and adaptations and *Song of India*" (ibid: npd). Fifteen years later, long after most people had forgotten him, Pandit's live concerts were little different. A program from a 1966 concert sponsored by the Los Angeles chapter of the American Theatre Organ Enthusiasts, is divided into seven parts, which appear more populist than the report of this earlier live concert. This concert was entitled 'An Evening of Musical Enchantment' and began with the theme music to *Musical Adventure with Korla Pandit*, a composition by Pandit entitled the *Magnetic Theme*, which he composed to open and close the program.

I

The Magnetic Theme

Overture "The Universal Language of Music" Opus I
Music of the Exotic East
Ragas Tallas and Talas
Flutes and Drums of India

II

The Academy of Motion Picture Themes
The Sound of Music   *Never On Sunday*
Climb Every Mountain   *Moon River*
Shadow of Your Smile Tarra's [sic] *Theme*
Smile

III

The International Interpretor [sic] of Music
A journey aboard the magic carpet of sound
Favorites from many lands Classical
Pop Rhythmic Orchestral

NEW SOUNDS IN MUSIC

Composer's Corner

No Love Is Lost   *The Banjello*
Rose of Descanso   *Once Again*
English Music Hall
French Trio Theatre

COMMAND PERFORMANCE

"A Treasure Chest of Musical Gems"
Encores and Requests Hits
Favorites of yours and mine, played on the heartstrings
of time

To Be Announced
"Your Wish is the Artist's Command"

Song of India

Theme   Finale

Judging by this program, and his recordings, most of Pandit's repertoire consisted of standards: show tunes, tunes from Hollywood musicals, other popular songs of the time. He wrote (or at least registered with Broadcast Music, Inc., or BMI) nearly thirty compositions, but as far as I can tell, none of these have entered any other musicians' repertoire. Still, this repertoire of standards includes most of the tunes usually considered as 'exotica', in the style of music that emerged in the 1950s. The "Exotica Standards" pages on the Internet (http://www.netrail.net/~bbigelow/stand-ard.htm), the most extensive treatment of this music in any medium to date[22], lists a number of exotica tunes organised by type. Pandit is only briefly mentioned, but he recorded works that would fit almost every one of these categories[23]:

  - The Hawaiian number: *Lovely Hula Hands*

- The Near Eastern number: *Misirilou, In a Persian Market*

- The Jungle number – *Moon of Manakoora*

- The Brazilian number: *Tico Tico*

- The Latin number: *Perfidia*

- The European cover song: *Autumn Leaves*

- The Foreign film theme: *Never on Sunday*

- The American film theme: *Moonglow, Exodus*

- The Sea song: *Red Sails in the Sunset, Harbor Lights*

- The Lecuona Song[24]: *The Breeze and I, Taboo*

- The Mancini Number: *Moon River*

Even though these were standards, Pandit seemed to think of the 'exotic' pieces as having real links to the peoples they were supposed to be from, or representing. Pandit says that he:

> ... *played music from every country, but the secret was: every number I played, I played it in a way that the people of that country would claim it as their own. I didn't do a European's version of a Hindi number, or a Chinese version of a French number, but I tried to capture the true feeling of every song I played so that people would recognize it as their* own *music. This was why I was able to transcend the differences of religion, race, etc., and have an audience that was a cross-section of the world.* (Pandit, 1994: 116) [emphasis in original]

The way he accomplished this was to stay away from music and sounds that most of his viewers would have found to be off-putting; instead, he cultivated musical exoticisms well within contemporary North American norms. The *Magnetic Theme*, for example, begins with a virtual catalogue of musical orientalisms[25], from near east to far east; it is mysterious, portentous; and it doesn't seem to have a meter (at least initially, in the introductory section):

Example 2. Pandit: *Magnetic Theme, opening.*

After the opening leap, the melody of the *Magnetic Theme* starts with a stepwise, upward movement from the tonic to the dominant, as if it must outline the building blocks of western tonal music before it can make a foray into the nether regions of musical otherness. In the music following the above excerpt, ornaments abound, as do the obligatory augmented seconds, followed immediately by a pentatonic passage, which is harmonised in parallel fourths. The rhythm starts, and we reach the *Magnetic Theme* melody, which foregrounds the augmented second (in the fourth complete measure):

Example 3. Pandit: *Magnetic Theme, melody.*

In one of the episodes of *Musical Adventure with Korla Pandit*, he appeared with an Indian male dancer, credited as Bupesh Guha, but while his dancing appears to be traditional, the music played by Pandit certainly was not – it comprised *Song of India*, from Rimsky-Korsakov's opera *Sadko*[26]. *Song of India* was popular among many musicians in the 1930s and 1940s and appeared in the musical films *Song of Sheherazade* (1947) and *Drum Crazy* (1959) (also known as *The Gene Krupa Story*). Versions were also recorded by Tommy Dorsey, André Kostelantz, and others.

Example 4. (see facing page)

Pandit's recorded version (on *Music of the Exotic East*, which has been re-released on *Odyssey*, 1996) is a bit different; he takes a few liberties here and there, omits some repeats, telescopes some sections, and perhaps most interestingly, adds a few embellishments that heighten the 'oriental' effect. The excerpt in Example 4 concludes in measures 26–7 with a simple downward motion that echoes the previous few bars. Pandit's version, while similar in this respect, nonetheless concludes:

Example 5. *Song of India, phrase ending, Pandit's version*

This makes Rimsky-Korsakov's rather mild chromaticism – which nonetheless is sufficient in its slip-slidey quality to signify the "orient" to most listeners, more exotic still within western idioms.

33

Example 4. Rimsky-Korsakov: *Sadko, Song of India*[27]

Some of Pandit's musical exoticisms have a clear lineage, going back to the popular songs of the very early part of this century. A song by Amy Woodforde-Finden and Laurence Hope, entitled *The Temple Bells*, makes use of the same kind of left hand ostinato in open fifths that pervade Pandit's own excursions into these styles (as we saw in the excerpt from the *Magnetic Theme* [Example 3, above]), beginning:

Example 6. Woodforde-Finden and Hope, *The Temple Bells, piano left hand ostinato, measures 3–4.*

and moving quickly, in both hands, to:

Example 7. *The Temple Bells, piano ostinato, measures 7–8.*

One of Pandit's 'eastern' 'exotic' numbers was entitled *Kashmiri Love Song*, (originally entitled *Kashmiri Song*), another song with music written by Amy Woodforde-Finden, composed in 1902. The words of this song refer to the actual story of a memsahib during the Raj, Adele Florence Cory, who pined for the son of a raja, even though she was married to an English army officer. Given this, she could hardly write the words under her own name, so they are credited to Laurence Hope. A further obfuscatory defence was Hope's claim that these words were originally Indian, a claim not believed by many, evidently. This song become one of the most popular songs of the early 20th Century, and was recorded by Yehudi Menuhin, Rudolph Valentino, Xavier Cugat, Maggie Teyte, John McCormack, Nelson Eddy, Percy Faith and more (Farrell, 1997: 110)[28].

Ethnomusicologist Gerry Farrell notes the way that *Kashmiri Love Song* signals its 'exotic' flavour in the introductory bars, which he says, "coincidentally or otherwise,

35

Example 8. *Kashmiri Love Song (from Farrell, 1997: 108)*

is the scale of *râg Bhaivrî*, one of the most famous and popular *râg*s in Indian music and the basis of a multitude of popular and classical compositions" (Farrell, 1997: 107). More interesting, however, is that this musical exoticism never recurs in the rest of the song, serving as "an oriental tag for the song that followers, a gesture without which the Indian ambience of the song would not come through, despite the subject matter of the lyrics" (ibid: 110).

36

Below is the original poem by Hope (1868):

'Kashmiri Song'

Pale hands I loved beside the Shalimar,
Where are you now? Who lies beneath your spell!
Whom do you lead on Rapture's roadway, far,
Before you agonise them in farewell?

Oh, pale dispensers of my Joys and Pains,
Holding the doors of Heaven and Hell,
How the hot blood rushed wildly through the veins
Beneath your touch, until you waved farewell.

Pale hands, pink tipped, like Lotus buds that float
On those cool waters where we used to dwell,
I would have rather felt you round my throat
Crushing out life; than waving me farewell!

It is striking that Pandit leaves the *râg* music out entirely – his version on *Music of the Exotic East* begins with the melody itself, which begins in measure seven of the above excerpt. This might be simply because there is no need to have an introduction when there is no singer, but, since Farrell has identified this introductory music as (by design or accident) an authentic *râg*, the fact that Pandit omits it limits his ability to portray an authentic Indian.

Recent developments

Throughout the 1970s and 1980s Pandit was largely unknown to most North Americans. Although the New Age movement (by which I mean a predominantly white, middle-class interest in spirituality and religious practices of the ancient past and of other cultures) began in the 1980s, it did not notice Pandit; he slowly worked his way into it and occasionally gave lectures on spiritual topics. But in the 1990s, the revival of interest in lounge culture[29] led to a rekindled interest in Pandit and his music. There are now 'zines devoted to Lounge/Exotica/Cocktail/Space Age Bachelor Pad music, which occasionally mention Pandit; there signs that lounge (as style) is entering mainstream consciousness, with a cover story in *Esquire* (Rothenberg, 1997), reviews in the *Wall Street Journal* (McDonough, 1997), and a spate of reissues[30]; and there are an increasing number of lounge colours, fonts and graphic design elements in television and magazine ads[31]. This new interest and profitability has resulted in a reissue by Fantasy of two albums, *Music of the Exotic East* and *Latin Holiday* (on one compact disc) entitled *Odyssey* (1996); and a new album, *Exotica 2000* was released on the Sympathy for the Record Industry label in 1996. Pandit appeared as himself in that paean to all that was campy in 1950s Los Angeles show business, Tim Burton's film *Ed Wood* (1994), composing one tune, *Nautch*

Dance, for the soundtrack. This revival has led to an occasional concert appearance in major venues; and in 1995 Los Angeles' *Buzz* magazine named him as one of the hundred coolest people in the city[32].

The lounge revival has also resulted in a tribute band called Karla Pundit, whose CD *Journey to the Ancient City* (1996) pokes loving fun at Pandit. The music clearly is meant as an homage – it is serious and sincere. A comment at the end of the liner notes reads: "[a]ll music was ... performed with the greatest respect for and as a tribute to Korla Pandit, its inspiration, and is in no way mean to belittle or ridicule his musical achievements" (Kaufman, 1996). Pundit, whose real name is Lance Kaufman, does parody Pandit in some ways, mainly in his talk about the music. The liner notes to *Journey to the Ancient City*, rather than employing something resembling Pandit's rhetoric of "the universal language of music" and love, instead parody the dry, descriptive style of a scientist, or perhaps more to the point, *National Geographic*, which would have been quite at home introducing an adventure program on 1950s radio. Also, Los Angeles-based lounge revivalist Joey Sehee helped resuscitate Pandit's career in the mid–late 1990s. Sehee produced Pandit's *Exotica 2000* (1996), and performed live with Pandit. Sehee also makes short films that affectionately lampoon lounge culture, in which Pandit occasionally made a cameo. However, both Pundit and Sehee are far from the centre of mainstream popular music.

Conclusions: staged authenticities, new age and agency

Attempting to understand Pandit as a social actor embedded in a particular time and place presents some difficulties. Partly this a result of the paucity of information about him, and partly also due to the peculiar historical moment he inhabited during his popularity (at the dawn of the television age, as a South Asian when there were few in the U.S.A., and as a kind of proto-New Ager). What seems to me to be most striking about seeing his television program and the marketing of him on his LP covers is the ways in which he was packaged for a mainstream American audience. The staginess of his (self-)presentation has some resonances, I think, with some of the issues surrounding tourism, even though, of course, there were no tourists around *Musical Adventure with Korla Pandit*. The nature of the program, however – even its title – evoked ideas of travel. Viewers were beckoned to visit Pandit as though he were in India, or at least, elsewhere; the moving clouds behind him contributed to the idea of motion away, or motion toward. As mentioned earlier, the program occasionally featured sets representing far away places, and 'exotic' dancers. And in these days, television itself was a technological adventure. We must remember, too, that in the late 1940s and early 1950s, travel itself was, for most Americans, prohibitively expensive; the industry was just getting off the ground following World War Two. David Halberstam recounts the fascinating history of the development of the Holiday Inn chain in the early 1950s, which filled a gap missing until this point: affordable, reliable, family motels for the growing American tourist industry[33].

One of the earliest theoretical works on tourism, Dean MacCannell's *The Tourist* (1976) proposes the notion of "staged authenticity", that is, that local peoples stage pseudo-authentic or superficial events and projections of their culture for tourists, helps understand some of the authenticising of Pandit – the turban most visibly[34]. Klaus Landsberg's injunction to Pandit never to speak is also important; one might think perhaps that Pandit did not speak English very well, but in fact his English seems to have been good and his accent slight. But what was perhaps most exotic about Pandit was that he was an exoticised Other who did not play exotic music, but, rather, played standards which employed familiar western devices that signify the exotic. He was not simply an Indian who played Indian music; he was an Indian who played American popular music standards with an occasional tinge of musical exoticism that was no more exotic than what many American musicians were performing at the same time. Even the Latin tunes Pandit played were standards; almost all of them appear in John Storm Roberts's book that examines the influence of Latin American musics on American musics (Roberts, 1985). Pandit was an Other who played the music of the Sames, music that staged authenticity for people from other places.

MacCannell writes in a more recent book that everyone is today a modern, caught up in a game of playing the roles assigned to them by modernity: ie Westerners are tourist-consumers, non-westerners are gazees, consumed, who have learned that they can profit from this role. He argues that "at the level of economic relations, aesthetic exchange (the collecting and market of artefacts, and so on), and the sociology of interaction, there is no *real* difference between moderns and those who act the part of primitives in the universal drama of modernity" (MacCannell, 1992: 34; emphasis in original). Perhaps, but we need to take this formulation further to understand what these social actors make of these economic relations, what they do with the cultural forms in this aesthetic exchange, and how they feel about these interactions.

Drawing on MacCannell's work, I think it is nonetheless possible to muster an argument that allows some degree of agency on the part of the producers of cultural forms. Korla Pandit's viewers and listeners must have expected, even demanded, that Pandit appear to be an 'authentic' Indian to them – demands that Pandit met in some ways and not in others; he doesn't merely 'stage' his authenticity: he juggles different images and impressions of authenticity in both his dress and music. Moreover, within the music he employs some western musical codes of oriental otherness, but the pieces Pandit played, whether by himself or others, fit squarely with 20th Century musical modes of the representation of the exotic oriental.

This does not mean, however, that Pandit, his music, and his discourse weren't accomplishing anything more salutary. Pandit's discursive affiliation with Paramhansa Yogananda marks an early espousal of what we might now call New Age viewpoints; I think this embrace provides a key to understanding him, and is perhaps where his real agency lies. And so I want to conclude by discussing Pandit's use of spiritual or metaphysical language, a language far different than that used by other lounge and exotica musicians to discuss music that was quite similar.

Pandit's album *The Universal Language of Music*, volume 1 (date unknown, possibly issued in the late 1950s or early 1960s), seems to be an attempt at extending his television show in its use of an announcer. This unnamed person introduces Pandit's tune *Trance Dance* with the words: "in far-off India the voice of the tabla drum speaks with resonant rhythm ... and the message is of love"[35]. In the background Pandit is playing simulated tabla drums on his Hammond organ, a technique he used frequently, judging by the videos.

It may be that the producers and directors at KTLA manipulated Pandit and his image – not permitting him to speak, highlighting, or perhaps even insisting on, the turban, filming him staring into the camera – but Pandit clearly believes in his music and in the spiritual power of music generally. While some of Pandit's metaphysical discussions may evoke cynicism in some readers, his messages are positive and empowering:

> [w]e owe it to ourselves to take time out, to quiet down and tune in to these vibrations [connecting all things] – and everyone can do it, not just the poet or the artist. Becoming more aware will make poets and artists out of all of us. (cited by Mitchell, 1995: 47).

The 1966 program from a live concert, mentioned earlier, contains a brief biographical message, which concludes:

> From there [the University of Chicago] to fame as a television artist his path was one of romance, intrigue and mystery, highlighted by the spiritual factor which underlies his main objective – expressing through the universal language of music the golden union of East and West.

Such rhetoric isn't that far from Paramahansa Yogananda's, who also spoke of music as a "universal language" (an idea with European heritage meant to forward the notion of the universality of Western European art music); as well as the importance of the union of East and West[36].

Before embarking for the U.S.A., Yogananda told a young boy that he was going to America, which he says the boy could hardly fathom:

> "Yes!" he tells the boy. "I am going forth to discover America, like Columbus. He thought he had found India; surely there is a karmic link between those two lands!" (Yogananda, [1946] 1981: 399)

40

This union of East and West, so important to Yogananda and Pandit, is, I think, central to understanding Pandit, the son of an Indian father and a French mother who has lived most of his life in the U.S.A. It is precisely the West's seeming inability to get beyond a dichotomised view of India – a view summed by the binary 'East or West' – that Pandit was attempting to circumvent in his music and his metaphysics: 'East *and* West', or even, as Yogananda named the magazine he began in 1924 (with the advice of the great horticulturist Luther Burbank), *East-West*[37].

Yogananda also argues for the universality of spirituality, a theme that Pandit also takes up. After docking in Boston on 6th October 1920, Yogananda gave a speech to the International Congress of Religious Liberals, a speech summed by the secretary of the American Unitarian Association (which had sponsored the Congress) in the following terms:

> *In fluent English and with a forceful delivery he gave an address of a philosophical character on "The Science of Religion," which has been printed in pamphlet form for a wider distribution. Religion, he maintained, is universal and it is one. We cannot possibly universalize particular customs and conventions; but the common element in religion can be universalized, and we may ask all alike to follow and obey it* (cited in Yogananda, [1946] 1981: 407, quoting *New Pilgrimages of the Spirit*, 1921).

In this era of multiculturalism or cultural relativism – in which most people would argue for differences between peoples, not commonalities among them – such a sentiment may strike us as naive or uncomfortably idealistic. But it is the recurring theme in Pandit's interviews. The interview Pandit gave in *Incredibly Strange Music* begins with this assertion:

> *More than 40 years ago I began communicating the idea of the* Universal Language of Music ... *transcendent sound which transcends all borderlines, expressing universal love. That was always my theme, yet I never spoke it in my more than 900 live television shows – it was expressed only through the* music (Pandit, 1994: 112; emphasis and ellipsis in original).

Later he states:

> *What I'm trying to communicate through music is true love and the divine consciousness (regardless of religious belief – that doesn't matter). TV isn't real, it's just light, and in my programs I was expressing love through* sound and light vibrations – *actually, that's what* we *are. We reflect light, and that's what determines what 'color' we are.* (ibid: 113)

It may be that the producers and directors of *Musical Adventure with Korla Pandit* fulfilled, perpetuated, or even helped form stereotypes of the mystical, exotic, Indian Other in order to stage authenticity – with Pandit's participation – but it was through

41

his own interpretations and manipulations of these stereotypes that Pandit was able to assert his ideas and beliefs, in music and words, and fashion a self as an Indian in America like Yogananda, a self he inhabited until his death.

Thanks to Sherry B. Ortner, Guthrie P. Ramsey, Jasbir K. Puar and Rosalind Morris for conversations helpful in writing this chapter.

Notes

1. I will not, however, consider one of the most pervasive stereotypes about Pandit that still circulates: that he and his music were mainly popular with suburban housewives – since there is very little evidence for this from the era of Pandit's television program (save for one article in *Down Beat* entitled 'Korla Pandit and Organ Attract Femmes to Video' [Holly, 1951]). Beyond this, there are only recurring rumours retold in the Internet newsgroups and mailing lists that talk about lounge and exotica musics, and the occasional reviewer of Pandit's concerts who brings up this notion. So rather than perpetuate a stereotype that is suggestive but unverifiable, I will let it be. (There are various arguments one could make about women's and girls' attraction to African-American culture in the 1950s. Wini Breines has written extensively about this [1992, 1994 and 1997]).

2. See most importantly Jackson (1985). Also, a recent collection contains several interesting articles; see Roger Silverstone (ed) (1997).

3. With the term 'cookie-cutter' I am referring more than anything else to those houses designed by William J. Levitt for mass production. Halberstam (1993) devotes an entire chapter to these so-called Levittowns. The classic text on these is Gans (1982). See also Kelly (1993).

4. We had one prominently displayed in the centre of my front yard in suburban Lansing, Michigan in the early 1960s.

5. According to Marty Jezer, perhaps oversimplifying a bit, this is because the U.S.A. still believed in its pluralism and the notion of the melting pot (1982: 195).

6. In a recent essay, Horace Newcomb (1997) takes issue with this narrative of the homogenisation of television through the 1950s, arguing that students of 1950s television should pay attention to the range of programs available, instead of the content of individual programs. This is a good point, but Newcomb's evidence doesn't support it as it might; he doesn't examine enough programs to escape the risk of over-generalisation himself, and one of the episodes in which he finds evidence of a radical politics could be interpreted differently. *Have Gun Will Travel* from the 1959–1960 season features our San Francisco-based hero, Paladin, rescuing his hotel's Chinese houseboy from the near-slave conditions of working on the railroad. In a scene to which Newcomb attaches much import (calling it "politically challenging, even politically risky" on p. 118), Paladin lectures the assembled workers on standing up for their rights. It seems to me though that Paladin's action is more paternalistic than anything else.

   George Lipsitz (1990) writes in 'The Meaning of Memory: Family, Class, and Ethnicity in Early Network Television' that such programs featuring ethnic Americans that survived later into the 1950s were made to bolster a growing consumerist ethnic.

7. See R. J. Smith's liner notes to *Mondo Exotica* (*Ultra-Lounge v1*) (Capitol). This is reprinted in Jones (1997).

8. This chronology is from Helweg and Helweg (1990). Immigration laws continued to change after this; see Helweg and Helweg (1990) and Jensen (1988), for information on immigration laws after this period under consideration.

9. The author interviewed over a hundred people, and learned that most couldn't name as many as four Indian political leaders; most knew only a dozen or so words of Hindi.

10. *House & Garden* (1949), December: 134.

11. As we periodically are. (See, for example, Jackson [1994] – thanks go to Jeff Taylor for telling me of this fascinating book.)

12. The term "otherworldly" seems to have been a favourite used to describe Indians in this period, for it occurs frequently. Another example occurs in Chester Bowles's 'The Brown Man's Burden Analyzed', in which he writes, "For better or worse, and despite their heritage of otherworldliness, the Asian people are now in a hurry" (Bowles, 1954: 30, 32). Bowles was ambassador to India from March 1951 to October of 1952.

13. An account of Shankar's tours can be found in Farrell (1997).

14. For other reviews see 'The West Sees the Real Hindu Dance', 1933; 'Dancing that Expresses the soul of India', 1933; 'Brown Dancers', 1937; 'The Past for the Present', 1948; 'Return of Shankar', 1950; and Sargeant (1950).

15. Or so he claims. I have not been able to verify this with the University of Chicago.

16. Used Korla Pandit LPs – now collector's items – turn up frequently, autographed (leading one to suppose that they were mostly sold at concerts).

17. *Return of Chandu* (1934) presented Lugosi in the title role.

18. This transcription omits the 'percussion' parts in Pandit's version that aren't used in the *Chandu* theme music, as well as a few ornamental touches.

19. A light orchestral composition by the English composer Albert Ketèlby (1875–1959), popular in the 1920s.

20. *KTLA at 45*, archived at the Museum of Television and Radio, New York City. Klaus Landsberg is much discussed by his co-workers in the chapter on KTLA in Kisseloff (1995).

21. According to various accounts, 3–5 minute shorts of Korla Pandit playing popular songs on a Hammond were often used as fillers on commercial TV in the south.

22. While perhaps not as long as Dylan Jones's *Ultra Lounge* (1997), it is more comprehensive in terms of repertoire.

23. There are a few categories Pandit's music doesn't fill, though since I haven't been able to hear all the recordings, it may have after all. These unfilled categories are: The Classical Kitsch Song; The R & B Number; The Leroy Anderson Number; The Juan Tizol/Duke Ellington Song.

24. Ernesto Lecuona was a Cuban musician and composer of many songs well known in the U.S.

25. For more on the musical orientalisms of the far and near east, see Scott-Maxwell (1997).

26. A work completed in 1896 about Sadko, a poor minstrel who wins the heart of the Princess Voolkhova, daughter of the King of the Sea, whom he loses through the power of his music which unleashes uncontrollable natural forces.

27. The words have been omitted.

28. Recently the song has enjoyed something of a renaissance among classical musicians, and so has been recorded by tenors John Aler, Robert White, Anthony Rolfe Johnson, Benjamin Luxon, and others. (In the U.S.A., it is even possible to purchase an arrangement for four flutes.)

29. An in-depth discussion of the current revival of lounge culture is beyond the scope of this chapter. For discussions of the lounge revival, see Chocano [http://www.salon1999.com/weekly/lounge 960826.html]; Ditchburn (1997); and Morris (1995).

30. The most noticeable of these is Capitol's Ultra-Lounge series, which has nearly twenty albums out, and has its own website at http://www.ultralounge.com.

31. One effect is that the price of Pandit's albums, on sale in the U.S. (and those of other musicians in this category) have skyrocketed; I have seen Pandit's LPs advertised on the Internet for as much as $60, and one LP reseller tells me that they usually go for around $30, autographed or not.

32. The reasons for the revival of lounge at this particular historical juncture are not entirely clear, and it would take too much space to go into them here. But most commentators note the importance of the publication of *Incredibly Strange Music* (of which volume 1 was published in 1993 and volume 2, which contains an interview with Pandit, in 1994), and Joseph Lanza's *Elevator Music* in 1994, which aided the entry of these nearly-forgotten musicians into the mainstream. There are other factors that are too remote from Pandit's history to recount here; see 'The Lounge Fad' (http://www.revoltinstyle.com/october/lounge/).

33. See Halberstam (1993) chapter 12.

34. See especially pp. 96–99.

35. *Universal Language of Music*, vol. 1, India, n.d.

36. See Yogananda ([1946] 1981: 546) for his description of music as universal.

37. The name of this magazine was changed to *Self-Realization* in 1948. Yogananda's followers to this day are an active group and maintain a book store called EastWest Books that features his works, among many others.

Discography

A compilation of Korla Pandit's albums *Music of the Exotic East* (1958) and *Latin Holiday* (1959) has been released on CD, under the title of *Odyssey*, on the Fantasy label (1996). His most recent recording, *Exotica 2000*, has been released by Sympathy for the Record Industry (1996)

Karla Pundit   *Journey to the Ancient City*, Dionysus (1996)

Various Artists   *Ed Wood* (Original Soundtrack), Hollywood Records (1994)

Filmography

Ed Wood (U.S.A., Tim Burton, 1994)

Kim (U.K., Victor Saville, 1950)

KTLA at 45. Program archived at the Museum of Television and Radio, New York City

Musical Adventure with Korla Pandit. Program archived at the Museum of Television and Radio, New York City

Webography

The Exotica Standards pages: http://www.netrail.net/~bbigelow/homepage.htm

Official Korla Pandit web site: http://www.spaceformusic.com/

Capitol's Ultra Lounge series site: http://www.ultralounge.com/

Chapter Two

UTOPIAS OF THE TROPICS

The Exotic Music of Les Baxter and Yma Sumac

REBECCA LEYDON

A defining feature of American instrumental pop music of the 1950s and early 1960s is its reliance on exotic references. The extraordinary recordings of Les Baxter and Yma Sumac are among the earliest and most successful examples of the genre. These albums were crucial for establishing the essential characteristics of the widely-imitated exotica style. Sumac's *The Voice of the Xtabay* (1950) and Baxter's *Ritual of the Savage (Le Sacre du Sauvage)*[1] (1951) inaugurated a nation-wide exotica craze, subsequently propagated by lounge acts like Martin Denny and Arthur Lyman. Some of the signature musical devices of this exotic music include Latin, Cuban, and African rhythms, exotic percussion, ostinato bass patterns, rich colouristic chromaticism, and, especially, textless vocalise, jungle noises and bird calls. For the American cocktail set of the 1950s, lounge music peopled the world with exotic friends.

The exotic musical elements are consistent with the atmospheres of 1950s cocktail lounges themselves, with their tikis, pseudo-Polynesian decor, and tropical drinks like the Mai-Tai. But the true home of lounge music is the suburban recreation room, and its dissemination is closely linked with explosion of domestic hi-fi audio technology in the 1950s. Hundreds of instrumental groups imitated Les Baxter's sound on elaborately packaged LPs, produced in "Custom hi-fidelity", "Dynacoustic", "Spectra-sonic","Orthophonic" and later "Stereo Action". Exoticism thus goes hand in hand with a seemingly contradictory technophilia and these two impulses interact in complex ways.

This chapter considers exotica's pioneers, Les Baxter and Yma Sumac. I want to explore how the music of these two key figures draws upon a repertory of specific musical codes that have signalled the exotic and the primitive in western music for centuries. These codes became especially prevalent in the late Romantic and early Modernist idioms, around the turn of the century. In the first part of this chapter I discuss some of these musical devices, tracing their origins in 19th Century Orientalism, their role in the French Impressionist and Primitivist schools, and finally their resurgence in the cocktail music of the 1950s. I want to argue that 1950s exotica takes over particular characteristics of late 19th and early 20th Century European concert music once that language ceases to be of interest to 'serious' composers in the high art tradition.

The ideological functions of these venerable musical codes are reactivated in their reception by post-war American suburbanites. In the second part of the chapter I show how Baxter and Sumac each fulfil a social need in recreating aspects of a particular musical style that is newly relevant and meaningful for a large audience in the 1950s. Exotica thrives anew, I believe, partly because the experience of post-war America re-enacts certain aspects of the European experience at the turn of the century. Each of these two historical moments is characterised by profound transformations in technology and its role in domestic life, while the growth of suburbs is a conspicuous aspect of life both in post-war America and in Europe – particularly around Paris – at the turn of the century. Exotica, I claim, is intimately connected with the experience of suburbia. The exotic musics that thrive at each of these historical moments, I believe, seek to work out a particular relationship between the *urban* and the *rustic*, between the high-tech and the primitive. Indeed, exotica is a fantasy that is embodied in the notion of suburbia itself.

I. *The Call of the Xtabay*: exoticism, primitivism, orientalism

> *The Xtabay is the most elusive of all women. You seek her in your flight of desire and think her as beautiful as the morning sun touching the highest mountain peak. Her voice calls to you in every whisper of the wind. The lure of her unknown love becomes ever stronger, and a virgin who might have consumed your nights with tender caresses now seems less than the dry leaves of winter. For you follow the call of Xtabay ... though you walk alone through all you days.* (Liner notes to Yma Sumac's *The Voice of the Xtabay* [1950])

In the West, the 'exotic' and the 'primitive' are closely related qualities that have been mapped onto a monolithic non-western Other. The conspicuous Orientalism of the 19th Century, of which Edward Said has made careful study, is one manifestation of the West's ongoing tendency to project a particular set of attributes onto an exotic other. Said understands the notion of 'The Orient' as a set of representations produced within the West itself. Independent of any particularities of geography or language or culture, the Orient is a collection of knowledges of the East, which, especially in the 19th Century, came to be regarded as authoritative and 'natural'. Said argues that this fiction of the Orient is implicitly counter-posed by another fiction, 'the West'; the meaning of the Orient and the meaning of the West do not inhere in either one, but arise out of a relationship of difference between them. For Europeans, the category 'oriental' has served to define for them what the West is and is not. The purpose of the Orient is to act as a repository of the West's own repressed desires and fantasies; the Orient thus becomes a reservoir for all that must be excluded from the definition of the western self. Moreover, as Said argues, particular fictions of the Orient have been used to justify and perpetuate the power relations between the West and *real* non-Western others:

> [t]he Orient that appears in Orientalism, then, is a system of representations framed by a whole set of forces that brought the Orient into Western learning, Western consciousness, and later, Western empire ... The idea of representation is a theatrical one: the Orient is the stage on which the whole East is confined. On this stage will appear figures whose role it is to represent the larger whole from which they emanate. The Orient then seems to be, not an unlimited extension beyond the familiar European world, but rather a closed field, a theatrical stage affixed to Europe ... In the depths of this Oriental stage stands a prodigious cultural repertoire whose individual items evoke a fabulously rich world: the Sphinx, Cleopatra ... settings, in some cases names only, half-imagined, half-known; monsters, devils, heroes; terrors, pleasures, desires. To this list I would add the Seraglio with its eroticized authority, its passionate heat and its sexual violence. (Said, 1985: 202)

Like the fantasy of the Orient of the 19th Century, the exotic and the primitive are not given facts of geography or history, available out there for observation, but rather they are constructs produced by and for the West itself. It follows that exoticism in music is rarely simply a matter of disinterested 'cultural borrowing'; on the contrary, the powerful fantasies of the exotic produced within western music are purposeful and motivated in complex ways. But the situation is even more complicated than Said imagines, because a fantasised exotic Other has served not only as a decisive marker of difference, but also as a powerful figure of *identification* for the western subject. Western listeners have often allied themselves with the personae of exotica: in queer and feminist listening practices, for example, the exotic can serve to validate one's of own sense of difference. A marked aspect of much post-war American music is the way that musicians – such as John Cage, LaMonte Young, Terry Riley and Steve Reich, to name a only a few – attempted to adopt and internalise non-western perspectives, and the way these musicians appealed to exotic musics as *authoritative*[2]. Thus, while the exotic other is certainly a construct produced by the self, it must also be understood as a fiction motivated by doubts and anxieties about the self. The exotic is more than just a titillating, irrational opposite that confirms the boundaries of selfhood; at the same time, it holds out the promise of a utopian wholeness.

Within particular musical styles, especially late 19th Century opera, early 20th Century concert music, and in post-war instrumental pop; the exotic has offered to the western listener an alternative subjective position. In the 1950s, for example, the elaborate fiction of the tropical paradise functioned as an exoticised complement to American suburbia: a colourful, dangerous, mysterious, heterogeneous Other which contrasted with the safe, predictable, homogeneous and sexually repressive environment at home. Certainly in the music of Les Baxter and other post-war pop musicians, the exotic is kept at a distance, confined to its theatrical arena, but at the same time it beckons, inviting the listener to escape into a fantasy of identification. The exotic embodies deep-seated contradictions and ambivalences: it is experienced as a self-conscious escapist fantasy but it is also a 'collection of knowledges' regarded as authoritative and natural; it is set of damaging stereo-types, a dangerous perpetuation of power relations, but, at the same time, it represents an implicit criticism of post-war America's drabness and homogeneity.

II. Musical indices of the exotic: an archaeology

> *Exotica, like the Tonga Room, thrives as an environmental recreation, a musical whirlwind tour inspired by the notion that the entire non-western world – from the dynastic palaces of China to the straw-hut promenades of New Guinea – really is an assortment of devil-masks, radiant volcanoes, coral reefs, stone gods, jungle rivers, and enchanted seas compiled from fantastic travel brochures.* (Lanza, 1994: 120)

Anyone familiar with 'world' musics of any sort and with the history of western music will have the impression that European composers have been either unable or unwilling to recreate anything close to an authentic likeness of non-western musical styles. Exotic quotations in western music are notoriously inaccurate with respect to their original sources. Until recently, this was partly connected with European listeners' and musicians' lack of experience with the actual sound of non-western musics, and exotic quotation would often have be accompanied by explicit verbal or pictorial cues. In his discussion of exoticism in 19th Century Music, Carl Dahlhaus remarks:

> *[b]oth exoticism and folklorism thrive on stylistic quotations interpolated into a polyphonic setting governed by the principles of art music. At the same time they flourish on an aesthetic illusion that arises when the defining features of music, painting, and literature intermingle: without a picture to pinpoint a milieu, or a caption to suggest a country of origin, the ethnic elements inserted into a European art composition are seldom distinctive*

enough to be pinned down to a particular locale, except perhaps in the case
of certain dances. (1989: 305)

Dahlhaus traces the proliferation of Oriental subjects in opera and concert music of
the late 19th Century. The way exoticism functions within these late Romantic
works, Dahlhaus notes, marks a shift in the nature of the exotic and its specific role
within the Western musical imagination. An occasional feature of 18th Century
opera, exotic elements, such as 'Turkishisms' (especially pseudo-Janissary music)
were primarily employed for comic effect. Dahlhaus observes that:

[a]esthetic and compositional norms were broken to create comedy as
measured against the rationality of European classical music; indeed,
ethnic peculiarities as a whole were regarded as accidental deviations,
occasioned by untoward circumstances, from the inherent rationality of the
human mind. (ibid: 304).

He contrasts this kind of parodistic use of the exotic with a more serious and dignified
exoticism characteristic of later 19th Century operas, such as Verdi's *Aida* and
Delibe's *Lakmé*. The penetration of the exotic into the deeper levels of musical
structure reveals itself in the new practice of colouristic harmony, which begins to
displace functional harmony in European music around this time. In this shift from
the exotic as comedy to a more complex and empathic exotic, Dahlhaus discerns the
"declining belief in a general and uniform rationality" (ibid) and the corresponding
emergence of an identificatory impulse toward the exotic.

Dahlhaus sees exoticism as closely allied with the nationalistic folklorism which
also arose in late 19th Century music. While these two '-isms' – the representation
of one's national identity and the depiction of an exotic other – may at first appear
antithetical, they are connected inasmuch as they employ the very same compositional means. In composers' desire to create and express an ethnic identity of their
own, they tend to draw upon exactly the same musical devices that convey foreign
exotic difference in other contexts:

Nineteenth century folklorism was linked with the idea of a national style,
turning national styles into artistic species of folk music and, conversely,
folk musics into national styles in embryo... [A] folk-music tradition never
represents one nation and one nation only. Moreover, any peasant music of
local or regional origin (or flavor) which has been transferred to the urban
bourgeois milieu where national styles are concocted will, when extracted
from its evocative theatrical or literary context in an opera or a symphonic
poem, be essentially no less "exotic" than an orientalism made congenial
and familiar by being adapted to the key schemes and instrumental timbres
of European art music. (ibid)

49

Dahlhaus proceeds to enumerate the particular musical devices that recur again and again as markers for the exotic, regardless of any specific ethnic orientation:

> [t]here is no tangible difference between the double bourdon of open fifths in the Chorus of Bayadères from David's Lalla Roukh, intended to depict an Indian subject, and the ones that paint a Jewish milieu in Gounod's Le reine de Saba, a Moorish backdrop in Saint-Saën's Suite algérienne (1881), or a Russian setting in Balakirev's folk-song arrangements. Nor can we raise the obvious rejoinder that musical elements only take on a distinctive national character in context, not in isolation. After all, it is no easy matter to see a definitive distinction between the combination of double bourdon, Lydian fourth, and chromatic coloration in the Jumping Dance of Grieg's purportedly Scandinavian Nordic Dances and Folk Tunes, Op. 17 (1870), and the similar stereotype combination used as an orientalism in the dance L'Almée from Bizet's Djamileh ... In neither case can the local color be localized in purely musical terms without a scenic or linguistic tag. Regardless of the milieu being depicted, exoticism and folklorism almost invariably make do with the same technical devices: pentatonicism, the Dorian sixth and Mixolydian seventh, the raised second and augmented fourth, nonfunctional chromatic coloration, and finally bass drones, ostinatos, and pedal points as central axes. (ibid: 305–306)

It is pointless to evaluate the degree of authenticity that such music achieves, for the purpose of exotic musical devices is not to render a faithful portrayal of one or another exotic source, but rather to serve as deviations from a 'normative' European idiom[3].

Colouristic chromaticism often goes hand in hand with the exotic; a favourite orientalist device of the 19th Century is the use of scale steps altered with respect to normative diatonicism. Regarding such altered scale degrees, Susan McClary observes:

> [w]hen listening to foreign musics, the Western ear usually notices that some of the pitches cannot be justified on the basis of tonal scales. These points of difference then become crucial as marks of identification. A composer can give the impression of exotic music – to peers, at least – by salting the score liberally with these fetishized pitches. To a musician whose native music is thus being imitated, for whom such pitches ordinarily operate within a cohesive network of relationships, the result is nonsense; but to the European listener, the imitation may sound even more "authentic" than the original, for it delivers a concentrated image of "difference," purged of all those elements that might have been perceived neither as intelligible nor as satisfyingly exotic. (1994: 54)

These "fetishized pitches" – the lowered seventh scale degree, the raised fourth, lowered second, and the altered sixth – are hallmarks of exoticism in the 19th Century, and they resurface in the popular exotica of the 1950s. McClary argues that this pitch-bending serves a utopian function: it reveals a teeming exterior world beyond the rigid perimeters of the rational tonal order. Literally speaking, altered pitches move into the cracks between fixed, equal-tempered diatonic scale-degrees and as such they allude to the presence of the entire pitch continuum. Pitch-bending can thus serve as a metaphor for excess and abundance, among other things, and it offers the listener an experience of utopian plenitude. At the same time, however, these symbols of license and excess also serve to perpetuate the idea of the exotic as essentially irrational and maladjusted. In place of the logic of the tonal system, what exotic music offers is rationality's opposite, sensuality. For western listeners, the binary oppositions of functional tonality and colouristic harmony, of diatonicism and non-diatonicism, tend to map onto a network of other binaries: western/non-western, rational/sensual, male/female, mind/body, and so on.

III. Fin de siècle exoticism

Dahlhaus identifies a shift in the relationship of the European subject to the exotic other that seems to be played out in late 19th Century opera, as exotic codes begin to penetrate to deeper levels of musical structure. Arguably, exoticism was one of the primary means by which functional tonality was dismantled at the turn of the century. It was that very repertory of musical devices signalling exotic difference that brought about the eventual undoing of unitary tonal identity in the late romantic idiom: colouristic harmony, chromaticism, bass drones, pentatonicism, and so on. In their 'discovery' of the musics of Indonesia, Africa, and the rural areas of Eastern Europe, European composers found vindication for their own post-tonal experiments, and these exotic musics were enthusiastically mined for their unusual rhythmic and harmonic materials. But these composers tended to fixate upon the same elements that were already available within the 19th Century orientalist idiom. The works of Debussy, Ravel, Stravinsky, and other early 20th Century composers, are often saturated with these devices.

What distinguishes the new primitivist and exotic styles that inaugurate the modernist idiom from 19th Century Orientalism is not necessarily a more authentic set of musical codes, but rather the fact that these codes find their way into the structural fabric of the composition. The ostinato, for instance, is the primitivistic device par excellence; in Stravinsky's Russian ballets, each of which features an exotic scenario, the ostinato becomes a fundamental structural principle governing the form. Some new exoticist devices do emerge, however, especially as composers begin to explore percussion sounds and new orchestral timbres. A favourite Impressionistic device cultivated by French composers Claude Debussy and Maurice Ravel was the use of textless choral writing, in which singers hum or sing neutral syllables "oh", "ah", etc. Debussy's *Sirènes*, from the three orchestral *Nocturnes* (published 1900),

51

is a well-known example. In this musical portrait of the myth of the Sirens, whose enchanting song lures unwary sailors to their deaths, Debussy represents this seductive music through the use of a choir of women's voices, humming – *bouche ferme* – at first, and later singing with open mouths on the syllable "ah". In *Sirènes*, Debussy restricts the choral writing to a limited melodic range, and the voices frequently oscillate between two adjacent pitches. The effect is very hypnotic. Ravel, in his ballet *Daphnis et Chloé* (1909–12), adopts the same technique for a mixed chorus of men's and women's voices. It is significant that both these works deal with mythological subjects from antiquity. In both, the 'invisible choir' is called upon to represent a remote, mythic time and place; the wordless voice intimates a pre-rational ancient past.

In some of his later compositions Ravel becomes more deeply involved in exoticism, with his gypsy-inspired *Tzigane* (1924) and the minimalistic *Bolero* (1928). A spectacular example is his three *Chansons Madécasses* of 1926 in which Ravel sets texts of an 18th Century poet, Evariste-Désiré de Parny, who purportedly translated poems originally written in India and based on Madagascan models. The French music critic Henri Prunières, commenting upon the premiere of the work, remarked: "[i]n these Chansons Madécasses he [Parny] has left us some small tableaus of the ideal life of the natives of the Great Isle, scenes of voluptuousness, of peaceable life and sometimes war against the oppressive whites" (1926: 60 – author's translation). The texts are intended to be sympathetic with the perspective of the natives. The second song, for example, begins with the line: "Aoua! Mefiez-vous des blancs" ("beware of the whites"). But the generic nature of Ravel's exoticism erases any particularities of the specific African locale. This fact is highlighted in Prunières' review: as he listens to a piece supposedly about Madagascar, Prunières claims "one thinks of Japanese paintings," and later "one is reminded of *graves mélopées oriental*", then "of the ideal Tahiti discovered by Piérre Loti, with its couples entwined under lianas and palms" (ibid). The piano, he wrote, evokes "strange sounds of percussion instruments of exotic countries" (ibid). The music is "sensuous" and "a picture of voluptuous sloth" that "renders to a marvel the mix of indolent gravity and sensuality which characterizes the oriental soul" (ibid). Finally he admits that Ravel "worries no more than Parny of geographic exactitudes and his savages could just as well be Maoris or Arabs or Malgaches"! (ibid).

It is remarkable how accurately Prunières' review prefigures the liner-note prose that accompanies the exotic albums which began to proliferate in the 1950s. Track titles often provide a linguistic tag suggesting a particular exotic referent, but these are irrelevant from a purely musical perspective. In instrumental pop of the 1950s, as in earlier concert music, exotic locales are musically interchangeable. If the diversity of place-names serves any purpose, it is to represent a kind of luxurious surplus, as listeners, are invited to consume what is advertised as an array of differentiated objects. We get this sense of a teeming world of musical possibilities in the liner notes to Baxter's 1955 album *Tamboo!* which read as follows:

> *Tamboo is the Haitian Creole word for drums ... and to the ears of the outside world, Tamboo seems the very keystone of native life everywhere. For all around the globe, drumbeats sound the provocative rhythms of dance of ritual, even of communication. In the tropics especially, drums set the tempo for exciting colorful movement – and from the insistent, tantalizing percussive sounds of these exotic lands, Les Baxter has composed a thoroughly romantic album.*

> *For Les Baxter knows a thing of two about transporting people, musically, to far-off places. The spirit of the tropics, from Mozambique to Maracaibo, is in his music with its array of unusual drums, mysterious bells, strange wooden instruments – all enriched in his fanciful arrangements, with the lustrous sound of many strings.*

> *The final effect that he creates is more than simply African and Latin-American; it is grandiose, extravagant African and Latin-American. It is music for every romantic daydreamer, full of the rich lure of the tropics and its fascinating drum call – TAMBOO!*

Tamboo!'s tracks include *Rio, Havana, Tehran, Mozambique*, and *Oasis of Dakhla*, but Baxter, like Ravel, isn't especially concerned with "geographic exactitudes". All the tracks utilise the same limited set of musical devices, techniques which closely resemble those used by Ravel. Especially conspicuous is Baxter's use of the textless choir – what Mickey McGowan has dubbed "pseudo-head hunter oogum-boogum" (cited in Juno and Vale, 1993: 104). Like the wordless choruses in *Daphnis et Chloé* and *Sirènes*, Baxter's 'native chanting' serves to position the exotic other in a mythic time and place[4].

IV. Post-war American exotica

> *Taking the various native idioms and translating them into breathtakingly ear-appealing vignettes, once again Mr. Denny stimulates the jaded palate of everyday civilization with music that is pure escape.*

> *Listening to the subtle blendings of rhythms and voices both human ... and instrumental, in Afro-desia, one feels that he is being allowed a rare glimpse into other cultures ... other rooms. We become armchair travellers with our magic carpet, our hi-fi (or stereo) equipment and this album. We see and feel the searing veldt ...the moody reaches of the jungle ... a tribal initiation fete and sheer encompassing beauty.[5] (Liner notes for Martin Denny's Afrodesia [1959])*

One path by which exotic devices make their way into the pop music vocabulary may be traced though Hollywood film scores, a repertory that had essentially preserved the late Romantic idiom long after it had ceased to be of interest to composers of serious concert music. In her study of music in classical Hollywood cinema, *Strains of Utopia* (1992), Caryl Flinn explores the pervasive Romanticism of American film scores of the 1930s and 1940s. Hollywood's adaptation of late 19th Century idiom, she argues, is closely connected with film music's utopian function. In studio films such as *Gone With The Wind* (1939) and *The Adventures of Robin Hood* (1938) orchestral scores by Max Steiner and Erich Korngold serve to construct an idealised irretrievable past. The late 19th Century idiom proved to be ideally suited to this function, partly because the style had, by the 1930s, become so unremarkable: film makers could count on the fact that its codes were already thoroughly internalised by listeners, and the music could go about its reparative work on "the fragmentation and lacks inscribed upon the 'corpus' of the cinema" without drawing undue attention to itself (ibid: 45).

As film music styles infiltrated the consciousness and styles of composers living in and around Hollywood, pop music incidentally absorbed the orientalist codes that were an inherent stylistic component of that 19th Century idiom. We can suppose that Baxter came by a measure of his exoticism in this fashion. Baxter arrived in Los Angeles in the late 1930s, where he enrolled in the music program at Pepperdine College. His piano lessons had began when he was five years old, and his studies at the Detroit Conservatory had led to plans for a career as a concert pianist. Once in Los Angeles, however, Baxter redirected his musical energies to other, more lucrative kinds of music making. A talented tenor saxophonist as well as a pianist, he performed at various clubs in and around Los Angeles, working with Ellington's clarinettist Barney Bigard, with Artie Shaw, and with the Freddie Slack orchestra. Baxter was also a very good singer, and he joined Mel Torme's group the Mel-Tones in the mid-1940s. Further vocal work came when NBC Radio hired him to sing in the vocal quartet which performed the Pepsodent jingle on the Bob Hope show. There, Baxter began to do arranging and conducting for the show, and eventually took over as musical director. Soon his conducting and arranging engagements expanded to include recording sessions at Capitol Records: Baxter worked on projects with Nat King Cole (including *Mona Lisa* in 1950), Bob Eberle, Frank Sinatra, and he produced a series of dance albums for the Arthur Murray dance studios.

Baxter's own work at Capitol begins with the 1950 release of his *Music Out of the Moon*, followed by a string of some twenty albums through the 1950s. Baxter's last LP for Capitol, *Sensational !,* was recorded in 1961, after which he moved to a series of less prestigious labels: Reprise (for *Voices in Rhythm* [1962] and *The Primitive and the Passionate* [1962], GNP/Crescendo (*African Blue* [1963]), and Alshire (*Million Seller Hits*, [1964] and *Que Mango!* [1970] , both with the 101 Strings orchestra). During the 1960s, Baxter's energies were primarily taken up with writing a series of film scores for American International Pictures. Baxter proved to be very much at home in this medium, scoring some 120 films throughout his career. Among his many noteworthy projects is the score for Ed Wood's *The Bride and the Beast*

(1958)[6] and other cinematic gems, including *Beach Blanket Bingo* (1965), *Bikini Beach* (1964), *Operation Bikini* (1963), *Dr. Goldfoot and the Bikini Machine* (1965), *How to Stuff a Wild Bikini* (1965) and *The Ghost in the Invisible Bikini* (1966)[7].

But Baxter spoke disparagingly of 'movie music' and, by comparison, considered his earlier work with Capitol Records in the 1950s to be of great personal and artistic significance. Indeed, Baxter claimed in an interview before his death in 1996:

> *I write difficult music. You know Stravinsky's Petrushka? I don't know of any scores as concert like and advanced as my scores. My scores were Petrushka – Stravinsky, Ravel. Other people's scores were movie music.* (cited in Smith, 1996: nd)

When Baxter claims to have transcended movie music, he identifies the Hollywood film-score style as a bankrupt idiom. He claims that his own music surpasses this idiom in the same ways that Impressionism and Primitivism supplanted the 19th Century idiom. Stravinsky and Ravel are indeed his kindred spirits in the sense that in the work of these composers exotic musical devices are transformed into vigorous Modernist techniques. Likewise, what makes Baxter's music more than mere chinoiserie is the degree to which exotic devices permeate the fabric of his work.

Baxter felt his own work was worthy of the concert stage, and he professed an intimate knowledge of the European orchestral repertory – a claim that is certainly born out in his expertise at handling the codes of *fin de siècle* exoticism. The French language sub-title of his second album, *Ritual of the Savage – Le Sacre du Sauvage* – is, of course, an overt reference to Stravinsky's *Le Sacre du Printemps*, and one which Baxter most certainly intends in all seriousness. "I refuse to cheapen my records," proclaimed the headline for an interview with Baxter in *Downbeat* magazine in 1953. "Les hopes eventually to go into full-scale classical writing for large orchestra and has already written several smaller pieces", the *Downbeat* correspondent reveals (unattributed, 1953: 3). In the interview, Baxter positions himself firmly in the high art tradition:

> *I've never believed in cheapening my music by going according to what some people think is public taste. I think that people will respond to quality in the song and in the arrangements. ...I believe that's what the public will buy. Under my contract with Capitol, I have complete freedom to do just about anything I want in my own way. When I want thirty musicians in the orchestra, I get thirty. I don't try to make fifteen musicians sound like two each.* (ibid)

Even if his link with Stravinsky and Ravel were only a conceit on Baxter's part, it was certainly reinforced in the marketing of his albums. Liner notes to *The Sounds of Adventure*, Capitol's reissue of Baxter's greatest hits ("twenty milestone selections") in 1969, read:

[a]ctually the Exotic Movement in music can be traced back to Ravel and Bolero - this composition had Parisian audiences in a frenzy in the year 1928. But "Exotica" was not heard in a popular sense until Les Baxter embellished the basic classical ideas with his own innovations ... Because of his constant contributions to the field of music, no one can forget that Les Baxter originated the Exotic Movement, although there have been many imitators ... He spends considerable time in Mexico and South America seeking out century-old manuscripts and storing them away for future use. He is considered an expert on Latin American rhythms and melodies. However, Les does not restrict himself to any one form of music ... Travel – an adventurous search for new sounds, new music – has become a part of Les' life.

V. Baxterisms

One obvious means by which Baxter maintains his ties to European concert music is through his continued reliance upon the resources of the traditional orchestral ensemble, enriched with saxophones, an assortment of percussion, and the Impressionistic shadow chorus. Additional forces are occasionally required, such as the electric organ featured on the *Jewels of the Sea* album (1960), the dulcimer and kazoos on *Ritual of the Savage*, accordion on *African Jazz* (1958), rock instruments – especially fuzz guitar- on the late *Que Mango!*, and the theremin on his very first album for Capitol, the groundbreaking *Music Out of the Moon* (1950)[8]. *Music Out of the Moon* is Baxter's proto-exotica work[9]. Along with the theremin it features an ensemble of piano and rhythm section, one harp, one French horn, a five-voice chorus. Theremin and voices interweave in a dreamy, ethereal texture. The track *Moon Moods* foregrounds the slithering vibrato of the theremin melody against some Ellington/Tizol-inspired conga rhythms, which suggest Baxter's debt to Afro-Cuban musics. This merging of the sounds of the tropics with the frontiers of solar system is a theme to which Baxter would return to on his *Space Escapade* album (1957). Although Baxter never wrote for the theremin again after this album, it is interesting that he should turn to it amidst these first stirrings of his exotic impulse. As one of the most sophisticated electronic instruments of its day, the theremin offered something like a perfect rapprochement between the high-tech and the primitive. The theremin is played without any direct physical contact to the instrument; as such it might be understood to represent a completely unmediated type of music-making, in which the motions of the body are directly translated into musical sounds. The theremin thus serves as a wonderful symbol for the kind of technological utopia that seemed imminent in the post-war period[10].

This sort of attempt to work out a relationship between the urban and the untamed takes several forms in Baxter's music. It can be discerned, for instance, in one of Baxter's favourite topoi: the busy foreign metropolis. Even in his most remote forays into the exotic, Baxter frequently recreates familiar images of the modern city.

Musical portraits of bustling agoras and congested traffic reconstitute a fantasised image of the American inner city in Baxter's *Busy Port* from *Ritual of the Savage*, *Hong Kong Cable Car* from *Ports of Pleasure* (1957), *Acapulco* from *The Sacred Idol* (1959), *Havana* and *Rio* from *Tamboo!*. These exotic cities are sites of copious plenitude, dream cities that combine exotic mystery with all the modern conveniences.

Alternatively, Baxter depicts ghostly abandoned cities, cities in ruins, the once-bustling metropolis engulfed by encroaching natural forces, as in the ephemeral *Sunken City* from *Jewels of the Sea* (1960) and *Lost City* from *African Jazz* (1958). By far Baxter's most frequently recurring pictorial theme is the jungle. The hugely influential *Ritual of the Savage* of 1951 marks the definitive inauguration of American post-war exotica. The liner notes introduce the album as "a tone poem of the sound and struggle of the jungle". Indeed, the twelve tracks are more properly twelve movements, with cyclic themes that return in each. Each movement has a programmatic title: *Busy Port*, *Jungle River Boat*, *Love Dance*, *Stone God*. The first track, entitled *Quiet Village*, was to become the anthem of Exotica. When Martin Denny recorded the piece in 1957, it remained on top-forty charts for thirteen weeks, and launched Denny's own successful recording career. I am aware of at least thirty-eight additional covers of *Quiet Village*, including versions by Ferrante and Teicher, The Surfmen (with Paul Horn, Milt Holland, Jimmy Rowles, et al.), The Fifty Guitars of Tommy Garret, Spike Jones, and even Vincent Bell on his *Pop Goes the Electric Sitar* album (1967).

What makes *Quiet Village* such a success, I believe, is Baxter's expert handling of the time-honoured musical indices of the exotic. Page 58 shows a transcription of the beginning of Baxter's composition; I want to point out on the score a few of the venerable musical devices that Baxter employs here. The piece opens with a modally-flavoured ostinato bass pattern – loosely adapted from the pizzicato string parts of the *Omens of Spring* in Stravinsky's *Le Sacre*. Muted strings enter at measure 5, and their slithering sustained melody, voiced in parallel triads, intertwines with the rhythmically precise, percussive ostinato. The melody is rhythmically and tonally fluid, its phrase-endings blurred with "feminine" cadences[11]. The modally-inflected seventh scale degree appears at measure 25, and the passage dissolves into nonfunctional chromaticism with the string of parallel triads at measure 34. Baxter's fondness for harmonic parallelism recalls the chord 'planing' so typical of Debussy and Ravel; parallel voicing continues at measure 41, where the melody becomes tonally remote, underscored with sonorities that suggest a whole-tone collection. At the same moment, destabilising syncopations appear in the ostinato, along with the enigmatic scale-degree #4.

All the music up to measure 48 acts as a large-scale structural 'upbeat,' prolonging a pseudo-dominant harmony which resolves to the C major harmony at measure 49. Here Baxter begins a new theme, with the violins playing in unison, while the piano introduces a third, inner layer to the texture, a repetitive rhythmic figure of block

57

chords. With the particular registral deployment of melody and accompaniment in this three-voice texture, Baxter is employing a surefire technique designed to induce a specific physical response from his listeners. The three layers of the texture here are rhythmically distinct: a slow-moving bass voice, the sustained legato melody gliding along above, and, in the middle register, a rhythmically active ostinato accenting the weak beats of the metric unit[12].

Baxter's Quiet Village – *opening section*

Baxter's Quiet Village – *opening section (continued)*

This layered configuration is a signature device for Baxter's music. While closely connected with layering techniques used in big band arranging, Baxter always gives the technique a decidedly exotic twist. Consider, for example, Baxter's *Papagayo* from *Jungle Jazz* (1959) in which three registers are deployed as follows: reiterated bass notes fall on the second beat of a slow quadruple meter; a faster-moving ostinato – piano and vibraphone playing in parallel fifths – occupies the middle register; soaring above is a woman's voice singing "ooh," her melodic line heavily laden with swoops and portamento. The tonality of this tune is quite complex, with each registral layer suggesting a different tonal centre. A similar situation arises in *Safari* from *African Jazz*. Here, again, repeated bass notes fall on beat two; a rhythmically fluid melody glides along above, first played by an accordion, later repeated by English horn; inner voices – clarinets in parallel sixths – play a subtly varied ostinato figure. In each of these cases, Baxter creates sharply differentiated layers in the texture, and he places parallel voicings and unusual repetitive figures into the middle register. Inasmuch as listeners experience the various rhythmic layers of a multi-part musical texture as analogues for the movements of their own bodies, these mid-range ostinati map onto the middle of the body, the torso and hips. Baxter's exploitation of the power of this middle line to engage the moving body proves him a consummate master of exotic codes.

Ritual of the Savage is a carefully constructed symphonic poem in which separate tracks are organically conceived as part of a unified whole. Each track on the album references some theme from *Quiet Village*, the first movement. *Jungle Flower*, for example, is interwoven with the rhythms from the piano at measure 49 of *Quiet Village*; in *Jungle River Boat*, and *Stone God*, Baxter develops variations on the ostinato theme from the beginning of the first movement. Passages based on interlocking fourths and fifths – especially those formed by scale-degrees 1 and 5, and 4 and flat 7- recur throughout the album, and predominate on *Busy Port*. Baxter's principle of a musically unified 'concept album' would come to characterise his best projects for Capitol Records[13].

Baxter's *Ritual* abounds with Stravinskyisms. Indeed, references to *Petrushka* appear throughout Baxter's oeuvre; two spectacular examples are the introduction to *Spice Island Birds* from *Ports of Pleasure* and the polytonal piano arpeggios on *Amazon Falls* from *Jungle Jazz*. Baxter is a versatile composer: he is equally at home in the post-war avant-garde idiom, as his atonal explorations on *High Priest of the Aztecs* from *The Sacred Idol* (1959) demonstrate; but it is the *fin de siècle* primitivist language that Baxter most often invokes.

While Baxter's reliance upon Stravinsky's musical vocabulary is interesting from a biographical perspective, what especially intrigues me is that these musical indices of the primitive and the exotic have such relevance for Baxter and his audience in the 1950s. *Quiet Village* sparked off the exotica craze that manifested itself in a proliferation of tiki bars across the nation – even in Disneyland, where Baxter's music was piped in to the Tiki Bird Room. Ultimately, though, it is in the suburbs that exotica found its broadest base. After all, a "Quiet Village" is precisely what suburbia promises: relief from urban chaos, a quiet pastoral setting. The contradictions inherent in suburbia – the fact that the idyllic simplicity of the suburban landscape is completely dependent upon the sophisticated technology of cars, freeways, access ramps, and fully electric kitchens – are mirrored in the music itself. It comes as no surprise that the craze for exotic music exactly coincides with a proliferation of pseudo-scientific discourse about hi-fi audio equipment. This activity reaches near pathological proportions in the pages of *Downbeat* magazine, where, beginning in September 1958, each issue presents the 'Stereo News' feature, devoted to the intricacies of supertweeters, proper speaker placement, turntable rumble and wow, and so on.

I see a striking parallel here with events at the turn of the century, when exoticism and primitivism seemed to go hand-in-hand with the musical avant-garde and with an unprecedented technological revolution. Writers of this earlier period frequently remark upon the intersection of the primitive and the modern. What seems to impress them is that at the very moment when western civilization was attaining its highest stage of development, artists and musicians spontaneously began to adopt primitivist techniques. As one writer put it:

> [t]he style most perfect in its regularity, the style of highest abstraction, most strict in its exclusion of life, is peculiar to the peoples at their most primitive cultural level. A causal connection must therefore exist between primitive culture and the highest, purest regular art form. (Worringer, 1908: 3)[14]

Here the primitive provides a positive figure of identification, a source of empowerment, used to vindicate the formal techniques of modern painting. In their 'purely aesthetic' use of primitivism, many modernists perceived an advance over earlier anthropological approaches to primitive peoples. Art critics like Roger Fry and Clive Bell encouraged a non-contextual approach to primitive objects by emphasising 'significant form' and 'universal' principles of design. Such attitudes were understood as socially progressive, even anti-colonial, because they elevated primitive culture to the same status as European art. Needless to say, the Europeans retained the power to grant or withhold that status. And while the modernists often seemed eager to recognise the achievements of primitive peoples, their desire to downplay cultural context and their insistence on autonomous forms made them insensitive to the colonial interests that had motivated contact with primitive peoples in the first place. In the shift from an ethnographic to an aesthetic approach, these political motivations are erased.

In the 1950s, the interpenetrations of the primitive and the high-tech were manifested in the design of record jackets for exotica albums. Conventions of iconography were consolidated rapidly and album covers rarely departed from a single simple design. Almost invariably, the cover features (1) a beautiful woman, whose gaze frequently meets the viewer's, paired with (2) some miscellaneous primitivist icon – an African mask, some drums, palm trees, a native hut, fruit, or some such item. Martin Denny's *Quiet Village* album acted as a much imitated model: on the cover appears the lovely

61

Sandy Warner, her body draped across a bamboo structure amidst a tangle of tropical foliage. (Warner's image was so frequently found on these record jackets that she came to be called "the exotica girl".) This unvarying iconographic format – women plus primitivist icon – is a hallmark of 1950s' exotica LPs.

But the reverse sides of many of these album covers present a very different set of images. Typically one finds there a wealth of information about condenser microphones, the electroplating and stamping process, frequency range, the Ampex model 300 tape recorder, acoustical distortion, groove dimension, and the optimum radius of curvature of the playback stylus. The back of the jacket is dominated by text, often accompanied by schematic diagrams, for instance of the Hertz scale. Among the most spectacular examples of this iconography are the elaborate gatefold LPs in the 'Phase Four Stereo' series, produced by London Records. Each album in the series features the usual 'winsome miss' on the cover, while the interior folios provide a meticulous and lengthy technical essay on minute details of the recording process.

Equally spectacular is Capital Records' special compilation *Full Dimensional Sound: A Study in High Fidelity* (1957?) which includes Baxter's *Quiet Village* as one of its tracks. The album is intended for the demonstration and evaluation of hi-fi equipment, and contains both popular and classical selections. An accompanying booklet features an essay on 'Fidelity and Illusion' by *High Fidelity's* editor Charles Fowler. The booklet begins:

> *Art and science are rarely as closely wedded as in the making of a record. Ever since the invention of the phonograph more than seventy-five years ago, engineers have been steadily increasing the beauty of recorded sound, providing us, in our living rooms, with an almost incredible wealth of musical enjoyment.*
>
> *Much of this immense achievement has taken place quite recently, and is reflected today in a rapidly awakening public interest in the latest equipment and techniques of sound reproduction. At the forefront of this interest stand the high fidelity enthusiasts, the audiophiles who find special delight in this marvellous combination of scientific skills with music's expressive power.*
>
> *This album has been designed for them. The record is the finest that can be made, for it is intended to be played on quality equipment. It meets the growing demand of high fidelity enthusiasts for a convenient means of demonstrating to themselves and to others the full range and capabilities of their sound reproducing systems.*

Helpful listening tips are provided for each of the fourteen tracks. Suggestions for Baxter's *Quiet Village* are as follows:

> *This is a good bass test track. In spite of the sweeping effect on the entry of*

the highs, balance is maintained throughout with a nice dominance to the
beating rhythm. The piano enters and still the overall level is held, for the
dynamic range is not broad. The orchestra sounds much larger than it is.
There are only nine strings – exotically colored by mutes – plus one bass,
harp, piano and two percussion.

Like the modernists who insisted that primitivist devices were purely formal, rather than representational, these kinds of liner notes utterly disavow the actual content of the albums. While jungle music came blaring over the hi-fi, liner notes persuaded the audiophile to concentrate on the quantifiable, non-representational properties of the sounds per se. One of the reasons this music language was so enduring probably has to do with the way its exotic codes were so often concealed beneath a formalist discourse, where they continued to operate in a covert manner.

VI. Yma Sumac and authenticity

In contrast to Baxter's instrumental music, it is almost unthinkable that any of Yma Sumac's albums could be subjected to a purely technical formalist reading. Baxter's music could lend itself to the techospeak of hi-fi enthusiasts, partly because his exotic references are ultimately non-specific. Baxter delivered credible exoticism, with great conviction, yet without any ethnic specificity whatsoever; something Martin Denny was also able to pull off in the later 1950s and early 1960s. Denny's work is really the chamber-music counterpart to Baxter's large-ensemble idiom: together they represent a subgenera of exotica that might be called 'pan-exotic'. This pan-exoticism should be distinguished from, on one hand, the 'pseudo-exotic' style of, for example, Hugo Winterhalter or Bert Kaempfert – a style that seems perpetually self-conscious of its own clichés[15] – and, on the other hand, the vivid realism of Yma Sumac, Korla Pandit, Sondi Sodsai, and other 'genuine' articles.

Unlike the formalism often connected with Baxter's music, in which representational aspects of the exotic are down-played for the benefit of the audiophile, Sumac's albums deliberately foreground the network of vivid images and associations inherent in the notion of the exotic. At least in terms of her marketing to American audiences, Yma Sumac was the real thing – marketed as an Incan Princess, no less! – and front and centre is the specific 'ethnicity' of the performer herself. Her album covers depict, not a generic exotica girl, but the singular persona of Yma Sumac. Singing both in Spanish and in her native Peruvian language Jivaro, Sumac claims to deliver an uncorrupted native musical idiom. Born Zoila Augusta Emperatriz Chivarri del Castillo in a small village in Peru, Sumac took her mother's name as her stage name when she began performing in the 1940s. Liner notes to the Coral Label recording *Presenting Yma Sumac* (1952), a compilation of early recordings made in Argentina in the 1940s, claim that she is directly descended, on her mother's side, from Atahualpa, the last of the Incan kings. The notes also say that she is "revered by her mountain people as a spiritual leader as well as a princess". Official

63

information on Sumac's biography is sketchy and impossible to verify, but her carefully-constructed stage persona is filled out with romantic stories of her youth in a remote mountain village. Liner notes from her first album for Capitol in 1950, *The Voice of the Xtabay* (henceforth referred to as *Xtabay*) describe her vocal talents in supernatural terms and provide her with a fantastical life history:

> *Small wonder that in the mysterious land of the Incas, Yma assumed an almost deified position as "the bird who became a woman," and "the voice of the earthquake." No one in her native village of Ichocan, 16,000 feet high in the Andes of Peru, had ever heard such a voice in human form when this "chosen maiden" sang at their annual festivals to the sun.*

> *No one in the big cities below had heard such a voice either. So when exciting rumours of her rare talent and beauty reached officials of the Peruvian government, they arranged to bring Yma Sumac down to the coastlands ... a decision that almost caused an uprising among some thirty thousand Indians over the loss of their revered ritual singer.*

On *Xtabay* Sumac sings a number of 'traditional' songs from her Incan heritage, including the hymn *Taita Inty*, that, the notes say, "dates back to 1000 B.C". The songs evoke a mythical paradise lost, of which Sumac herself is a surviving artefact.

Paradoxically, the more Sumac's authenticity is reinforced, the more she seems to relinquish her discursive authority. Sumac's 'voice' – her real subjective presence as a performer – is somehow eerily absent. Even her recent 'interview' in Re/Search's *Incredibly Strange Music* consists of a pre-written text supplied by her manager Alan Eichler. Unlike the interviews with other exotica originals Juan Garcia Esquivel and Martin Denny in the Re/Search volumes, Sumac provides a precomposed monologue, in which she sometimes even refers to herself in the third person (eg "[a] lot of famous rock'n'roll people – I never remember their names – have come to see Yma Sumac" [ibid: 46]).

This absence of agency is a necessary condition of her authenticity, and it characterises her persona from the outset. She is "discovered" in a remote mountain village by Carlos Moisés Vivanco, composer and "world's foremost authority on ancient Inca themes" – according to liner notes on *Xtabay*. It is Vivanco, the expert (actually Sumac's husband for a time), who brings her to the attention of the civilised world. Meanwhile, Sumac's own incredible singing voice is stripped of its objective authority, partly because it emanates from a feminine body is which is obliged to contain it. With each effort that goes into the careful construction of her stage persona, Sumac forfeits her right to represent herself; her albums must therefore be supplemented by a body of authoritative critical appraisal. The rear-cover text of *Xtabay* declares:

> *When you play the records in this album, prepare for an exotic musical*

experience – a voyage of discovery into a new land of sound. For you have never in your life heard anyone sing like Yma Sumac.

"There is no voice like it in the world of music today," says Glenn Dillard Gunn of the Washington-Times-Herald. "It has greater range than any female voice of concert or opera. It soars into the acoustic stratosphere, or it plumbs sub-contralto depths of pitch with equal ease. Such voices happen only once in a generation."

In Buenos Aires, La Prensa said, "The greatest musical revelation of our times."

In Rio de Janeiro, O Globo commented, "Yma Sumac dominates the artistic sensibilities of all Brazil with her magic and divine voice . . . the problems of our modern world are forgotten through the magnetism of this fabulous gift which comes to us, directly descended from Atahualpa, last of the Inca kings."

And in Los Angeles, Albert Goldberg of the Times said: " . . .to hear her weave that fantastic counterpoint over the complex rhythms of her accompaniment is at last to experience something new in music."

Everywhere the story has been the same. Yma Sumac is more than a great singer; she is a major discovery in the word of music; an unbelievable creation of nature in voice, face, and form.

The authenticity of the music, then, is closely tied to Sumac's status as a "creation of nature".

In the end, however, it proved impossible to resist deconstructing Sumac's "authentic" persona. A widely-circulated story has it that Sumac was actually a native of Brooklyn, and that her real name was Amy Camus[16]. This story, perpetrated by the notorious Walter Winchell in his syndicated column as early as 1951, has persisted precisely because Sumac's exotic persona is so flawlessly constructed in terms of her handling of the representational codes. Perhaps it is just a bit too heavy-handed; and, unlike instrumental music which can be subjected to a formalist reading, Sumac's vocal music cannot be so easily detached from its network of extra-musical associations.

Sumac's voice was celebrated for its freakishly vast range. Liner notes on *Xtabay* read:

... for how is it possible for one voice to plumb the lowest depths of the vocal range with moving timbre and richness ... then, in a few dazzling steps, to "soar into the acoustic stratosphere" with thrilling clarity and brilliance?

65

> *Yet it is all one voice – one alluring young woman – with over four octaves at her command!*

Her range has been variously reported as anywhere from four octaves (in liner notes to her albums), to five octaves (Juno and Vale in *Incredibly Strange Music Volume 2*), to a preposterous eight octaves (the authors at www.planetout.com). My own empirical listening has revealed that Sumac only rarely moves outside of a three octave range, from the F below middle C to the F three octaves higher. She reaches a low E flat on the track *Taita Inty* on *Xtabay*, and gets out a low D as the last note of *Jungla* on *Mambo!* (1955) On *Ataypura* on *Xtabay* she nearly gets the high F# during her extended improvisation over the chorus of jungle noises; and on the remarkable *Chuncho* on *Inca Taqui* (1951), Sumac emits a sustained noise -if not an actual tone – somewhere in the vicinity of the A above this. Nevertheless her vocal range is indeed exceptional; it is shown to especially good effect on *Jungla*. The track begins with sequentially rising statements of a melodic figure; transpositions of the melody – a six-note figure that outlines a perfect fourth – gradually climb from the bottom of her low register all the way up through her three glorious octaves, while Billy May's orchestral accompaniment correspondingly builds in intensity to the apex of the tune. But Sumac's most striking vocal acrobatics are her unusual effects of timbre – her growling, her vibrato, her gasps and groans. A good illustration of her colouristic resources is *Goomba Boomba* on *Mambo!* The piece opens with a four-measure ground-bass ostinato that is repeated four times by the orchestra alone. Each repetition adds a new layer to the accompaniment, before Sumac finally enters with a deep, chest-voiced "Huy!!" She then sings the first strains of her melody in an unearthly rasping *sprechstimme*, punctuated by husky laughter and breathy gasps. Sumac juxtaposes this material with her sparkling *coloratura*, and she switches back and forth between the two with remarkable agility.

Baxter assisted Vivanco in the production of Sumac's first album for Capitol in 1950. *Xtabay* was an international success, and was released in a variety of formats: a 10-inch LP, as well as a pair of 78s, and a boxed set of 45 rpm records. In 1956 Capitol reissued the album as a 12-inch LP. Its sleeve notes emphasise that

> *Much of the credit goes to him* [Baxter] *for his capacity to retain the essential spirit and character of the native music in all its thrilling authenticity. In collaboration with Maestro Vivanco he has woven fragments of traditional themes, native chants and forbidden ritual into tapestries of sound that are as fresh, new and exciting as the beautiful Yma Sumac who sings them.*

Having recently completed *Music Out of the Moon*, Baxter no doubt approached *Xtabay* with the sound of theremin still fresh in his ears; each of his two original compositions on the album – *Xtabay* (subtitled 'Lure of the Unknown Love') and *Accla Taqui* ('Chant of the Chosen Maidens') – exploits Sumac's status as a kind of human theremin. Baxter's characteristic exotic devices are conspicuous on *Xtabay*:

Sumac begins the piece with a repeating melodic figure, scale degrees #4 – 5 -flat 7 – 6 -#4, dwelling upon all the "fetishized pitches" and skirting the diatonic scale-degree 5. *Xtabay* abounds with familiar Impressionistic devices of harmony and orchestration, especially chord planing, and the ethereal writing for the muted strings. Baxter's writing for the harp and flutes and the pentatonicism on *Accla Taqui* similarly invokes a *fin de siècle* exoticism. Sumac does sometimes work with a more specifically Latin-American idiom in Vivanco's compositions – for instance, *Monos* and *Ataypura* – but even these songs draw heavily upon Impressionistic techniques of harmony and orchestration[17].

Sumac's albums, then, share a basic exoticist musical language with Baxter's. But in contrast to Baxter, Sumac puts a great deal of effort into constructing an exotic that is not only tantalising and mysterious, but also decidedly dangerous. For example, her photographs on her album covers do not resort to the appetising docility of Sandy Warner; on the contrary, Sumac is a fearsome sight. The cover of *Legend of the Jivaro* (1957) shows her in the throws of some supernatural sortilege, crouched over a steaming cauldron and looking upward with a diabolical gaze. On *Legend of the Sun Virgin* (1951) she points her impervious, smouldering gaze directly at the viewer, while on *Xtabay*, where she sports an enigmatic metallic headdress, she seems powerfully entranced by something somewhere off behind our right shoulder. Sumac's exotic arena can be a place of erotic violence; liner notes to *Legend of the Sun Virgin*, for example, play up the cruelty of primitive ritual:

> *The ancient Incas worshipped the Sun God and the Moon Goddess Quilla. Every year the most beautiful maidens were selected to become Virgins of the Sun, serving in the convent which rivalled in splendor the Inca's palace. The sacred flame was entrusted to the virgins and if by neglect it was allowed to go out, it was believed that some terrible disaster would follow. The Virgin assumed holy vows which bound her to the temple service. Should she prove unfaithful to her vows, she was buried alive, while her lover was strangled, and the village which he belonged razed so that no stone stood upon another.*

This notion of primitive rituals and superstitions that plays such an important role in much of Sumac's music points toward another aspect of *fin de siècle* primitivism. At the same time that primitivist devices were regarded as a 'purely aesthetic' set of formal techniques by some writers at the turn of the century, the same devices could be utilised for their specific representational power. Another purpose of the exotic at the turn of the century seems to have been to serve an identificatory function for artists increasingly alienated by technology. Many of the modernists harboured fears of dehumanisation, of the loss of autonomy that accompanied the increasing mechanisation encountered in everyday life. For them, the image of the primitive could thus serve as a symbol for a repetitive machine-like existence[18]. Now the primitive is conceived as mindless figure, automatically playing a part in mysterious rituals without rational understanding or control over his environment. The condi-

67

tion of the modern artist, as a cog in the machinery of the modern world, was thus sometimes imagined as analogous to that of the inhabitants of a primeval pre-technological landscape. For example, Hermann Bahr, a champion of Expressionism, wrote in 1916:

> [p]rimeval man sees lines, circles, squares, and he sees then all flat, and he does so owing to the inner need of turning from the threat of nature away from himself... As primitive man, driven by fear of nature, sought refuge within himself, so we too have to adopt flight from 'civilization' which is out to devour our souls. ([trans. T. Gribble] cited in Harrison and Woods [eds] 1992: 118)

I believe exotica enthusiasts of the 1950s shared with modernists like Bahr a sense of identification with a technologically backward primitive, a figure at the mercy of incomprehensible natural forces. As a kind of automaton, mindlessly playing a part in pagan rituals, this exotic other resonates with the cold-war anxieties of Americans at a time when all aspects of technology advanced at a bewildering pace, be it hi-fi or convenience foods or atomic energy.

To make matters worse, Americans were informed by their contemporary social critics that they were, in fact, routinely subjected to mind-control in the form of subliminal advertising. Vance Packard's *The Hidden Persuaders* was a best seller in 1957. The book begins with the startling claim that:

> Large-scale efforts are being made, often with impressive results, to channel our unthinking habits, our purchasing decisions, and our thought processes by the use of insights gleaned from psychiatry and the social sciences. Typically these efforts take place beneath our level of awareness; so that the appeals which move us are often, in a sense, "hidden" .... it seems to represent regress rather than progress for man in his long struggle to become a rational and self-guiding being ... Gone are the days when scientists confined themselves to classifying manic depressives, fitting round pegs in round holes, or studying the artefacts and mating habits of Solomon Islanders. These new experts, with training of varying thoroughness, typically refer to themselves as 'motivation analysts' or 'motivation researchers'. (1957: 3)

Packard amasses anecdotal evidence confirming the vulnerability of ordinary Americans at the mercy of cunning and unscrupulous motivational researchers. Beginning with pseudo-Freudian premises, Packard urges his American readers to picture themselves as pre-rational beings, despite their space-age pretensions. Throughout the book, an image of the American middle class emerges in which the ordinary consumer takes on attributes of the uncomprehending primitive, duped by the technologically superior marketing-strategist. Packard's popularisation of the notion of a modern American id closely parallels the growing interest in exotica in the 1950s, and the appeal of, for instance, Sumac's music is probably partly connected with its capacity to represent 'the primitive within'. It offered a vivid means of picturing the tumultuous primeval desires that allegedly lurked beneath the rational conscious minds of ordinary suburbanites.

VII. The decline of the exotic

Yma Sumac's celebrity was relatively short-lived, at least in the U.S.A. After her appearance in a few films – Paramount's *The Secret of the Incas* (1954) and *Omar Khayyam* (1957) – and a period of performing in Eastern Europe and Russia in the 1960s, Sumac withdrew from performing for many years. She attempted, briefly, to reach a rock audience with her album *Miracles* on London Records in 1972, but the album was deleted after its first pressing, apparently at the insistence of Sumac who disliked the cover design (which departs markedly from the usual conventions of exotica iconography: it is a peculiar drawing of a giant electric guitar floating down a canal towards a poorly executed likeness of Yma's torso coming over the horizon). Two years prior to this, Baxter's *Que Mango!* had been released: a collection of compositions and arrangements for the 101 Strings orchestra. Here Baxter attempts to blend his signature devices of exotica with a 'neo-anglo contemporary' sound. *Tropicando*, for example, recycles melodic material from *Cuchibamba* off *Tamboo!* along with the ostinato figure from *Simba* – here played by fuzz guitar – and a bass line adapted from the opening of *Quiet Village* (essentially the same ostinato figure but with its elements rotated into different registers). While this track proves that Baxter's language was remarkably adaptable to the new easy-listening context, the album itself was destined for department-store budget bins and supermarkets. Exotica was by this time a dead language.

Conclusion

In this chapter I have tried to contextualise the work of exotica's pioneers within the orientalising traditions of the exotic. Baxter's and Sumac's music engages a rich historical practice in which the primitive and the exotic are represented through a specific set of musical devices: expanded percussion resources, textless vocalise, layered ostinati, chord-planing and colouristic chromaticism, melodic emphasis on non-diatonic scale-degrees and particular techniques of orchestration. The infusion of these musical practices into the North American popular music vocabulary coincides with the emergence of suburbia and a radical reconfiguration of the notions of urban and rural. And as suburban audiophiles reconstructed their living spaces around sophisticated futuristic technologies, they turned to a music that spoke of places and people that somehow lay beyond the reach of that technology. In their listening habits, exotica enthusiasts enacted a fantasy in which an uncorrupted exotic other is preserved. In turn, the imagined personae of exotic musical landscapes could serve as figures of identification for listeners on a number of levels. I maintain that

69

the formalistic technospeak surrounding the hi-fi culture in which exotica thrived served to disavow these embarrassingly representational aspects of the music, but that these images and fantasies of the primitive and the exotic are a central aspect of its reception.

Notes

1. The front cover of the original vinyl release includes the French language translation of its title – in bracketed, small font-size – as a sub-title.

2. See Chapter Three for discussion of Steve Reich's adoption of non-western techniques.

3. A good illustration of Dahlhaus's argument is the opera *Carmen* by the nineteenth-century French composer Georges Bizet. Indeed, the musical codes that are employed in the exoticisation of the opera's main character are precisely those indices enumerated by Dahlhaus. Carmen's signature device is nonfunctional chromatic colouration, what Susan McClary has called her "chromatic excess" (1992: 51) a device foregrounded in the sinuous chromatic melody of Carmen's famous *Habañera*. Its primary purpose in the opera is to contrast sharply with the character Don Jose's bland diatonicism, and to imply musically the gulf separating the two characters socially and psychologically.

4. McClary points out how Carmen's exoticism has been variously perceived by listeners as a faithful representation of Spanish music, as Gypsy music in particular, as authentic Arabic music, and, finally, to the ears of most Spanish audiences, as singularly French music. Thus the ethnic orientation of the music is by no means self-evident, but rather fluctuates according to the perspective of the audiences themselves. It is known that Bizet did consult some 'real' Spanish musical models for the opera: Carmen's *Habañera* , for instance, is based on the song entitled *El Arreglito* by the Spanish composer Sebastián Yradier. But, as McClary observes, Yradier himself never intended to give voice to his own Spanish ethnicity with this composition. In fact the song was meant as a characterisation of Afro-Cuban music, the 'Creole' music that Yradier encountered during his travels in Latin America. In Bizet's opera, then, the exoticism of the *Habañera* is, in a sense, already twice removed. The intended Spanish flavour of the work does not inhere in the music itself, but requires the linguistic tag, the libretto, to make the ethnic reference explicit for the listener. What makes the *Habañera* a successful piece of exoticism is not any particular Gypsy-like or Spanish quality; it is Bizet's effective employment of stock devices available in the 19th Century idiom. (See McClary, 1992).

4. A more immediate cause of the sudden popularity of the textless choir was the American Federation of Musicians recording strike in 1942. In his battle against 'canned' music, federation president James C. Petrillo had barred musicians from performing in recording studios. Because vocalists were not union members, they were frequently called upon to recreate the sustaining sound of orchestral strings.

5. Baxter's Impressionistic chorus is a widely imitated technique in 1950s' exotica, one for which Martin Denny shows a special fondness. These liner notes to Denny's *Afro-desia* closely parallel those of Baxter's *Tamboo!* in their promise of a vast world of musical possibilities.

6. Wood's extraordinary film represents a distillation of some of the emblematic themes of exoticism. When Laura and Dan get married, and Laura begins to show an unnatural interest in Dan's pet gorilla; it is revealed through hypnosis that Laura was, in fact, Queen of the Gorillas in a previous incarnation.

7. Baxter himself took on the occasional acting gig; he appears briefly in *Untamed Youth* (1957), starring Mamie Van Doren.

8. Originally released as a three disk 78rpm set in 1947 (label unknown).

9. *Music Out of the Moon* enjoyed modest but enduring success; it is purported to be the best-selling

theremin album in history. According to Joseph Lanza (1994), a devoted fan of the album was Neil Armstrong, and Lanza reports that the astronaut suggested the album be played over NASA's communication systems during his Apollo missions in the 1960s (ibid: 114).

10. See Hayward (1997) for a further account of various uses of the instrument.

11. 'Feminine cadence' is a term, now fallen out of common parlance, formerly used to denote a resolution to tonic harmony that falls on the weak part of a measure. I include this note because, while I encountered the term quite regularly as a student myself, my own undergraduate music students seem never to have heard of it; the pun in Susan McClary's book title, *Feminine Endings* is lost on them.

12. At measure 49 and following, I understand the smallest metric unit to be four half-notes, or two bars; that is, the music is really in 4/2 time despite my notated meter signature of 4/4. To get a sense of the hypermetric grouping here, try conducting this passage.

13. For instance, introductory brass fanfares tie together various tracks on *Ports of Pleasure*; and themes based on interlocking perfect fourths are woven throughout *Tamboo!*

14. Another great example is Clive Bell's *Aesthetic Hypothesis*, originally published in 1914. Bell claims that photography has rendered representational art obsolete, and therefore artists are free to focus on the 'true' subject matter of art: A significant form":

     Most people who care much about art find that of the work that moves them most the greater part is what scholars call 'primitive'. Of course, there are bad primitives [But] *as a rule primitive art is good – and here again my hypothesis* [that art has is about significant form] *is helpful – for, as a rule, it is also free from descriptive qualities. In primitive art you will find no accurate representation; you will find only significant form ... [E]ither from want of skill or want of will, primitives neither create illusions, nor make display of extravagant accomplishment, but concentrate their energies on the one thing needful – the creation of form.* (cited in Harrison and Woods [eds] 1992: 114)

15. To my ears, the archetype of the 'pseudo-exotic' style is Bert Kaempfert's album *Music of Far Away Places* (1965), particularly his irrepressibly German arrangement of *A Little Street in Singapore*, or the ear-appealing *Mambossa*, surely among the most *wunderbar* renditions of a mambo ever recorded.

16. Following her performance at the Montreal Jazz Festival in June 1997, however, I can report that Sumac does speak English with what sounds like a Peruvian accent, and also that she claimed to be "not yet 70 years old, thank God" at the time.

17. It should be emphasised that French composers are, in any case, largely responsible for the creation of a 'native' Spanish musical idiom: a whole set of 'Iberian' musical devices can be traced back through Ravel and Debussy to Bizet's *Carmen*, and this pseudo-Spanish Impressionistic style was subsequently cultivated by Latin American composers such as Villa-Lobos and Ginastera.

18. Nancy Berman's doctoral dissertation, 'Modern Primitive: Stravinsky and the Rite of Spring' (McGill University, forthcoming) addresses this issue.

Discography

A selection of Les Baxter's best known exotica material from the 1950s is collated on the double CD *The Exotic Moods of Les Baxter*, Capitol Records (1996). *Colours of Brazil* and *African Blue* have been re-released on an eponymous (single) CD, GNP Crescendo (1991). Scamp Records have also issued *Que Mango* on CD (1996) and a previously unreleased recording, *Lost Episode* (1995).

Yma Sumac's albums *The Voice of the Xtabay* and *Inca Taqui -Chants of the Incans* are collated on the (single) CD *Ymac Sumac... Voice of the Xtabay*, The Right Stuff (1996). The same label has also re-released *Fuego del Ande*, *Mambo!*, *Legend of the Sun Virgin* and *Legend of the Jivaro* on individual (eponymous) CDs (1997).

71

Chapter Three

MARTIN DENNY AND THE DEVELOPMENT OF MUSICAL EXOTICA

SHUHEI HOSOKAWA

In this chapter I raise questions about aesthetic and symbolic aspects of the production and consumption of musical exotica during the 1950s-early 1960s. Focusing on Martin Denny, a musician renowned for his lifelong commitment to the form, and the style of musical exotica his work pioneered and exemplified, I analyse the manner in which exotica and the exotic relate to tourism; the asymmetric power relations between the West and the rest of the world; and developments in sound technology during the period in question. This leads me to refute the contention that exotica is simply a naive and superficial evocation and imitation of faraway places and people. Instead, I contend that it is a complex form premised on a play of subtle sound textures which condense various (aural) stereotypes within an unobtrusive style designed to be easily consumed and appreciated.

Exotica v the vanguard

In 1973, after learning Balinese gamelan and Ghanaian drumming, the composer Steve Reich scrutinised the relationship between western and non-western music from a composer's point of view and argued that the most interesting approach to non-western music for composers is the adoption of elements of the structure and thought underlying non-western musical styles and techniques. He contrasted this to imitating the non-western *sound*, which he characterised as:

> *... the simplest and most superficial way of dealing with non-Western music since the general sound of these musics can be absorbed in a few minutes of listening without further study. Imitating the sound of non-Western music leads to 'exotic music': what used to be called 'Chinoiserie'.* (1974: 40)

Reich's engagement with non-western music coincided with a new direction in ethnomusicology which emphasised performance and learning rather than transcription and analysis. In contrast to imitative exoticism, Reich advocated a creative treatment of non-western music, which he explained in the following manner:

> *...one can create a music with one's own sound that is constructed in the light of one's knowledge of non-Western structures... This brings about the interesting situation of the non-Western influence being there in the thinking but not in the sound. This is a more genuine and interesting form of influence because while listening one is not necessarily aware of some non-Western music being imitated. Instead of imitation, the influence of non-Western music structures on the thinking of a Western composer is likely to produce something genuinely new.* (1974: 40)

Reich thus juxtaposes the "simplest and most superficial" type of musical production with "a more genuine and interesting form of influence". His works in the mid-1970s undeniably evidence an emphasis on non-western structure, rather than on non-western sounds[1].

For Reich, "non-western music is presently the single most important source of new ideas for western composers and musicians" (ibid: 38). His appraisal of non-western sound as the ultimate means for salvaging western art music is typical of the (standard) non-reciprocal aesthetic relationship between the West and the non-West, that is to say that the West can learn from the rest of world while the latter should – ideally – keep away from western contamination. Appropriations of non-western sound produce what some may dichotomise as the artwork *inspired* by non-western music, as opposed to the exotic piece *imitating* it. Both types, however, are addressed to a western audience – be it elite or mass – in concert halls or in hotel lounges. Though they may not sound the same, both presuppose western consumption. This is not to say that both are of an equal status, either aesthetically or commercially. Rather, it is my assertion that the blanket denigration of certain forms of exoticism obscures a relevant framework within which to conceive the exotic according to its own logic and the context of its production and consumption. Musical exotica, I will argue, does not imitate the non-western sound[2]. If chinoiserie sounds imitative, it is because that particular sound matches (all-too-perfectly) the western imagination and expectation of the relationship between certain sounds and their associative geographies. The question is, what kind of aesthetic transformations of 'alien' sound can conjure familiarity for western listeners? And, if this process is a part of the domestication of faraway cultures, what kind of politics lurks beneath the surface of the sound?

What is exotica?

The history of exotic music is at least as long as that of colonialism itself (Gradenwitz, 1977; Bellman (ed), 1998). Even if we limit our scope to 20th Century North

American popular music, we can easily make an extensive list of compositions, from Jelly Roll Morton's *Spanish Tinge* to Madonna's *La Isla Bonita*, from Duke Ellington's *Far East Suite* to Hank Snow's *The Rhumba Boogie*. However, such compositions are not usually categorised as exotica. Therefore, the simple evocation of the mood of distant places is insufficient to characterise a work as exotica. It is different from exotic jazz, Latin rock and other fuzzy combinations of established styles with exotic elements. The popularity of musical exotica may be better understood in the context of the North American entertainment industry that distributes and recycles ethnic and geographic stereotypes around the world.

In order to clarify this discussion, the term 'exotica' is taken here to designate the imaginary and intentional construction of non-western sound arranged and/or performed for western audiences. As the definition of 'The West' becomes increasingly problematic in an age of mass migration and the fusion of cultures, the notion of (a) 'non-western sound' may also seem antiquated. Nevertheless, there is still a certain consensus concerning *us* and *them* due to fixed ideas of geography, race and culture. Empirically, exotica is represented by such musicians as Ethel Azama, Les Baxter, Martin Denny, Russ Garcia, Arthur Lyman, Korla Pandit, Tak Shindo, Sondi Sodsai, Yma Sumac and Si Zentner. Although these musicians have worked in different contexts, they share some common traits. Signed by major labels such as Capitol or Liberty in the 1950s, they tend to be primarily recording artists/arrangers with jazz and/or film music backgrounds, or else, the exotic female singers produced by them (except Tak Shindo, who is a Japanese-American koto player, and Korla Pandit, an Indian-American Hammond organ player). To some extent, exotica can be considered a sub-set of the broader category of what was once called 'elevator music', and is now often termed 'muzak'. This broad genre and style is designed to be unobtrusive by virtue of its familiar – often deliberately clichéd – melodies, harmonies and structure; its lack of aggressive dynamic effects; its usually low playback volume; and its consequent low attention, subconscious or (even) subliminal hearing (see Gibian, 1984; Lanza, 1994). In order to explore the precise nature of the sub-set of exotica, I will now turn to a discussion of the work of Denny, whose musical production has – at least prior to its recent revival as a form of kitsch retro-chic – been critically marginalised.

Martin Denny, pianist, composer and arranger, was born in New York in 1911 and grew up in Los Angeles. In the 1930s he toured South America with a white dance ensemble, the Don Dean Orchestra, for more than four years. After his service in the U.S. Air Force during World War II, he studied piano, orchestration and composition at the Los Angeles Conservatory of Music. In 1954 he first travelled to Honolulu under contract to Don the Beachcomber's (later Duke Kahanamoku's) resort where he regularly appeared over the course of ten years. In 1955 he set up his own group and signed a contract with Liberty Records. The following year, when his quartet opened the Shell Bar in Hawaiian Village in Honolulu, a renowned tourist spot run by the industrialist Henry J. Kaiser, he discovered an audience for aural exotica. His original quartet consisted of Arthur Lyman on vibes, Augie Colon on bongos, John Kramer on bass and Denny on piano. (Lyman left to form his own group in 1957 – with his album *Taboo* subsequently selling two million copies – and was replaced by Julius Wechter). The band's reputation grew quickly and they performed in Las Vegas before recording a debut album, *Exotica*, in Honolulu, during December 1956. The LP, released in 1957, sold about 400,000 copies and resulted in Denny securing a prestigious mainland appearance later in the same year, during the Bing Crosby Golf Tournament at Pebble Beach. A single from the album, a cover of the noted Les Baxter composition *Quiet Village*, also reached Number One on the U.S. singles charts.

In the sleeve notes to his album *Ritual of the Savage* (*Le Sacre du Sauvage*) (1952), Baxter described (his original version of) *Quiet Village* in the following terms:

> *[t]he jungle grows more dense as the river boat slowly makes its way into the deep interior. A snake slithers into the water, flushing a brilliantly plumaged bird who soars into the clearing above a quiet village. Here is a musical portrait of a tropical village deserted in the mid-day heat.*

Unlike Baxter's original suite, with full orchestra and percussion – "a savage symphony of brass and cymbals" (Lanza, 1994: 122) evoking a jungle world – Denny's slower version, with added bird calls, conjures up a hotel lounge decorated with tropical fare[3]. In 1959 Denny's ensemble won the *Billboard* magazine award for 'Most promising group of the year' and he was also nominated for 'Pianist of the year'. He has lived in Honolulu for over forty years and has recorded thirty-nine albums which have sold in excess of four million copies worldwide. Although he semi-retired in the 1980s, he, and most of his original musicians, re-grouped in 1990 to make the album *Exotica '90* with a young Japanese producer, and toured Japan.

Denny has described his brand of musical exotica as "a combination of the South Pacific and the Orient ... what a lot of people *imagined* the islands to be like" but has added "it's pure fantasy, though" (1993: 142). On the sleeve notes of the first album, *Exotica*, he defines his music in another way: "[w]e establish a mood by stressing melodic content and highlight it with novel effects". In the liner notes to *Enchanted Sea* (1959), Denny's ninth album, a collection of tunes related to travel and the sea, Ira Cook, a Los Angeles disc jockey, discussed the effect Denny's music has on listeners and argued that:

> *[i]n every arrangement the Martin Denny group has ever played, the interested listener discovers something new each time he hears it – a descriptive chord, a bird call, an animal noise, a soft note – all the brilliant individual fragments that blend into the Martin Denny sound at first hearing.*

> *This is not my opinion alone. The same enthusiasm is apparent in letters from my listeners who welcome and appreciate the relaxation they find in*

75

Martin's music. And in today's world of nervous tension and jitters, relaxation is something we certainly need more of... Notice, if you will, his Sentimental Journey to swinging, modern, oriental country; the rippling waves Beyond The Sea (La Mer); the upbeat original Flotsam and Jetsam; the wind and spray splashing Beyond the Reef; the soft, gentle and Enchanted Sea.

THIS is music.

These descriptions point to exotica having several distinct aspects:

(1) Geographically, exotica focuses specifically on the South Pacific, the 'Orient', and on islands in general (rather than on continents and deserts).

(2) Aesthetically, it is orientated more towards *mood* and *effect* than towards structure and thought.

(3) Epistemologically, it comprises a fantasy of travel, an aural simulation of imagined experience of transport to exotic lands (an aspect which is intended to relax listeners).

I shall return to these points later.

The basic instrumentation of the 'Martin Denny sound' comprises the piano, the vibraphone (or marimba), the upright bass, and percussion. Occasionally, instruments such as strings, drums, chorus, sitar and Moog synthesiser are added. Denny's piano style is reminiscent of the 'cool' jazz approach of George Shearing (the combination of piano and vibes, four-beat walking bass with or without quiet brush work on drums) but the frequent use of marimba instead of vibes differentiates Denny's style from that of straight jazz. The piano-and-marimba ensemble is an alternative to George Shearing's hallmark piano-and-vibes sound and enables Denny to produce a mixture of 'cool' *and* 'exotic' moods. This is due to the dual associations of the marimba. It sounds western by dint of its western tuning and non-western due to its wooden percussion sound. This ambiguity makes the instrument marginal – and primarily a curiosity – in both western art and popular music. In the case of Denny's music, this ambiguity can be drawn upon to link the West with the Orient[4].

More important than the use of the marimba, however, is the use of Latin percussion instruments which do not necessarily keep a Latin beat. Denny himself explains that his earlier experience as a pianist for over four years in South America sharpened the Latin feeling of his sound, making his music more vivid: "[i]f you take Hawaiian music alone, it lulls you to sleep – whereas Latin has exciting rhythms; it has a *beat!*" (1993: 142). His Latin beat is not, however, as intense as in mambo or cha-cha, for example. More akin to a dance band in night clubs and hotel lounges, his syncopation – softly augmented by maracas, bongos and congas – sounds modest and moderate.

It is not particular rhythmic patterns but the use of 'tropical' percussion that produces a 'Latin' atmosphere. This is particularly evident in his albums. *Latin Village* (1963), for instance, a collection of Mexican (*Angelito*), Cuban (*Malaguena* [sic]), Brazilian (*The Girl from Ipanema*) and Hollywood-style (*Flying Down to Rio*) tunes, was recorded while bossa nova was in vogue in the USA[5]. According to the sleeve notes:

> *[t]his perennial appeal* [of Latin American music] *is doubled when Martin Denny plays the music, because he brings to Latin music new and unusual harmonies and rhythms, making it an entirely new and fresh listening experience. His classic interpretation of "Quiet Village" is a great example; it set a whole new trend in Latin American music.*

At this point it might be concluded that exotica is simply a variation of Latin music ("with new and unusual harmonies and rhythms"). This is partly true since the 'Latin', even more than the Hawaiian music, has been privileged in musical exoticism in the U.S.A. since the mid-19th Century (most prominently in the work of creole composer-pianist, Louis Moreau Gottschalk)[6]. But this characterisation is also partly false, since the appeal of Denny's sound does not primarily come from its Latin element but from a more diffused exotic quality. As Denny has stated:

> *[w]e distinguished each song by a different ethnic instrument, usually on top of a semi-jazz or Latin beat. Even though it remained familiar, each song would take on a strange, exotic character.* (1993: 144)

Thus, the 'Latin' in Denny's musical vision is more susceptible to different 'flavourings' than jazz (and thereby functions as a key element in his musical cocktails). Denny describes the sound of his version of *Quiet Village* as follows:

> *"Quiet Village" has a compulsive jungle rhythm to it; the bass has a hypnotic effect almost like Ravel's Bolero. On top of that are layers of exotic percussion, plus the sounds of the vibes, the piano, and (of course) the bird calls. It all adds up to a modern sound that evokes some very primitive feelings.* (1993: 148)

Denny's reference to the bird call sounds on the track is far from incidental, since these remain his most distinctive and evocative musical trademark.

The aesthetics of bird calls

One of the most immediately perceptible differences between the versions of *Quiet Village* recorded by Les Baxter and Martin Denny is the latter's use of vocal bird call impressions to evoke what we might term *jungleness*. Performed (principally) by August (Augie) Colon, they have become the essential signature of musical exotica. According to Denny, his use of these represents an interaction between both human and nature, and between the musicians and the audience of the Hawaiian

Village resort. According to an account he published in 1993, one night, large bullfrogs in a pond next to the bandstand croaked during a performance. When the band stopped playing, the frogs stopped croaking. Checking to see if this was merely a coincidence, Denny repeated the same tune and then the frogs started croaking again. Then, as a gag, some members spontaneously started imitating bird calls, much to the rest of the band's amusement. The next day one of the guests requested the song with the birds and the frogs. The band then began to deliberately imitate frogs and birds. Each chose a different bird call, while Denny produced the croaking sound by holding a guïro (a grooved cylindrical instrument of Afro-Cuban origin) up to the microphone and rubbing a pencil in the grooves. The tune augmented in this way was *Quiet Village* and the arrangements were subsequently recorded on the best-selling single[7].

This well-known account demonstrates how the specific institution and location of the tropical lounge, and specifically its open-air ambience, made it possible to incorporate such a seemingly mundane device as bird calls into the band's (already) exotic sound. Such an improvisation, Denny believes, would not necessarily have happened in a (North American) mainland context (1993: 143). In this regard, Hawai'i offered him not only a variety of instruments but also the relaxed setting conducive to the creation of unusual and spontaneous sound effects. This account raises two issues. One concerns the meaning of sound effects in music, and the other, the nature of bird call impressions.

The effect of bird call impressions may be better understood when we compare it to ornithological *descriptions* in western music language (for example, the use of the piccolo in Prokofiev's *Peter and the Wolf*, the clarinet in the Beethoven's *Pastoral Symphony*, or the piano in Messiaen's *Les Oiseaux Exotiques*), and to the sound effects in various pieces such as Tchaikovsky's *1812 Overture* (the cannon) and Varèse's *Ionisation* (the siren). By comparing the bird calls with the use of the voice and/or conventional instruments to produce approximations of avian utterances, it becomes clear that bird calls do not simply *express* but *exemplify* the bird. These two modes of denotation are here used in the sense indicated by Nelson Goodman's statement that a "line drawing of softly draped cloth may *exemplify* rhythmic linear patterns" whereas "a poem with no words for sadness ... may in the quality of its language be sad and poignantly *express* sadness" (1978: 12, my emphases). In other words, the bird calls are to descriptive pieces as taxidermy is to sculpture. Messiaen, for example, does not intend to *imitate* but rather to *translate* bird calls into western sonority – just as an artist like Picasso embodies the figure of bird with bronze (rather than with bird feathers). The bird calls, or stuffed bird, *show* rather than *represent* what the bird is.

In terms of sound effects, the bird call imitations sound more like the cannon in Tchaikovsky's belligerent *1812 Overture* than the siren in Varèse's percussive *Ionisation* because they *denote* 'bird' literally (like the cannon in *1812* denotes the Napoleonic Wars) rather than simply being used for their aural specificity. For

Varèse, the siren does not refer to the mechanical life of a factory, for example, but is used as an instrument capable of continuous glissando. Varèse experiments with the everyday device to expand established musical language and to break down the outmoded distinction between noise and music (like the percussive use of a type-writer in Erik Satie's *Parade*). This type of experiment bears little resemblance to Tchaikovsky's intentions in using the cannon. In a nutshell, the Denny band's bird calls are extrinsic to the musical texture but denote something concrete. Unlike Tchaikovsky's rather abrupt intervention of the cannon, however, they are more than a poor substitute for the 'real'. Rather, they are central to Denny's sound since they connote the imaginary place of the jungle, the essential signification of exotica. Or perhaps it is from the parasitical positioning, their *riding on the back of* the sound, that the bird call imitations affect the whole signification of Denny's music. As Denny has insisted, the exotic bird calls are the essential hook of his oeuvre (1993: 143).

Whereas 20th Century western avant garde music may have been searching for what might be termed a *pure* aesthetics of sonority through the use of everyday objects popular culture has also developed, so to speak, a *spurious* aesthetics of heteroge-neous sounds. Put another way, while the work of avant garde artists such Pierre Schaeffer and Pierre Henri in the 1950s – in a style often referred to as *musique concrète* – attempted to crystallise pure sound by disassociating 'found sound' from its referents and origins; sound effects used in 20th Century popular music, (largely) try to *retain* as many associations as possible.

Since the 1930s, radio drama and animated cartoon film soundtracks have deliber-ately juxtaposed human voices, music and sound effects in order to give the audience a means by which to visualise a particular scenario and/or location. To this end, skilled artisans have learnt how to make and use various sound effects. But in a purely musical setting, despite the increasing use of a variety of percussion instru-ments after jazz and rumba became popular, sound effects were considered to be nothing but comical devices. This approach was exemplified by the Spike Jones Orchestra, who used buckets, cans, train whistles, neighing, croaking, chirping sounds etc. The humour of the Spike Jones Orchestra lies in the bizarre combinations of 'tuned' noise (eg melodious gargling) and 'untuned' instruments (eg the tuba out of tune) in the blend of regular orchestral performance and more conventional and/or cinematographic sound effects. In this manner, for audiences, the Orchestra effec-tively performs an animated film soundtrack, with the visual dimension implied rather than actual. This aspect can be seen as a key to establishing the Orchestra's performances *as* humorous – with the audience anticipating, visualising (and thereby providing) the 'sight-gags' to the soundtrack. In terms of comparisons, the Martin Denny sound does not function in as overtly humorous a manner as Spike Jones; not simply because Denny is more 'serious' than Jones but because the visual evocation in his music is more sensual than humorous.

Bird call impressions are practiced in many parts of the world, both 'undeveloped' and modern. They involve various combinations and/or co-ordinations of the mouth, throat, tongue, fingers, breath and voice. There is little evidence that such impressions are formally taught, or set down in how-to-do manuals. People tend to learn them through lessons from elders or other accomplished individuals, or else by chance, as Augie Colon did (Denny, 1993: 148). While this bodily-produced sound practice forms a part of daily life for some hunting peoples, it is merely a gag for urban and/or industrialised societies, one which usually surfaces in the form of strange talent competitions in colleges or on radio or television (and, previously, on the vaudeville/music hall circuit). Birdsong itself is generally considered to be pleasing rather than comical, but its imitation is understood differently. Unlike extended vocal expressions in contemporary music, bird calls are too directly denotative to be recognised as an artistic expression in themselves. They might be as ancient as shamanistic spells or speaking-in-tongues but they bear none of the mystery of these forms[8]. They are not a sign to be interpreted but a signal whose designation is already incorporated within the sound. Bird calls are easily identifiable (although few can identify the species imitated), particularly within the context of a musical arrangement[9].

Exoticism in the age of stereo reproduction

The popularity of the 'Martin Denny sound' owes much to the stereo recording technology that had just appeared on the market when Denny started recording. According to Denny, "[p]eople were interested in sound *per se* – and that included my so-called 'exotic' sound ... I guess I just happened to be there at the right time" (1993: 144). The sleeve notes for his early records invariably emphasised the type of technology used. For example, the sleeve notes to the original monophonic version of the *Exotica* album (1957)[10] state that the album was recorded with:

> ...*the ultimate in High Fidelity... LIBERTY'S SPECTRA-SONIC-SOUND is a process which incorporates the use of an advance design of the famed Telefunken microphone in conjunction with Altec Lansing power amplifiers and Ampex Recorders... For best results, use the RIAA equalization curve. Frequency response is from 40 cps. to 15,000 cps.*

The sleeve notes for Denny's first (recorded-as) stereo record, *Exotica Volume II* (1957), boasted of the even greater technological advances, claiming:

> *This is a STEREOPHONIC, TWO-CHANNEL, non-compatible long play record, utilizing Westrex 45–45 stereophonic disk cutting system, to be reproduced with a stereophonic cartridge only.*

> *"EXOTICA – VOL.II" was recorded through the WORLD'S ONLY TRANSISTORIZED STEREOPHONIC MULTIPLE-CHANNEL recording system. ...Liberty's new STEREOPHONIC SOUND features a fully TRANSISTOR-*

IZED multiple-channel system which incorporates the use of specially designed multiple-track, synchronous Ampex Recorders, producing a frequency response from 20 cps. to 20,000 cps.

When *Exotica Volume II* was released, stereo recording was so expensive that only a few select artists could use the technology. Recordings made with stereo had to be both commercially viable and have an aesthetic rationale for its use. Leopold Stokowski, for example, was one of the earliest artists to record in stereo because – besides having maintained a huge degree of popularity amongst the American classics audience since the 1930s – he was particularly interested in the separation of right and left channels. His aim was to visualise the spatial arrangement of an orchestra in collaboration with engineers (McGinn, 1983; Hosokawa, 1990: 86–90).

New technology gratified the audiophile by its ability to produce sounds such as a bird (apparently) flying from right to left channels, endless patterns of waves breaking on Waikiki Beach, tramcars passing rapidly on the street, impressive gongs with full reverberations or the subtle sounds of 'singing bamboos' in full detail. With each new technological innovation (stereo, quadrophonic stereo, compact disc and so on), sound effects recording (thunder, waterfalls, stream locomotives, car races...) has been a crucial means by which to test the performance of a new device. The percussion ensemble was another trial for the new technology because of the technical difficulty involved in reproducing its discrete pulsive and dynamic sound elements. In western aesthetics, percussion (with the exception of tuned instruments like the timpani) lies somewhere between music and noise (as sound effects rather than instrumental devices). Since the medieval carnival, the untuned percussion sound made by available objects has been seen as confrontational to the social order represented by commonly understood notions of 'music'.

As Attali (1985) has argued, percussion itself can be thought to threaten (conventional) music. But the audiophile (ie sound-conscious individual) does not necessarily prefer listening to music (understood in its narrowest definition), or, even, to organised human sound. Such individuals may wish to be exposed to a variety of sound sources. Denny's works were therefore addressed in large part to an audience of audiophiles (which grew rapidly due to factors such as an increasing number of new sound technologies and the diffusion of greater economic affluence). As the liner notes of *Exotic Percussion* (1960) declare:

[t]he audiophile will be delighted with the technical perfection and the wide selection of the sound spectrum presented in this unique album. The exacting reproduction of these rare instruments with their odd overtone colorations makes this album a truly exciting experience for the sound-conscious individual. The stereo fan will discover that the stereophonic version of this album is recorded in the most dramatic manner, providing new and exciting sound thrills.

The development of sound reproduction apparatus in the 1950s was intimately related to the emergence of new technologies for sound production such as tape splicing, overdubbing and transistor sound generators pioneered, for example, by Les Paul, Lennie Tristano and Karlheinz Stockhausen (although Denny's work obviously did not have such futuristic implications as electronic music had). Unlike these devices for new types of studio performance, the 'Spectra-Sonic-Sound' Denny used was designed directly for reproduction by audiophiles. Its technology was consumption- (rather than production-) orientated. Technological reproduction of the primitive, or hi-tech exotica, corresponds with the notion of 'East meets West' encompassed in the following statement from the *Exotic Percussion* liner notes: "he uses the exotic instruments of the *East* to play the beautiful melodies of the *West* and the *twain* meet in a rare combination of magnificent sound". The *East* provides the "exotic instruments" and "odd overtone colorations", while the *West* structures these into "beautiful melodies" and the "exacting reproduction". The relationship between the "twain" is neither reversible nor reciprocal[11]. However, such rare, strange sounds are (necessarily) not totally unfamiliar to western ears. On the contrary, exotica plays upon particular expectations on the part of the audience regarding what the 'primitive' sounds like[12]. To some extent, such preconceived notions developed out of film and television representations of the exotic. The contemporary musical language used to create the exotic in mass media was also undoubtedly affected by 19th Century European music, Tin Pan Alley, jazz, Afro-Caribbean genres and so on. What distinguished the exotica of the 1950s was the technological enhancement and sophisticated mise-en-scène, the rendering of the exotic as comfortable.

The uneven and irreversible position of East and West mentioned above is also reflected in the nature of the resort club experience. This is characterised by the provision of up-to-date equipment and facilities in a (stereo-)typically exotic environment. Such amenities are indispensable to tourists, whether they arrive by armchair or jet plane. After discussing Denny's albums from the perspective of an armchair audience, I will now turn to the hotel context in which he most often performed.

In the hotel lounge

The impact of tourism on traditional music has recently begun to be explored (see, for instance, Kaeppler, 1988). Ethnomusicologists have traditionally blamed tourism (and/or economic development) for the western 'contamination' of non-western music resulting in the watering down of traditional forms, the production of localised imitations of western styles and the development of forms of musical syncretism. Recently, however, some ethnomusicologists have begun to rethink tourism as a type of cultural transformation brought about by processes of contact and/or the secular pilgrimage of the leisure activity. But the impact of tourism on *non*-traditional music has, as yet, been little examined.

Hawai'i is one of the greatest laboratories for tourist music in the world, and the history of hula – and the whole amalgam of culture in the islands – could not be written without reference to the impact of tourism. In her book *Paradise Remade* (1993), Elizabeth Buck provides the following insights into the cultural appropriation of a paradise by the capitalist (North American) mainland economic system:

> [a]lmost everything in Hawai'i communicates through a system of codes
> that tourism, and the public and private institutions that support tourism,
> have constructed over years of selling Hawai'i as paradise ... The produc-
> tion of paradise is an all-encompassing code that revalues everything in the
> islands, imposing social relations and codes of behavior on the total struc-
> ture of the islands ... It is the logic that says locals cannot surf where tour
> boats want to go, that local residents must suffer the noise of sightseeing
> helicopters or the fumes of tour buses, that golf courses are more productive
> than agriculture. (ibid: 180)

Despite her criticisms of the cultural logic of early and late capitalism, Buck also observes that:

> [a] hegemonic Western culture dominates the islands, but it does not totally
> control the discourse of culture ... Hawaiian culture is both residual in its
> ties to the past and oppositional in its critique of the existing social structure
> of the islands and its projections of the future. (ibid: 183)

Finally Buck reads the music of Hawai'i as an *intertext* that keeps on transforming itself along with the continuous changes in "ideological, economic, and political structure of the islands" (ibid: 190), "an intertext where Hawai'i, the West, and the social context of the present continuously interact to construct, deconstruct, and reconstruct the myths of Hawai'i" (ibid: 191).

Buck's conclusion may be pertinent to music *in* Hawai'i as well, even when produced by a New Yorker. Denny played in a place typically peopled by outsiders and had little or no contact with local tradition such as the hula and Hawaiian chant. When he mentions "Hawaiian music", he exclusively means *hapa-haole* songs such as *The Queen Chant (Lili'u E)* and *Wedding Song (Ke Kali Ne Au)* (both included on *Exotica Volume II*). Furthermore, he never included ukulele or slack key guitar in his instrumental line-ups, two instruments central to the sound of contemporary Hawaiian music. What exotica represents is not so much Hawaiianness but *para-dise-ness*. For Denny, Hawai'i is simply one imaginable earthy paradise. What is at stake in his live performance is the ability to associate Hawai'i with any sort of paradisaical fantasy in the minds of tourists visiting the islands – tourists who have just been released from their daily routines into (keenly anticipated) environs such as daiquiri lounges. In this regard, they are no longer 'armchair travellers' but cane-chair 'travellers'. As the sleeve notes to Denny's *Afro-desia* album (1959) remark:

> *[t]aking the various native idioms and* translating *them into breathtakingly ear-appealing vignettes, once again Mr. Denny stimulates the jaded palate of everyday civilization with* music that is pure escape. (my emphases)

The essence of exotica is thus based on the "translation" of "native idioms" into "ear-appealing vignettes" or already-known stereotypes. The encounter with what the tourists have already known, empowers the "pure escape" from "everyday civilization" of the tourists, who feel all the more the sense of belonging to home (the West in our case) by being conscious of exotic pleasure. According to the sociologist John A. Jakle:

> *[t]ravel tested the individual's* sense of belonging to community. *It enabled self-confirmation through various degrees of socialization en route, and through* a heightened sense of homecoming. *Travel sparked the acting out of fantasies. ... [T]ourism [is] not merely ... a superficial spending of leisure time, although tourism has its superficial dimensions, but rather, [is] a form of social glue that binds modern society together. Tourism is a principal means by which modern people define for themselves* a sense of identity. (1985: 10, 22, my emphases)

Denny's performance also evoked this "sense of identity" by providing the expected pleasure for customers.

As the sleeve notes to his *Primitiva* album (1958) stated: "[w]atching them [ie the band] perform is a treat to the eye as well as the ear because of the excitement expressed in their ballet of motion". The experience of both seeing and hearing unusual instruments used in Denny's show contrasts greatly with that of simply viewing such 'oddities' in exhibitions at venues such as Honolulu's Bishop Museum. Audiences could delight in the "ballet of motion" created by the percussionists as well as in the peculiar look and sound of Burmese gongs, wood chimes, wind chimes and boo bams ("tuned sections of bamboo with skins as percussion heads" (ibid)). Denny acquired this array of instruments through art collectors, occasional travellers and associates who worked with airlines (among others). His concern was not with authenticity, in terms of the original use and meaning of the instruments, but rather with the sound they produced.

There are similarities between the way Denny appropriated distant cultures and the practices of the ethnomusicologist or the museum curator, who also remove 'primitive' objects from their original contexts with the more benign intention of researching and publicising these unique and/or 'endangered' cultures[13]. Denny's use of Burmese gongs has, of course, nothing to do with reproducing real Burmese music just as listening to and/or performing the saxophone (or cymbals) does not neces-sarily imply experiencing Belgian (or Turkish) culture as such (the saxophone was invented by a Belgian and cymbals have been identified as originating in Turkey). In contrast, the audience of exotica – live or on record – will neither confuse the music with something Burmese nor take the illusion for reality. They simply enjoy listening to the unfamiliar twist added to a familiar Latin-like jazz. Perhaps Denny (and his audience) do not *understand* Burmese culture as deeply as the ethnologist or the local habitants. But even with a deeper understanding of each exotic culture he has used, his music would presumably not have changed. He is, as are most tourists, *effect-orientated*. He likes, therefore he uses. His aesthetics have deter-mined which exotic instruments he will use and which he will not. This is not unlike the case of Steve Reich and many other non-western-inspired artists.

In terms of Buck's discussion of the cultural logic of capitalism, tourist music *in* Hawai'i is no less important than music *by* local performers. Yet, it should be added that many of Denny's band members were actually Hawaiian: Chinese-English-Ha-waiian, Puerto Rican-Hawaiian, Chinese-Hawaiian, Korean-Hawaiian and so on (Denny, 1993: 144). Denny himself moved to Honolulu and became *haole*. Does not such racial diversity represent (one) Hawaiian-ness, despite the fact that the band played non-Hawaiian music? If vernacular cultural practices such as *hula* and chant drew on purist ideologies of the island culture, Denny's multi-racial band may deconstruct the essentialism that is maintained by local tourism itself.

Buck notes that, in the ethnically diverse culture of Hawai'i, the white culture alone has no annual celebration of arrival or commemorative museum event of its own:

> *[e]ven though the* haole *population does not constitute a majority of the islands' people and its people are as foreign as any of the Asian cultures that now reside here, Western culture – specifically* [North] *American culture – is so dominant it has no need to call attention to itself or construct itself as different; it is simply the taken-for-granted touchstone against which all other cultures construct their unique ethnic identities.* (Buck 1993: 182–3)[14]

This may explain the absence of ethnographic investigations into the Diamond Head piano bar's regular renditions of *My Way* or the Sheraton-based combo's nightly rendition of *Ebb Tide*. These are some instances of what I refer to as the impact of tourism on non-traditional music. Denny's music belongs to western culture, in spite of, or rather because of, its exotic gimmicks. But it is not simply the "taken-for granted touchstone" against which diverse cultural identifications are measured. White culture itself is not as monolithic as many ethnic studies presume. Questioning the taken-for-granted conditions of white culture is necessary for an understanding of issues of ethnicity in Hawai'i.

85

Denny played primarily in hotels or lounges in resort cities. His live music practice was determined by this performance context and is characterised by:

(1) Its commercial orientation, its attempt to deliver a predictable, acceptable sound.

(2) Regular nightly performance schedules comprising two or three sets of 45 – 60 minutes, each divided by 20 – 40 minute intermissions.

3) Performance at a low volume, with gentle sonorities and a familiar repertoire.

(4) Performance to an audience who were often diverted in their listening and/or engaged in parallel listening whilst chattering and drinking.

(5) An audience composed of members of an affluent leisure class.

The first three elements concern production, whereas the last two concern consumption. Of course the former conditions interact with the latter ones. Ola Stockfelt has proposed a cogent theory of "adequate modes of listening" that argues that the situation in which a listener encounters music is more significant than either the nature of the music itself or the listener's (preconstituted) cultural identity (1993: 157). Thus, concert hall listening – concentrated, autonomous and/or structural listening – is only one of several possible listening strategies, and has no more innate value (or validity) than the very different listening strategy appropriate for background listening in shopping mall. In this manner, Denny's music should be understood within its context – as hotel/lounge music – and in terms of appropriate listening strategies. Denny's sound was highly suitable for hotel music and thus, rather profitable. Many artists went on to imitate him and exotica became something of a fad. Denny has said however that "I don't hold it against them" [because] "imitation is the sincerest form of flattery, they say" (1993: 144).

Visual exotica

Besides the visual attractions of his live performance, Denny's albums were often discussed in terms of their abilities to evoke vivid visual images for their listeners. As James Michener, author of *Tales of the South Pacific*, wrote in the sleeve notes to Denny's *Hypnotique* album (1959):

> [t]his is music to see – and on this record there are many new sounds that will force the listener to create his own word pictures. It's music to feel – and Denny is careful to provide in his orchestrations the specific sound of things banging into other things, or scraping across them, or being struck by a human hand.

Similarly, the anonymous author of the liner notes for *Afro-desia* maintained that:

> *[l]istening to the subtle blendings of rhythms and voices both human... and instrumental, in AFRO-DESIA, one feels that he* [sic] *is being allowed that rare glimpse into other cultures... other rooms. We become* armchair travellers *with our magic carpet, our hi-fi (stereo) equipment and this album. We see and feel the searing veldt... the moody reaches of the jungle... a tribal initiation fête and sheer encompassing beauty. Here, in all honesty, has been recreated that marvellous* lost universe of fantasy - *completely appealing, impeccable in its taste and typically Martin Denny!* (emphases mine)

The sensations of seeing and feeling evoked in Denny's music draws on its effect-orientation, as mentioned above, and on its descriptive (synaesthetic) force to associate the sound with exotic déjà-vu in the minds of "armchair travellers". The "magic carpet" transport relies on the listener's previous knowledge of associations of sound and geography acquired through films, television, photography, literature and so on.

The album jacket is one influential factor guiding the fantasy. Denny's first dozen albums have a Caucasian model, Sandy Warner (nicknamed 'The Exotic Girl'), on the cover. As Denny has recalled:

> [art designers] *always changed her looks to fit the mood of the package. For instance, we called one album with an African sound* Afro-desia, *and... Sandy dyed her hair blond for the photo session; she's seen against a background of colorful African masks. When we did* Hypnotique, *which is surrealistic, she had dark hair. For* Primitiva *she was photographed standing waist-deep in water.* (1993: 144).

Exoticism consistently conjures up a (masculine) image of female sensuality and Denny's work is no exception to the rule. According to western aesthetics, the soft and tender timbre of exotica is apt to be related to femininity rather than to masculinity.

The second factor designed to channel the listener's imagination involves evocative song titles whose key words denote particular attributes. Drawing on Denny's repertoire alone, these include:

(1) General concepts (*Exotica, Primitiva, Hypnotique, Return to Paradise, Paradise Found, Stranger in Paradise*).

(2) Specific toponymies (*Hong Kong Blues, On a Little Street in Singapore, Port au Prince, Bangkok Cockfight, Tune from Rangoon, Manila, Congo Train, American in Bali*).

(3) Fauna and flora (*Lotus Land, Jungle Flower, Gooney Birds, Bamboo Lullaby, Flamingo, Cobra, Tsetse Fly, Sugar Cane*).

(4) Religion and mystery (*Stone God, Jungle Drums, Buddhist Bells, Mau Mau, Vovdoo* [sic] *Dreams*).

(5) Vague mysticism (*Ma'chumba, Mumba, Simba, Aku Aku*).

(6) Islands and the sea (*Busy Port, Ebb Tide, Island of Dreams, Escales, Harbor Lights, Trade Winds, My Isle of Golden Dreams, Beyond the Reef, Cross Current, The Enchanted Sea*).

As the French musicologist Françoise Escal (1990) argues, the title is the "paratext" that brings the interpenetration between the sound and the verbal into play: "it functions as 'shifter and modulator' of listening" (1990: 294, my translation). The title (re-)presents a certain coherent bloc of sound and conditions the mode of listening: "the title anticipates the work, it programs the listening thereof" (ibid). This is especially true of a 'descriptive piece' without whose title the listener might not recognise the 'picture' inscribed in the sound that does not contain the verbal concept in itself.

Toponymies act as powerful stimulants to imagine unknown places[15]. If the title of a certain piece is 'Manila', the listener is transported to the Philippine metropolis (and not Bangkok or Jakarta), although he or she may be incapable of distinguishing one city from another nor understand which elements of the piece allude to Manila.

Nature and mystery are inter-related with exotic perceptions of otherness. In Denny's music these elements are described by bird calls, the marimba, the gongs and/or the congas. The musical trope of mysticism is closely related to scenes of ritual savagery in exotic films – such as the various *Tarzan* movies – where the tribe chants and dances to strange percussion accompaniments.

Denny's privileged link with island and sea partly comes from his base in Hawai'i, since the majority of his audience would expect to listen to something associated with their own touristic expectation and experience. The concept of the island – particularly the Pacific island – established in modern western popular discourses intimately connotes female sexuality[16] because, from *Robinson Crusoe* to *The Bird of Paradise*, the unexplored island is (metaphorically) there to be conquered and penetrated by man (see Williamson, 1986; AA.VV. 1987: 82). The title is all the more definitive to the fantasy in that music is, in classical western aesthetics at least, essentially an a-referential mode of expression.

The end of exotica

Although Denny continued releasing albums and playing at famous lounges, albeit intermittently, through to the 1990s[17], his heyday ended in the early 1960s. It was at this time that he began to record less original material. During the 1960s he appeared to follow a standard recipe – take whatever tunes you choose, then cook them with Latin seasoning, add exotic topping (and bird calls) and your dish is ready. Compositions such as *Blowin' in the Wind*, *Harlem Nocturne*, *Take Five* and *Route 66* were all turned into exotica in this way. Once this recipe was routinised, exotica became nothing more than a standard arrangement technique applicable to any tune regardless of its origin, title or implied imagery.

Unlike Les Baxter, for instance, who continued working on cinema (mostly B-movie) soundtracks after his success with a series of exotica albums had peaked, Denny has not changed his style throughout his career. His trademark Latin-tinged sound was therefore somewhat double-edged. It appealed to a wide audience but at the same time it tended to be mannerist. When universalised, the exotic evocation in Denny's sound became dissociated from the geo-imaginary specificity because the aural difference between the West and the rest of the world was neutralised. The armchair travellers lost their (imaginary) destinations.

One of the clearest reasons for the declining popularity of exotica was the ascension of rock. The late 1950s/early 1960s was a time when film music with sweet string cascades, such as Victor Young's *East of Eden* (1955), Percy Faith's *Love in a Summer Place* (1959) and Henry Mancini's version of *Moon River* (1961) could be number one hits at the same time as the markedly different sound of rock and roll tunes. Denny remembers the period with nostalgia:

> ... *popular music has changed; now it's all 'rock.' But in 1958 Dick Clark, who had the hottest TV show in the country for teenagers, had me on his show.* (1993: 148)

Denny's band had a greater appeal for the old guard than for the emerging audiences interested in electrified and Afro-American-influenced music. The decline of Denny's popularity was not only the result of changing musical tastes, but also of the mutation of exotic imagination in the U.S.A. Visions of the earthly paradise of the South Pacific disintegrated in the wake of H-bomb trials in the region. Africa was liberated from western sovereignty and East Asia became synonymous with transistors and motorcycle manufacturing or, above all, a battlefield for nothing. It is no coincidence that exotica was favoured in the years between the Korean War (1950–51) and the Vietnam War (1964–1971). While the former war brought familiarity with East Asian cultures for many American soldiers, most of whom did not finally lose faith in the 'American way' or pride in their home country (and who brought back souvenirs from wherever they were stationed[18]), the latter war, as has been represented in many novels, films and studies, was so purposeless that the whole nation lost its self-confidence. It is U.S. citizens themselves who destroyed not only the real territory of other people but also the oriental fantasy and mystery of their own.

89

Denny's popularity occurred towards the end of an era when the jungle was not as frightening and cruel as in Vietnam, and before the 'Orient' was substituted by the much less fantastic – and much more geo-political – name 'Asia'. In her book on the history of representations of East Asia in Hollywood cinema, Yumiko Murakami has argued that "exotic Orientalism has been favoured since the early silent movies" (1993: 8, my translation) and that:

> ... it is not until the late 1960s that the 'Oriental' paradigm gradually disappeared and became replaced by the notion of 'Asia' and the 'Asian'. Underlying this shift was the impact of the Vietnam War. In this period, the U.S.A. confronted a new 'Asia' which could not be subsumed within the established, fuzzy notion of the 'Orient'. (ibid)

The shift in western paradigms away from Orientalism to a new, less romanticised concept of Asian identity paralleled the gradual decline in popularity of musical exotica.

Even if western (and Japanese) tourists still keep on searching for paradise in Hawai'i, Bali, Tahiti and The Seychelles (chasing a sweet fantasy based on white supremacy and the stereotyped Other), typical products of 1950s Broadway and Hollywood, such as *The King and I*, became impossible when the Americans met with the 'Asia' behind the 'Oriental' mask. Orientalist musical devices, such as pentatonism, complete parallel fourths, the use of bamboo and wood percussion instruments and the gong, suddenly dropped out of vogue (to become as nostalgically retro as the original 1950s Latin-style music central to Denny's own sounds). While the sitar enjoyed brief success in late 1960s western pop, drawing on its hippy associations, Indianism did not displace the long-standing popularity of Orientalism. Armchair travellers did not connect with Indianism in the same way as did the counter-culture since they were not concerned to discover their 'true selves' or to question the material life they enjoyed. The aesthetics of exotica were not compatible with Indianism (see Reck, 1985: 90ff).

So paradise was lost and exotica disappeared. While Denny had plenty of imitators in the 1950s and the 1960s he had no clear successor in the 1970s[19]. Now, western musicians such as Ry Cooder and David Lindley, among others, engage with musical otherness by collaborating with foreign musicians, by emulating non-western music and by creating accomplished syncretic forms (which, at their best, show a confluence of rhythmic pattern, interpenetration of heterogeneous instruments, technical versatility and intellectual flexibility). Nowadays, western consumers no longer associate Africa and the Pacific simply with 'primitive' chants and percussion but the intricate musicality of various genres of world music.

Exoticism lingers on, of course, just as tourist pursuits of paradise continue to thrive, and as enchanting images of different cultures are disseminated by mass publicity, adventure videos and other artefacts of popular culture. But the phase of exoticism has shifted, at least in musical domain. As a result, Denny's once fashionable music is now thought to be less banal than "incredibly strange"[20] (and is therefore once again fashionable with a cultural in-group who have redeemed and embraced such musics and leisure pursuits[21]). Historically, the end of its first period of popularity served to mark a limit, a crisis and a turning point of exoticism and notions of earthly paradises. The simplistic dismissal of "exotic music" offered by theorists such as Steve Reich does not adequately explain the gratification offered by exotica in the 1950s (and in the 1990s). For this we have to look to the convergence of factors I have outlined above. The very complexity of exotica marks its appeal.

Thanks to Claire Butkus, Philip Hayward, Will Straw and John Whiteoak for their comments on an earlier version of this chapter; and to Robert Carlberg for discographic information.

Notes

1. See Mertens (1983) for further discussion. It should be noted that his distinction between exotic gimmickry and artistic creation is, however, not new since music critics have often employed rhetorical dichotomies such as Imitation v Inspiration and Kitsch v Originality.

2. Note, for example, that Hawaiian vernacular music does not use imitation bird calls, neither does Chinese traditional music use bamboo percussion – exotica musicians do.

3. Also see Chapter Four for a musicological analysis of Denny's version of the composition and a comparison to Arthur Lyman's 1959 version.

4. The marimba was also featured by Herb Alpert and the Tijuana Brass during the same period (indeed, Julius Wechner, vibes player in Denny's quartet on several of Denny's early recordings, later joined the Tijuana Brass). However, the instrument's use in this context has different associations by dint of the Tijuana Brass's address to Mexican-derived music.

5. The bossa nova boom in the U.S.A. is illustrated, for example, by the track *Bossa Nova Baby*, released as a single by both The Clovers and Elvis Presley in 1963 (four out of twelve tracks in *Latin Village* are indeed Brazilian). *Spanish Village* (1964), a sequel to *Latin Village*, included several Mexican tunes (*Cielito Lindo, Maria Elena* and so on); North American ones referencing Hispanic themes (*In a Little Spanish Town*) and the Brazilian composition (*Samba de Orfeu*). It seems that 'Spanish' and 'Latin' are almost interchangeable in the musical lexicon of exotica.

6. See Chase (1987); Starr (1995); and Tatar (1987) for further discussion. (Also note that Van Dyke Parkes recorded versions of Gottschalk's compositions *Night in the Tropics* and *Danza* on his 1998 CD *Moonlighting: Live at The Ash Grove*.)

7. The bird calls were so impressive that Les Baxter asked Denny to send the tape of bird calls and he used it himself (Denny, 1993: 147). Baxter's live recording of *Quiet Village* on *The Lost Episode of Les Baxter* (1996) indeed features the bird calls. Sometimes the record company pressured Denny to use more birds to the extent that Denny reacted angrily that "I'm not selling bird calls – I'm selling music!" (ibid: 148).

8. Joseph Beuys' performance of vocalising a coyote was a particularly remarkable exception to the anti-mimetic tradition of 20th Century art. Recent New Age culture and Green sensibilities have boosted the popularity of animal 'songs' – most notably birds and whales. Charlie Haden has responded to this by composing a piece entitled *Song of A Whale* in which the jazz bassist imitates the voices emitted by whales by playing his bass with a bow.

9. Bird calls have surfaced in a number of popular music tracks including, the Young Rascals' *Groovin* (1967) and the Beatles' *Good Morning, Good Morning* (1967). What distinguishes

Denny's sound from such songs is his attempt to *integrate* the bird calls into the musical texture in order to produce an exotic effect. The bird calls are not a residual device used to denote a certain narrative situation but are actually a part of the music itself.

10.   The stereo re-recording was issued in 1959.

11.   In the sleeve notes for *Exotic Percussion*, Denny also notes that:

The cultures of the Orient have produced many musical instruments which, though they may sound strange to our ears, possess beautiful and exotic sounds. It has long been one of my desires to apply these rare sounds to our own music... The instruments heard here were selected because of their beautiful and distinctive sounds and the manner in which they blend together. Although some are not exclusively oriental, all have a quality not usually associated with our music.

The sharp distinction between *us* and *them*, between the familiar and the unusual, repeats the well-known dichotomy of exoticism. It is notable that Denny poses himself as able to "blend together" instruments from disparate traditions in (a new form of) "our own music" . Some of the "not exclusively oriental" instruments Denny uses comprise the Mange Harp, designed by J. C. Deagon, which simulates the sound of keyboard instruments such as the harpsichord and celeste; and curiosities such as "piccolo xylophones" and "celestette". Despite their exoticism, these are all tuned to western pitch in order to allow the arranger to "blend [them] together" with standard instruments. (Poly-pitch may be allowable for the avant guard but it is still an anathema for lounge music.)

12.   Stephen W. Foster (1982) argues that it is the *interplay* between the familiar and the exotic which constitutes the latter:

The unfamiliar implies an openness that invites symbolic associations and articulations. In the process of making the unfamiliar comprehensible, what is familiar is defined anew by being associated with the remote, and so a relation, however erroneous, is set up between the exotic and the commonplace. (1982: 22)

In this statement, Foster rightly identifies the exotic as a symbolic-interpretative element which seems to assimilate cultural difference or at least to create the illusion of doing so.

13.   The museum, a holy place for anthropology, art history and organology, has itself been put under critical scrutiny in recent years (see Ames (1992); Clifford (1988) [Chapter 10]).

14.   By the same token, Grenier (1989) remarks upon the absence of studies on MOR or white middle-class music in academia and emphasises that scholars have been primarily interested in music with social, racial, political, geographical, ethnic, gender, or aesthetic specificity. Grenier also argues that the "silence surrounding the musics of dominant groups" (ibid: 137) suggests that scholars assume an "authenticity" for the music of specific groups which they do no assume for the music of dominant ones. The musical style discussed in this article certainly falls into the latter category.

15.   The magical power of toponymies for stimulating the imagination of unknown places has been often mentioned.since Proust's Normandy tramway (in *Recherche du Temps Perdu*), where the names of each small station constitutes the town itself rather than a sign thereof. Each name conjures up in the mind of Proustian traveller the different images of people's life in each town, regardless of whether he has been there. The name fixes and frames the fantasy and notion of unknown places. This Proustian concept of toponymic reference is applicable to the listeners of exotica.

16.   As recent press advertisements for a Guy Laroche fragrance had it: "Woman is an island. Fiji is a perfume" – the two nevertheless being associated.

17.   With *Enchanted Islands* (1993) being his latest recording of new music at time of writing.

18.   Two of the Japanese songs recorded in Denny's early albums – *China Nights* and *Soshu Night Serenade* – were first exported to the U.S.A. by returning soldiers. The latter song, included on

Exotica II, is not credited to its composer, Ryoichi Hattori, but only to an American arranger. In this manner local composers are often overlooked – and therefore literally *dis*-credited – and their works represented as 'folk songs' whose authorship is obscure. *Soshu Night Serenade* is but one of many examples of colonial usurpation of copyright.

19.   Aside from Haruomi Hosono who developed a style influenced by Denny, but using electric instrumentation, in Japan in the 1970s. For further discussion of Hosono's work, see Chapter Five of this volume.

20.   Featured, as it is, in publications such as *Re/Search: Incredibly Strange Music* (1993).

21.   See for example the discussions in such fanzines as the U.S. publication *Tiki News*.

Discography

Scamp Records have released a number of Denny's original albums, including: *Exotica* and *Exotica Volume II*, released as a double CD entitled *The Exciting Sounds of Martin Denny – Exotica I & II*; (1996); *Afro-Desia* (1996), *Hypnotique/Exotica 3* (1996) and *Quiet Village/The Enchanted Sea* (1996).

There are a number of Denny compilation CDs available, including *Exotica: The Very Best*, Rhino Records (1990) and *The Exotic Sounds of Martin Denny*, EMD/Capitol (1996), which includes previously unreleased tracks.

Chapter Four

TROPICAL COOL

The Arthur Lyman Sound

JON FITZGERALD AND PHILIP HAYWARD

Introduction

This chapter analyses the musical and cultural significance of the work of Hawaiian recording artist Arthur Lyman in the 1950s–1960s. Our discussion of Lyman's oeuvre complements Shuhei Hosokawa's exposition of key aspects of musical exotica, with particular regard to the work of Martin Denny, in the previous chapter. Given the broad similarity of Lyman's musical approach to Denny's, we do not attempt to duplicate such general analyses here. Rather, we locate Lyman's career and musical style(s) within the context of post-War Hawai'i and the Hawaiian cultural 'Renaissance'; offer a set of musicological analyses of recordings central to Lyman's oeuvre; and compare and contrast aspects of Lyman's work with Denny's.

I. Locating Lyman

Analysis of Lyman's work within the context of post-War Hawai'i involves the negotiation of a number of cultural complexities. Fundamental to these is the disjuncture between Lyman's music, his identity and identification as Hawaiian, and the recent cultural history of Hawai'i – most particularly, the revival and re-assertion of indigenous Hawaiian culture which produced the Hawaiian cultural Renaissance of the 1970s and 1980s.

The Hawaiian Renaissance resulted from the increasing marginalisation of indigenous Hawaiians from economic, social and political power in the Islands in the immediate post-War period, as North American and Japanese capital, institutions and residents moved into Hawai'i (and particularly into Honolulu/Waikiki), accelerating and intensifying a process which had been under way since the early-mid 1800s. One major factor in the wave of offshore investment in the 1950s and 1960s was the Islands' (renewed) fashionability as a tourist destination. This in turn derived from a further convergence of factors, including publicity over Hawai'i's push for statehood and its achievement of this in 1959 (see Bell, 1982); the rise in living standards and disposable income amongst the North American middle-classes; and the development of relatively inexpensive air travel between Hawai'i and continental America.

One effect of Hawaii's increasing integration with the culture of North America was the increased dissemination and popularity of continental popular music. By the 1960s, those styles of Hawaiian music which had enjoyed a local (and global) 'golden' period of popularity in the 1930s–50s[1], had fallen into a decline on the islands, squeezed out of radio playlists and sales charts by pop and rock music produced in North America[2]. If the 1930s–1950s can be considered as the 'Golden Age' of Hawaiian music, then the 1960s were its 'Dark Age'. One significant statistic in this regard, is that during the period 1960–70 the proportion of Hawaiian music played on local radio dropped as low as 5% (Tartar, 1979: xxvi).

Responses to, and explanations for, this decline were various. At one extreme, some local commentators saw contemporary recordings of traditional Hawaiian music as increasingly archaic (and even embarrassing) for contemporary audiences. As Hawaiian-resident composer, arranger and record producer Jack De Mello argued in 1962 (characterising contemporary recordings of traditional Hawaiian music in a highly contentious manner):

> [n]o longer is the recording industry interested in producing so-called "authentic Hawaiian music" performed with a primitive sound; with faulty chord construction and untrained singers hidden in maze of gourds, drums and a battery of guitars. Time was when such a "local" sound was considered authentic. But the tourist record buyer, as well as the kamaaina [local], now looks for professional performance as well as quality of sound and technical excellence in the recordings. (1962: 21)

For De Mello, this excellence was epitomised by the "new and exotic sounds" of Lyman and Denny (ibid)[3]. Six years later, a *Billboard* magazine special report on the state of the Hawaiian music industry stated that "many" contemporary Hawaiian musicians believed that Hawai'i should "shirk off the old, welcome the new, the mod, the modern, the Mainland[4] sounds and styles" (Tiegel, 1968: 18). Like De Mello's earlier article, this survey also identified Lyman and Denny as instrumental in expanding the sonic potential of Hawaiian music (with their "crystal clear recordings [and] utlization of sound effects"); and concluded that "the enthusiastic spirit of young performers" might soon produce music which would allow Hawaiian traditions to be left behind (ibid).

Such perceptions served to inscribe and, arguably, accelerate the decline in popularity of established styles of local music. Indeed, by the early 1970s advocates of local music culture perceived the situation to be so dire that George Kanahele wrote a celebrated article in the *Honolulu Advertiser* which opened with the attention-grabbing claim that:

> *Popular Hawaiian music is in its death throes. Add it to the necrology of Hawaiiana, for soon it may be buried alongside the ancient mele.* (1971, cited in Kanahele, 1979 [ed]: 115)

One outcome of Kanahele's (cultural) 'call to arms' was the establishment of the Hawaiian Music Foundation in March 1971. This organisation went on to act as a key agency in the revival of traditional Hawaiian music performance, recording, training and promotion during the decade[5].

Lyman's position in this was complex. In one sense, his musical exotica was an element of that musical invasion of Hawaiian radio and music venues which was marginalising traditional styles of local music[6]. On the other, he was a local performer, performing a local version of the (emergent) global genre of musical exotica which – in his version, at least – drew on a range of Hawaiian musical traditions. Lyman was born on Kauai, the northernmost island of the Hawaiian archipelago, in 1936. Like many contemporary Hawaiians, Lyman was of mixed extraction, in his case, Hawaiian, French and Chinese. After moving from Kauai at an early age he grew up in Honolulu and became part of the incipient local surf/leisure scene around Waikiki[7] and began playing vibes (vibraphone) in small Honolulu clubs while still a teenager. The Honolulu that Lyman relocated to was one which was on the threshold of a marked and multi-faceted modernisation (yet another stage in Hawai'i's transition from a discrete Pacific culture to a contemporary, highly porous and fluid society) which was to have marked effects on the cultural and tourist orientation of the Islands.

Lyman first came to public attention as a member of Martin Denny's ensemble. Lyman played with Denny from 1955–56, featuring on Denny's internationally successful debut album *Exotica* and its hit single *Quiet Village* (1957), before leaving, along with bassist John Kramer, to form his own ensemble with percussionist Harold Chang and keyboard player Alan Soares. The ensemble's *Taboo* album (1957), and the title track, released as a single, emulated Denny's debut by becoming major hits in North America (and, to a lesser extent, internationally), with the album going on to sell over two million copies[8]. Like Denny, Lyman approached musical exotica as an enterprise in which musical styles and instruments from various cultural contexts could be unproblematically accessed, in the manner of a quintessential postmodern bricolage, to form a new – and pluralist – syncretic identity. In this regard, it is possible to see Lyman's music as constituting an attempt to produce a modern, multi/pan-cultural Hawaiian musical identity at a time of increased modernisation and further internationalisation of the Islands. His music was, therefore, a direct response to the same sets of pressures and upheavals that the Hawaiian Renaissance movement arose out of. The crucial difference was that Lyman enthusiastically *embraced* change and modernisation.

Many of the contradictions and ambiguities in Lyman's work are crystallised in the music and packaging of his album *The Legend of Pele*, recorded in 1957. The legend of the goddess, Pele, who supposedly lived in the volcanic crater of Kilauae, is a central one in the mythology of Hawai'i's pre-colonial society, and is well known throughout the islands (and features in many tourist-orientated publications)[9]. The album's lengthy sleeve notes relate the legend, ending with the dramatic passage:

> *The preparation of a great eruption began. Down thousands of feet in the pit, lava started to boil. The land about began to tremble and the entire surroundings took on a crimson glow. Fountains of fiery lava shot high into the air, tumbling down and searing the earth for miles around. Those who were present whispered in awe, "Aia Pele!" – "There is Pele!"*

> *Casting aside her cloak of molten lava, she displayed herself as the ever-glorious fire goddess with all the flame of youth, beauty, love and passion. In this fantastic setting, Pele knows all. She has been, is and always shall be, in the pantheon of Hawaiian worship, the Deity most revered and at the same time most dreaded.*

> *Pele Pele E Pele E...*

These passages present a powerful account of the legend of Pele[10]. In this way they can be seen as a positive contribution to the dissemination of Hawaiian mythologies in a popular cultural context. However, this aspect is given a dramatically disruptive and transformational twist by the album's cover design. Its image features a spectacularly buxom, blonde, pale-skinned female, representing Pele, rising in flames from a pool of molten lava. The choice of such an identifiably Aryan figure to symbolise a (specifically) Hawaiian goddess underlines the manner in which the album's designers and/or Hi-Fi Records (the Los Angeles-based company for whom Lyman recorded until 1964) perceived both Lyman and the album as primarily targeted at a tourist/international/North American audience (rather than addressed to a Hawaiian audience with their own distinct cultural sensibilities).

Similarly to the visual packaging, the album's title track takes a culturally pluralist approach to representing its subject. Instead of any studious reworking of Hawaiian music traditions, Lyman's track incorporates indigenous elements (most prominently, a recording of traditional Hawaiian vocal incantations) into a re-working of an earlier, European, musical representation of primitive, passionate exotica –

Spanish composer Manuel de Falla's dynamic *Ritual Fire Dance*[11]. The choice of this composition as the basis for Lyman's piece of florid Hawaiiana is significant since, as James Parakilas (1998) has detailed, de Falla's composition, and, indeed, his broader career, can be characterised in terms of its "auto-exoticism"; its reworking/re-indigenising of French musical conventions of exotic Spanishness[12]. Parakilas asserts a significant position for this approach with regard to contemporary local-national musics; identifying de Falla's project as marked by his "conscious[ness] that it was through exoticism that [Spanish] musical traditions had been transformed into modern ... music" (1998: 188)[13] – a characterisation also clearly applicable to Lyman's own musical vision.

II. Cool jazz

In various interviews Lyman has identified his early, formative musical interest as big-band jazz. He has also recalled that he taught himself to play music as a child by playing along with Benny Goodman records and learning Lionel Hampton vibraphone solos by performing them on a toy marimba in his bedroom[14]. Influenced by other jazz players, such as Trummy Young and, particularly, the West Coast style of jazz popularly referred to as 'cool', he began playing jazz in small clubs in Honolulu in 1947, before linking up with Denny in 1955. Cool jazz was a style which developed on the U.S. West Coast in the late 1940s. Its approach was predicated on a controlled and restrained musical style which, while often complex, had minimal melodic ornamentation. Bruce Johnson has characterised it in terms of its "deliberate sparseness and the attenuation of the expressive dimensions of the music" (e-mail to the authors 19/5/97). For its players and aficionados it was also characterised by a sartorial style and attitude which similarly expressed composure, hipness and sophistication as markers of generational/sub-cultural difference and modernity. In its most self-consciously artistic instances, such as the Modern Jazz Quartet, it even aspired to a contemporary classicism, one premised on the restraint of its instrumental style.

The vibraphone – as it name suggests – is an instrument which features a heavy vibrato effect. Indeed, this is its central feature, the vibrato being innate to its sound rather than an optional aspect. The instrument was invented in the mid-1920s, and comprises a series of metal bars, ascending in pitch, connected to resonating metal tubes which the performer plays by striking them with sticks known as 'hammers'. Hampton played a leading role in establishing the instrument as an accepted member of the small jazz ensemble – via a series of seminal recordings with the Benny Goodman Quartet (beginning in 1936)[15]. The sonority of the vibraphone was well-suited to cool and 'third stream' jazz, and Milt Jackson's virtuosic work with the Modern Jazz Quartet helped to consolidate the place of the instrument within 1950s' jazz.

While Lyman's music was clearly influenced by the musical styles and general ethos of cool jazz, it blended this aspect with elements of Hawaiian culture (both traditional and syncretic). This was reflected in the instrumental line-up of his band (which played together until the late 1960s) comprising Lyman on vibes, Harold Chang on percussion, Alan Soares on keyboards and John Kramer on double bass, guitar and ukulele[16]. Lyman's oeuvre reflected the band's location in an environment which was increasingly international; where Honolulu was a cultural hub, and where the band's own cultural plurality became the basis for a new musical expression. The style Lyman developed was far removed from any model of the (relatively simple) syncretic combination of a (notionally) 'pure' indigenous music and imported/imposed western forms. Rather, it was a more pluralist style, mediated through jet/cruise tourist culture as it moved through the lens and gateway of Honolulu – and specifically Waikiki. It can be characterised as a local creolisation of musical styles and influences produced by an ensemble whose own identity was also creole[17].

III. *Taboo*

Lyman's *Taboo* remains his best-known and most commercially-successful album. Its cover design combined two seemingly paradoxical but inter-linked facets of musical exotica: a powerful primitivism and (for the time) a high-tech production context – primeval forces as opposed to sophisticated human modernity. Unlike the demure cover of Denny's debut – showing a young woman gazing out from behind a beaded curtain – the front cover of *Taboo* comprises a vividly coloured image of an erupting volcano and lava flows (referencing the volcanoes of Hawai'i). The rear cover features a detailed description of the recording venue and technology used on the album. Like all Lyman's recordings for the Hi-Fi label in the period 1957–64, the album was produced by Richard Vaughan in the Henry J. Kaiser Dome, an aluminium structure constructed outside the Hawaiian Village Hotel in Honolulu[18]. Similarly to Denny's early albums, *Taboo*'s cover notes detail the precise recording equipment used and stress the album's appeal for audiophiles[19]. Vaughan's sleeve notes state that:

> [t]he Dome is a half sphere, seating about 1500 persons and is used for live entertainment and movie showings. We chose this place for our recordings because the half-sphere shape has no peaks and allows a pleasing, easy sound reproduction with natural room acoustical three second reverberation.

Daniel Caccavo, the re-mastering engineer on the 1996 CD reissue of the *Hawaiian Sunset* album, states in its CD booklet notes that this reverberation is "quite unique" -specifying that "it has a nice 'flutter' to it [which] is particularly effective for percussion instruments", creating a richness and 'breadth' to the sound. (Caccavo has also added that the result is "very modern sounding" [ibid])[20].

99

The reverberative qualities of the recording venue are a distinctive element of the classic Lyman sound, since the majority of tracks on his HiFi albums were recorded live, in single takes with minimal post-production. This aspect is emphasised in the *Taboo* sleeve notes, which state that due to the recording process used "perfect sound reproduction [was] achieved". This reference to the perfection of the sound reproduction refers to the producer's attempt to produce as faithfully 'transparent' a recording of the spatiality and balance of instrumental voices – as heard performed live – as possible[21]. The arrangements featured on *Taboo* (and subsequent albums) complement the audiophilic emphasis of the sleeve notes through a series of subtle and/or often dramatic combinations of musical elements[22].

Given that the membership and instrumental line-up of Lyman's band was stable during his seminal period of musical production (1957–64), and the acoustic quality of the venue remained unaltered, there is a consistency of acoustic quality to his work in the period in question which marks his recordings out from albums recorded by other artists using different studios, producers and/or individual musicians (etc.) Consequently, the following sections analyse and evaluate Lyman's work from a primarily musicological viewpoint (rather than combining this with an analysis of the [differential] acoustic dynamics of individual recorded sound productions).

As the following analysis details, *Taboo's* title track – an arrangement of a Lecuona/Stillman composition previously covered by Les Baxter on his *Caribbean Moonlight* album (1956) – exemplifies the qualities which Lyman became renown for. Lyman's version features a highly sophisticated musical arrangement which serves to complicate any blanket dismissal of his work as a predictable, simplistic style of easy-listening music. This is not to fall into any crude argument that complexity necessarily represents refinement and/or aesthetic excellence/'superiority'; but rather to make the point that musical distinctions within the broad genre of exotica are evident.

The opening section of *Taboo* immediately invokes an exotic, island-type setting by employing a sustained 'conch shell' sound, followed by the establishment of a regular rhythmic pattern augmented by a series of bird calls (an immediately recognisable aural marker of late 1950s' musical exoticism). The conch shell call is pitched on the note E, which is the fifth or dominant note of A minor (the key of the ensuing section). The repeated rhythmic pattern highlights the distinctive sound of the *guiro*, under which the bass plays a slightly syncopated two-bar figure (see Example 1). After the repeated rhythmic pattern is established, Lyman introduces the main melody on vibes. The opening phrase of this theme consists of a minor pentatonic melodic idea harmonised by a part a third below (see Example 2), and supported by the i chord (A minor). This section of the theme circles around the dominant note (E), which was first introduced by the conch shell. The second phrase of the melody provides a four bar 'answer' to the opening phrase. It is also built from the minor pentatonic scale and employs an identical rhythmic pattern to the opening phrase; and the lower harmony part is now placed at a sixth below the melody. This phrase is supported by the sub-dominant (iv) chord – D minor.

Example 1.

To this point then, the music is even and predictable – employing the seductive tone of the vibes; a smoothly flowing melody; a regular rhythmic pattern on percussion; the consonant sound of third and sixth harmonies; and 'primary' chords (i and iv).

When the ensuing phrase moves to the dominant chord (E), Lyman introduces several prominent new features. Most notable is the disruptive role played by the

Example 2.

acoustic piano, which has a 'surprise' entry on the weak (second) beat of the bar, disturbing the serenity of the preceding section. A number of elements accentuate this disruptive function. The clear, vibrato-free tone of the piano contrasts markedly with the tone of the vibes, as does the accented, percussive-style part given to the instrument; the volume of the piano part is also sufficient to overpower the other parts momentarily, and the piano tends to push ahead of the beat in an almost impatient manner. At the same, time the vibes part introduces a distinctive 'oriental' flavour by employing the sound of the perfect fifth interval between the upper and lower part of the parallel major chords (see Example 3). The piano figure rises in pitch with each repetition, creating a build-up of tension, before release is provided by a return to A minor and repetition of the first eight bars of the original melodic material.

Lyman is not content to allow the listener a complete return to the serenity of the opening melody, however. After the eight-bar repetition, he ends this section of the music by creating a variation of the opening melodic phrase. This variation involves a repetition of the leaping fifth of the opening melodic idea, followed by a varied ending to the phrase. Lyman also re-introduces the contrast provided by the acoustic

Example 3.

piano, which doubles the vibe melody at certain points. In addition, Lyman's arrangement features bird calls prominently – placing them on the last beat of a number of bars.

The ensuing section provides a marked contrast with the preceding section by employing percussion instruments exclusively; changing from a 4/4 to 6/8 feel; and changing key (from A minor to F major). The section begins with a conga-like sound which outlines an F major triad played with a distinctive rhythmic figure (see Example 4). Other parts are added to create a basic rhythmic groove, and subsequently Lyman introduces an increasing level of rhythmic complexity by inter-

Example 4.

Example 5.

posing additional irregular rhythms. After establishing the F major tonality of the section, Lyman introduces an element of dissonance by featuring a tuned bongo part which alternates the pitches G and F# as the section progresses.

The third section returns to a 4/4 feel and, like the second section, opens with a prominent melodic motif performed by tuned percussion (see Example 5). As Example 5 illustrates, the rhythm part is now simple, on-beat and regular. This main melodic percussion motif can be heard as outlining either (or both) a Dmin7 chord or an F major triad (the pitch of the first note is not completely clear). The tonality of the section becomes clear upon the entry of the original melody from the opening section, which is now played by flute in D minor. This time the theme is given a more 'primitive' quality – performed by the 'exposed' solo flute accompanied only by percussion – and the melody receives a slightly freer, quasi-improvisatory treatment. Backing harmony is more drone-like in character, with percussion instruments outlining a static sense of D minor. The more modern pop flavour, which was evident in the opening section – through the use of a bass line, additional vibe parts and clearly articulated chord changes – is absent. As in the preceding section, Lyman introduces a slightly dissonant flavour in the bongo part by again featuring the semitone movement between G and F#. When the music moves to the dominant chord (A major), the arrangement more closely parallels the opening section – with the acoustic piano employed in a dramatic fashion for contrast, and a perfect fifth part introduced below the melody.

The fourth and final section, like the second, employs a change of tempo and is based around the sound of percussion instruments, which play numerous overlapping rhythms. The tonality of the piece remains D minor, and there is an overall feel of two beats in the bar. Once again, however, Lyman creates a sense of ambiguity – this time by moving between an even subdivision of the beat (implying 2/4) and uneven subdivision (implying 6/8). The rhythms include a number of rapid-fire patterns which help to propel the music to a sense of climax, accentuated by the inclusion of human voices for the first time in the work. Lyman again pays careful attention to the subtleties of instrumental (and vocal) balance, with only a hint of the human voices allowed to permeate the complex percussive texture. The result of this subtlety is to make the impact of the voices more, rather than less powerful. Equally subtle is the ending, in which Lyman allows the instruments and voices to appear to trail off into the distance rather than attempting to resolve the work with some final dramatic musical statement.

It is important to note that Lyman pays careful attention to overall structure in his *Taboo* arrangement – demonstrating a sophisticated understanding of the way in which melodic, harmonic, rhythmic and textural/timbral elements can be employed to produce a satisfying balance of repetition and variety, and to create a coherent overall musical form. For example, Lyman employs changes of time signature and tempo for each of the four sections of the arrangement, and alternates sections which contain mostly regular, predictable rhythms with those which incorporate more complex and irregular patterns. Regular rhythms are employed in those sections (one and three) which feature prominent melodic ideas, while the percussive sections involve more complex rhythms. Melodic ideas are prominent in the first and third sections, but absent from the second and fourth sections. When the opening melody re-appears (in the third section), it is played on flute and subjected to some variation, while the piano motif and perfect fifth intervals function as a link between sections one and three.

Lyman also displays a particularly sophisticated awareness of harmonic structure. The tonality of the first three sections (A[m], F, D[m]) can be seen to outline D minor – the ultimate tonal 'goal' of the work. In addition, Lyman's alternation of major and minor tonality between sections demonstrates an understanding of the concept of superimposed triads (see Example 6), and he provides a subtle manipulation of dissonance in what might be seen as a playful use of the G-F# movement, both in relation to the F and D key areas. This contrast also functions as an audible link between sections three and four. Percussion parts are given prominence via their volume level within the sound mix, while Lyman also uses timbral contrasts (eg vibes/piano; vibes/flute; melodic instruments/percussion) to introduce variation and

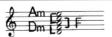

Example 6.

to create an element of surprise at certain points. Distinctive percussion motifs are present throughout, and a wide variety of percussion instruments is employed overall.

Taboo served a model for a series of other accomplished 'jungle'-style compositions in Lyman's oeuvre (such as *Bwana A* [1957], *Jungle Drums* [1963] and *Blue Hawaii* [1961]) – which feature bird calls, extensive percussion sections, marked tempo changes, solo flute melodies etc. These aspects, also present in Denny's work, provide a strong sense of 'jungleness' and the exotic which provides an injection of 'hot' elements to the cool jazz roots of his style. As signature elements to late 1950s' exotica, which rapidly became much imitated and clichéd, they also constitute a specific historical marker to the particular exotic imagination of 1950s'/early 1960s' continental North America, attuned (largely by Hollywood cinema and literary fiction) to think of primitive cultures as marked by drums in the night, and by teeming, abundant tropical nature and the supposedly 'hothouse' passions of those who inhabit such terrains.

IV. Orientalism, mellifluence and jazz

As our analysis of *Taboo* identifies, the track is marked by an imaginative and sophisticated musical arrangement and demonstrates Lyman's highly-developed sense of instrumental colour and musical contrast. However, the 'jungle' sub-genre of exotica only constituted one element of Lyman's oeuvre. As in Denny's work, orientalism was also prominent category. Compositions arranged in this manner commonly employed descriptive titles which signalled their orientalism (eg *China Clipper* [1957], *Ottome San (Japanese Drinking Song)* [1958] and *March of the Siamese Children* [1962]) and often incorporated oriental elements such as pentatonic scales, parallel fifth harmonies, Burmese gongs etc.

China Clipper exemplifies Lyman's approach to this (sub-)genre, combining oriental elements with a swinging jazz section to create a musical hybrid. The introduction presents a prominent oriental-sounding 'circular' melodic motif (see Example 7) played at a slow tempo and augmented by a variety of distinctive percussion sounds (xylophone, Burmese gong etc.). The oriental flavour of the motif is enhanced by parallel perfect fifth intervals, and there is an interesting mild dissonance created by featuring the sound of the D (2nd) and F (4th) notes over the tonic C. Mild dissonance

Example 7.

is also present in the subsequent melodic phrase, which features both major and minor second interval relationships at certain points, as well as bass movement (Bb-Eb-Bb-C) against a static upper melodic part.

Lyman introduces two surprise elements in the beginning of the second section. The first involves a sudden establishment of a very fast 4/4 swing tempo. The second is more subtle, and is achieved by repeating the final melodic motif several times and then changing the bass note to a repeated G. This technique results in a sense of tonal ambiguity. Is the note G which ends the first section to be heard as the fifth of C minor (as in the opening) ? Or now as the tonic in G minor ? This ambiguity is further accentuated by the ending of the subsequent phrase once again in C minor. The section then settles into fairly predictable up-tempo, swing jazz in C minor – featuring a walking bass line; short syncopated melodic/rhythmic statements and answering drum fills; a typical fast-swing hi-hat pattern; an improvised vibes solo with a 'comping' rhythm section; and a return to the opening 'head' which was presented at the beginning of the section. Once again, however, Lyman deliberately disrupts the flow of the music, creating an additional element of surprise. This time the disruption involves a return to the slow tempo of the opening and to the second melodic motif, after which the original motif finally re-appears. The Burmese gong is then used to end the piece. Lyman therefore creates a cleverly constructed mirror-image form – with the major themes presented in reverse order after the vibes solo.

Lyman's liking for evocative, impressionistic instrumentation, tonal variety and musical surprises (detailed in the analyses of *Taboo* and *China Clipper* above) is evident in a large proportion of his arrangements, from the more 'exotic' through to those identified as more 'traditional'. *Dahil Sayo* (1957) provides a good example of the way in which Lyman manipulates 'traditional' material to create an interesting and distinctive musical arrangement. Lyman's version of *Dahil Sayo* comprises three discreet sections which are each characterised by distinctive rhythmic features, creating variety and complexity within an otherwise predictable and repetitive framework. The first section employs an underlying Latin-style bass rhythm (see Example 8), while the second section involves both a change in the rhythm pattern and the introduction of a number of new percussion instruments. The third section

Example 8.

Example 9.

highlights a new rhythmic pattern, played in staccato fashion upon the acoustic piano (see Example 9), whose clear tone provides a marked contrast to the vibrato-laden sounds of the vibes.

Lyman's jazz background is evident in most of his arrangements, with jazz elements ranging from rhythm section grooves through to call/response sections and extended solo improvisations. In some songs (eg *China Clipper* [1957], *Cubana Chant* [1959] and *Love for Sale* [1963]) jazz elements take a very prominent role, clearly shifting the focus (at least temporarily) from 'exotic' elements towards the jazz groove itself and associated instrumental solos. Yet, despite his obvious liking for musical contrast and variety (and jazz), Lyman sometimes presents inherently appealing material in a simple uncluttered, and often highly 'catchy' format. Indeed, it is somewhat paradoxical that Lyman's two most popular (and, arguably, most effective) arrangements, *Taboo* and *Yellow Bird*, are at opposite ends of the arrangement spectrum.

In contrast to the complexity and sophistication of *Taboo*, *Yellow Bird* (which reached #4 on the U.S. singles charts in 1961), is notable for its mellifluousness – the smooth simplicity and predictability of the arrangement – and eschews the surprise elements and structural complexity evident in *Taboo* and *China Clipper*. In *Yellow Bird* the appealingly simple, conjunct and smooth-flowing melodic ideas are given a prominent role. Symmetrical four-bar melodic phrases feature throughout, apart from the addition of an extra bar towards the end of the B section. The consonant and predictable sound of the third interval is regularly employed to harmonise the melody, while the vibrato-laden sounds of the vibes, marimba and organ are augmented by tremolo effects on xylophone, and enhanced by the specific reverberative qualities of the Kaiser Dome, to produce the evocative 'shimmering' sound which characterises the work. *Yellow Bird* uses a simple, clichéd harmonic scheme, involving only the primary triads in D major, and the rhythm is smooth, unaccented and predictable. The song follows a simple ABABA structure and dynamics are muted throughout. In contrast to the sophistication of *Taboo*, *Yellow Bird* is an appealing example of the effectivity of a simple, repetitive melodic and rhythmic pattern.

V. Lyman and Denny

At this point it is perhaps timely to reflect on the still-common perception of Lyman as a Denny imitator – ie of Denny as the innovator and Lyman as the copyist. Aside from questions as to the problematic nature of innovation and originality in popular music (not to mention whether these have ever been essential for commercial and/or critical success); the particular nature of Lyman's departure from Denny's ensemble merits attention. When Lyman left Denny's ensemble in 1956 he was also accompanied by bassist John Kramer, effectively splitting the band in two. In this manner, it is possible to argue that the departing members were as much 'entitled' to the sound as Denny and the new members who replaced them[23]. In addition, it is readily apparent that Lyman's arrangements generally involve much stronger contrasts (in relation to timbre, texture, rhythm, dynamics etc) than Denny's, and, in that sense, represent a further development of the 'exotic' style of arrangement, rather than a simple imitation. Although it is beyond the scope of this chapter to present a detailed comparison of Denny and Lyman's work, some insight into their different arranging styles can be gained from a brief examination of Denny's (seminal) hit arrangement of the Les Baxter composition *Quiet Village* (1957)[24] and Lyman's version, recorded two years later[25].

Denny's introduction to *Quiet Village* begins with imitation bird calls, after which a bass motif is introduced on piano and string bass (see Example 10), accompanied by a prominent rhythmic figure (see Example 11). The acoustic piano takes the role of main melodic instrument throughout the ensuing section, while percussion instruments continue with the figure illustrated in Example 11. In the second section, the prominent percussion motif of Example 11 ceases. The piano plays a new, more rhythmic, block-chord theme, and is joined by a new counter melody which features the vibes. The sound of the acoustic piano still remains dominant in the recorded sound mix however. This section follows an internal AABA form and also features some new percussion sounds – bells, gongs etc. The final section can be described

Example 10.

Example 11.

as an 'outro', and mirrors the introduction by featuring bird calls, the bass theme, and the rhythmic figure of Example 11.

Lyman's introduction begins with the same bass motif employed by Denny, but in Lyman's arrangement the motif is played on the string bass alone, and the bird calls and rhythmic figure of Example 11 enter after the bass figure. Lyman employs the soft tones of the vibes and flute when he introduces the melody of the ensuing section. In addition, Lyman features a delicate counter-melody on celeste and glockenspiel throughout this section. In the second section, Lyman removes the rhythmic figure of Example 11, and introduces the acoustic piano on the bass motif. The piano enters loudly and plays in an accented staccato manner – thereby providing a marked contrast to the soft, sustained tones of the opening section. Lyman, like Denny, also uses the piano for the new, more rhythmical block-chord theme, but he features the counter-melody in this section much more prominently than Denny, and he also uses tremolo effects to highlight the contrast between the

107

piano motif and the counter theme. Lyman also uses dynamic contrasts, prominent percussive sounds and rhythmic motifs to create the effect of a new, contrasting section for what is the 'B' part of the AABA internal structure embodied in Denny's second section. In addition, Lyman removes the piano from the final 'A' of the AABA and features the sound of the vibes on the counter-melody, thereby creating further variety. Lyman's 'outro' is also less of an exact copy of the introduction than Denny's.

This brief analysis demonstrates that Lyman's arrangement of *Quiet Village* is considerably more varied than Denny's; and illustrates Lyman's liking for sectional changes and his clever manipulation of tonal and dynamic contrasts to create aural complexity. For example, while Denny uses the sound of the acoustic piano through-out the his arrangement, Lyman chooses the soft tones of the vibes and flute as continuing elements. As a result, when Lyman ultimately introduces the piano, along with tremolo effects on marimba, it provides a change of instrumental colour lacking in Denny's arrangement. Lyman subsequently employs strong dynamic contrasts to create interest, in contrast with the evenness and predictability of Denny's arrange-ment. Denny does create some variation by using an assortment of percussion sounds, but even in this area Lyman's arrangement is more distinctive – utilising a wider range of contrasting sounds, and featuring the percussion more prominently in the sound mix. Overall then, while Denny's arrangement has a sense of continuous flow, Lyman's version of *Quiet Village,* like many of his arrangements, embodies several distinct sections which are defined by changes in instrumentation, dynamics and rhythm – all qualities which work against the easy-listening orientation of Denny's principal work.

This specific analytical comparison identifies aspects of the essential distinctions between Denny's and Lyman's styles. Despite dismissals of Lyman as a 'Denny imitator', their recordings have notable differences which suggest that Lyman's work, in significant part, falls outside the general characteristics of Denny's oeuvre (identified as standard/exemplary musical exotica) as discussed by Shuhei Hosok-awa in Chapter 3. In particular, given what might be seen as the extra musical complexity of typical Lyman arrangements (as compared to Denny's), it is interest-ing to speculate as to whether the popularity of Lyman's work was actually hampered by the fact that, in terms of musical style, it lay somewhere between the categories of Dennyesque exotica and cool jazz (with too much variety and contrast for the former; and too many exotic elements for the latter). As a result, Lyman's work can be perceived to have become increasingly tangential to Denny's drift to a formulaic MOR style (described by Hosokawa in Chapter 3 as a standard 'recipe') from the early-mid 1960s; thereby ensuring Lyman a marked decline in sales and slide into (semi-)obscurity following his prominence in the late 1950s[26]. (This is not to suggest that Lyman himself did not increasingly repeat standard musical formulae as the 1960s progressed; but rather that even his more predictable output still retained a significantly different inflection to Denny's.)

Conclusion: re-locating Lyman

In 1959, Lyman addressed the musical traditions of his homeland and recorded an album entitled *Hawaiian Sunset*. This included versions of traditional Hawaiian compositions (such as *Im Au Oe*, *Hulawe* and *Waipio*) and hapa haole standards (such as *Sweet Leilani*, *Song of the Islands* and *Mapuana*). The album re-read various Hawaiian (and Hawaiian-associated) styles of music, through Lyman's established approaches to arranging (ie jungle, jazz, mellow etc.). To complement the album's theme and range of material Lyman included several traditional Hawaiian instruments commonly used to accompany hula performances – such as the *ipu* (a percussion instrument constructed from two hollowed out gourds), *puili* (a split bamboo rattle) and *uliuli* (gourd rattle)[27] – along with the established instrumental line-up of his band. One instrument significantly left out from the ensemble on the album (and all his other recordings) is the steel guitar. This omission is all the more notable since many of the compositions re-arranged by Lyman on the album are best known in – and closely associated with – the use of the steel guitar as a lead instrumental voice.

On *Hawaiian Sunset*, Lyman 'compensates' for the absence of the steel guitar by replacing it with the vibes. His melodic lines on this instrument do not simply provide an alternative melodic lead, they effectively 'impersonate' many of the melodic styles and standard generic ornamentations associated with Hawaiian-style steel guitar playing. The major difference, and major revision of musical sound involved, is the replacement of the prominent glissando of Hawaiian steel guitar music – with its highly emotive, melancholic and/or melodramatic instrumental affectivity – with the 'cooler', more 'controlled' and instrumental effect of the vibes' vibrato (emphasised by the Dome's distinct acoustic qualities, as discussed above). This substitution exemplifies one of the key tenets of cool jazz – as defined by Johnson – its "deliberate ... attenuation of the expressive dimensions of the music"[28].

While the vibes had occasionally been used in combination with the steel guitar in various Hawaiian music ensembles since the late 1920s[29]; this instrumental substitution is one of the most distinctive aspects of Lyman's reworking of Hawaiian musical style(s), and dates back to the development of the original 'Martin Denny Sound' in the mid-1950s, when Lyman was a key member of Denny's band and instrumental in designing 'his' sound. Indeed, Denny has himself identified Lyman's instrumental contribution as marking, affecting and characterising "the transformation" from traditional Hawaiian music to contemporary exotica (cited in von Stroheim: npd). With particular regard to Denny's work, we might also understand this to refer to a transformation from a musical form premised on its dramatic expressivity to one premised on its easy-listenability.

Having stressed the difference – and different affectivities – of the vibes as a 'replacement' for the steel guitar, it should also be noted, paradoxically, that the vibes' innate vibrato can also be seen as complementary to elements of traditional

Hawaiian music; since traditional vocal chants, 20th Century singing styles, slack-key and steel-guitar music (along with traditional instruments such as the *'ohe kani, hano* [nose flute] and *ukeke* [musical bow]) – all of which enable prominent use of vibrato. In Lyman's music however, the vibrato does not embody a highly personal performative quality but rather (antithetically), a precisely controlled and (material-mechanically) 'pre-programmed' feature of instrumental design. The vibes' vibrato is, therefore, sonically similar but highly different in stylistic significance and signification. It is as archetypally 'cool' as cool jazz itself, an instrumental effect rather than a player's own stylistic expression of emotion and/or emphasis. In this regard, the use of the vibraphone as a lead melodic instrument, playing melodic lines closely modelled on standard steel guitar phrasing, represents a distinctive extension of established genres of Hawaiian music and presents *Hawaiian Sunset* as a show-case for the possibilities of such an instrumental approach.

Although *Hawaiian Sunset* was the only album Lyman recorded specifically dedicated to Hawaiian compositions, one of his most revealing – and in many ways self-defining – recordings was his own composition *Aloha-No Honolulu*, included on the album *Colorful Percussions* (1962). 'Aloha', perhaps the best-known Hawaiian language word, has a cluster of meanings associated with love, affection, warmth and generosity. The title of the composition applies these feelings to the city of Honolulu and, understood in the sense of the classic Hawaiian *himeni* (hymn) *Hawai'i Aloha*, also connotes a love of place/land. Appropriately in this regard, the track begins with a slow, almost sombre melody played over a simple chord progression built from primary triads – evoking the dignity of traditional Hawaiian music. However, as in much of Lyman's work, the sense of serenity is soon interrupted and replaced; in this instance by a more rhythmically-oriented section.

The second section of *Aloha-No Honolulu* continues the chord progression of the opening section, but becomes marked by a regular repeated rhythmic accompani-ment figure in 4/4 time which abruptly changes the mood of the piece. When the third section is introduced, there are two new prominent elements. Firstly, the tempo changes again, into a jaunty, up-tempo duple feel (somewhat incongruously) more typical of 'hillbilly' music; and secondly, Lyman modulates from the C major key of the opening two sections into F major for the final section. Despite these relatively radical changes, Lyman maintains a sense of continuity by continuing the actual chord progression of the opening (but now in F), and by maintaining the original rhythmic figure (but now played in up-tempo duple feel). The piece therefore conveys the sense of rapid alteration within a continuing, accelerating, dynamic. The composition ends in an oddly unresolved fashion (for Lyman) by petering out with a repetition of the third section – as if suggesting an unresolved, to-be-continued and/or problematic, transitional identification for the city of Honolulu which the track alludes to.

Despite Lyman's endeavours to address aspects of traditional Hawaiian music on *Hawaiian Sunset*, and on tracks on subsequent albums, his work has rarely, if ever, been considered by local critics within the (continuing) tradition of contemporary Hawaiian music in the Islands. Underlining his 'invisibility' in terms of dominant local histories is his omission from George Kanahele's 543 page encyclopedia *Hawaiian Music and Musicians* (1979). While a nine page section is devoted to the work of British band leader Felix Mendelssohn (whose ensemble featured vibes and accordion alongside steel guitars) (ibid: 241–249) , there is no individual entry on Lyman. Similarly, while the Index lists Bing Crosby as referred to in eleven entries, there is no individual reference to Lyman's work (even in passing)[30].

Despite the awkwardness and/or tangential nature of many aspects of Lyman's work to the Hawaiian Renaissance, this chapter argues that the revival in popularity of musical exotica in the 1990s might be an appropriate moment for a re-examination and reappraisal of Lyman's career and oeuvre from a number of positions. Indeed, it might be argued that his work merits attention for its musical accomplishment and – precisely *due to* – the very problematic nature of its political and cultural symbolism. The point is not so much to try the awkward feat of attempting to redeem Lyman within an indigenous Hawaiian context (and/or 1990s' perceptions of political correctness) but rather to more clearly identify the reasons for his marginalisation, the awkwardness of his 'fit', to any histories – dominant or otherwise[31].

Thanks to Amy Ku'uleialoha Stillman for her insightful comments on an earlier draft of this chapter[32] and to Rebecca Coyle, Marie-Louise Clafflin and John Marsden for various other assistances.

Notes

1. See various entries under country names (eg England, Holland, Japan etc.) in Kanahele (ed) (1979); and Coyle, J and Coyle, R (1995) and Hosokawa (1994), respectively, for individual studies of studies of its success in Australia and Japan.

2. In 1961 Elvis Presley, then at the peak of his popularity, visited the island to star in Norman Taurog's film *Blue Hawaii* (which included songs such as the hit single *I Can't Help Falling in Love*, Presley's version of the Hawaiian standard *Aloha Oe*, the title track [recorded by Lyman in the same year with an almost paradoxically intense 'jungle' arrangement] and the novelty number *Rock-a-hula Baby*). Featuring generous expanses of Hawaiian scenery, and with Presley playing the role of a travel agency employee, the film was highly effective as an extended tourist promotion aimed at the North American market.

3. De Mello's own work as a producer combined (westernised) orchestral arrangements and clear separation of audio elements on a series of albums produced for the Honolulu-based 'Music of Polynesia' label from 1968 on.

4. As Amy Stillman has pointed out, the very use (and concept) of North America *being* a "*main*-land" for Hawai'i, reflects a colonialist ideology which views the Islands as peripheral to a continental centre (e-mail to the authors 21.2.98).

5. See the entry for the Hawaiian Music Foundation in Kanahele (ed) (1979) (115–120) for an account of its work in the 1970s.

6. In the decade between the late 1950s and late 1960s Lyman played a residency at the Hawaiian Village Hotel's Shell Bar, when he was not touring on the mainland.

7. See von Stroheim (1995: 14).

8.   Lyman's profile in Hawai'i was boosted by his ensemble being employed as house band on the popular TV show *Hawaiian Eye* in 1958–59, backing vocalists such as Connie Stevens and Robert Conrad.

9.   For a more detailed account of the legend of Pele see Colum (1937).

10.   They also continue a theme presented on the cover of Lyman's hit album *Taboo*, with its lurid colour cover image of a volcanic lava-flow and a sleeve notes which states: "Awesome, vibrantly beautiful, primitive, the great volcano – parent of the islands, symbolises the Paradise ... known as the Hawaiian Islands"; and the cover of *Yellow Bird*, which features a dramatic lava spurt.

11.   NB The album's track credits also reference a previous arrangement of the composition by jazz flautist Herbie Mann as the model for the Lyman ensemble's version.

12.   As he also argues, this musical approach offers "one of the earliest case studies of the condition, common to musicians in many parts of the world today, of being able to produce a marketable art only by exoticising oneself and one's culture" (Parakilas, 1998: 139).

13.   Indeed, as Parakilis identifies, De Falla was explicit in acknowledging the debt owed by Spanish composers to Claude Debussy for re-attuning them to aspects of traditional Spanish music (ibid: 188–189).

14.   Sleeve notes to his 1975 album *Puka Shells*.

15.   Hampton's later album, *Golden Vibes* (196?) showcases his virtuosity on the vibraphone and offers a number of points of comparison to Lyman's own work.

16.   Several of the band also had multi-instrumental talents and played other instruments on recordings – Lyman played occasional guitar and percussion and Kramer contributed flute and clarinet parts. Several early recordings also featured guest musician Chew Hoon Chang on flute and harp.

17.   See the Introduction to this volume for a discussion of musical creolisation and syncretism.

18.   The Dome, like the radio station KHVH, was established by Kaiser, a millionaire industrialist, to promote and popularise his tastes in local culture.

19.   Indeed, Steve Hoffman has noted that the particular sound quality of Lyman's early recordings facilitated their use as "demonstration discs" for "proud new phonograph owners" in the late 1950s and early 1960s (Hoffman: npd).

20.   It is worth noting however that Lyman has subsequently disparaged the acoustic properties of the dome – stating "the HiFi sound ? Yuck ! Kaiser Dome, it bounces back" (cited in von Stroheim: npd). And Daniel Caccavo has conceded that, for all the acoustic 'liveliness' of the venue, and its character on recordings undertaken there, he "could certainly understand how [the reverberations] might be hellish for the musicians" (ibid).

21.   The sleevenotes' reference to the high-tech apparatus employed in the recording emphasises this aspect, specifying use of "three AKG Austrian microphones" (a medium-high cost and quality model) and a "custom built Ampex portable three-track one-half inch magnetic tape recorder" (half inch tape, as opposed to the then-standard quarter inch, giving added detail and quality of recorded sound).

22.   These were worked-up and tightly rehearsed by Lyman and his band in advance of recording sessions at the Dome. Given their use of a sound stage (half) open to the environment, the band used to record at night, commencing at 3am, when the area was quietest. As Lyman later recalled:

      All we did was roll our instruments across to the Aluminium Dome. At 2 o'clock in the morning we'd go out and eat breakfast, 3 o'clock we'd come back in and start recording. That's a good time, cause you're warmed up. We would work 'til 9 o'clock (a.m.). (cited in von Stroheim: npd).

23.   It is also worth noting that Lyman's new ensemble, with the addition of Alan Soares (keyboards and percussion) and Harold Chang (percussion) was entirely Hawaiian in composition.

24.   NB Baxter's original version of this composition is discussed in Chapter Two.

25. Indeed, it might be argued that Lyman's re-arrangement of Denny's hit is a pointed rejoinder to the notion of him being a Denny 'copyist', offering, as it does, a clear indication of their stylistic difference.

26. Lyman's work was better received in Japan, which he first toured in 1964 and again in 1970. His style of exoticised Hawaiianna was familiar, and thereby appealing, to Japanese audiences through factors such as their familiarity with the vibraphone in Japanese Hawaiian music; their awareness of the (so-called) Jazz Hawaiian' style developed by guitarist Buckie Shirakata's band; and through the previous mediation of Hawaiian music through the work of various Japanese-Hawaiian performers in the 1930s and 1940s. In this regard, Lyman's vibes-orientated exotica had a notable predecessor in the work of Eiichi Asabuki. Best known as a steel guitarist , Asabuki came to the guitar after a career as a well-known xylophonist in the 1920s and popularised the vibraphone in the 1940s, performing it with his seminal band the Kalua Kamaainas. In the Japanese context, at least, *Hawaiian Sunset* gets closest to bridging the essentially infra-referentiality of 1950s/1960s musical exotica and a specific indigenous-derived musical tradition.

27. Lyman also played slack-key guitar on *Hilaawe* – but in a flamenco-esque style at marked odds with the instrument's traditional applications.

28. Op. cit.

29. Including the U.S. group Earl Burnett and his Biltmore Trio (late 1920s/early 1930s), British ensemble Felix Mendelssohn's Hawaiian Serenaders (late 1930s to early 1950s) and Japan's Buckie Shirakata and His Aloha Hawaiians (mid-1920s to mid-1950s).

30. Whether deliberate or not, this omission can be seen to be a response to those early 1960s critics – such as De Mello (1962) – who identified Lyman (and Denny) as exemplars of "professional performance ... quality of sound ... and technical excellence" in contrast to what they perceived as the crudity of "so-called 'authentic Hawaiian music'" of the time (ibid: 21).

31. It should also be noted that the marginalisation of Lyman also extends to broader cultural histories; despite his affinities with cool jazz; regular performances with mainstream jazz musicians such as Dave Brubeck and Shorty Rogers; and his recording of the heavily Hampton-influenced *Leis of Jazz* album (1959); his work was never perceived to have 'crossed-over' into the jazz mainstream by journalists and/or aficionados. Jazz histories, overwhelmingly disdainful of exotica, have also completely ignored his own – admittedly modest – contributions to the cool jazz genre.

32. Our acknowledgement of Amy's insightful critique of an earlier draft of this chapter should not be understood to represent any kind of unqualified endorsement of this final version on her part. The arguments and analyses of aspects of the cultural history of the Hawaiian Renaissance are ours alone.

Discography

Twenty five of Lyman's best known tracks recorded for Hi-Fi Records in the period 1957–64 are collated on the CD *The Exotic Sound of the Arthur Lyman Group*, DCC Jazz (1991). Rykodisc have also reissued a series of Lyman albums including *Taboo* (1996), *Taboo 2* (1997) *Hawaiian Sunset* (with additional tracks) (1996), *The Legend of Pele* (1996) and *Yellow Bird* (1997).

Chapter Five

SOY SAUCE MUSIC:

Haruomi Hosono and Japanese Self-Orientalism

SHUHEI HOSOKAWA

Rock has colonised our unconsciousness – Wim Wenders

Introduction

In Chapter Three I discussed how Martin Denny popularised a form of exotica in the period between the Korean and Vietnam wars. The rising popularity of electric and Afro-American-influenced music, along with changes in the exotic imagination of white Americans (who constituted the majority of Denny's audience) brought about the decline of the form. In the late 1960s the fantastic Orient and notions of the 'tropical' were gradually replaced by more geo-politically charged perceptions of 'Asia', 'Africa' and 'The Pacific Rim'. Only tourists visiting Honolulu had a chance to attend Denny's live performances and his name was soon forgotten by the mainstream music industry.

But Denny and exotica die hard. In the mid-1970s his sound was suddenly resuscitated: this time not in the U.S.A. but in Japan, on the opposite shore of Pacific. The agent of his revival was Haruomi Hosono, born in Tokyo in 1947 and best known internationally as the founder of the Yellow Magic Orchestra. This chapter analyses the manner in which Hosono appropriated the Denny sound in order to recall and examine the U.S. occupation of Japan as the founding moment of rock in Japanese culture; to explore how orientalism can be inversely adapted by its object; and to explore the manner in which the self-occidentalisation and self-orientalisation of Japanese culture is fundamental to the construction of its identity.

In this chapter I analyse the intertextuality of his trilogy of albums: *Tropical Dandy* (1973), *BonVoyage Co.* [*Taian Yôkô*] (1976) and *Paraiso* [*Haraiso*] (1978) – often referred to by Hosono as the 'Soy Sauce Music' series. Hosono's choice of 'soy sauce', the English language term for the Japanese national seasoning *syôyu*, for the trilogy, suggests a strategic ambiguity for both its Japanese producer and audience. Hosono's designation reflects the fluctuating identity of the music recorded and is thereby emblematic of Japan as seen from the West. The Trilogy comprises a complicated play on styles and discourses, made by a North American-influenced Japanese rock musician mimicking the exotic image of Japan and the Japanese made by previous North American musicians and composers.

Countering Orientalism

The anthropologist James Clifford (1988) has discussed the manner in which a Nigerian tribe imitated western anthropologists as part of a festival. During the festival, an individual wearing a straw hat pretended to write on a sheet of paper about what he was witnessing. Clifford interprets this as an ironic gesture of resistance to the asymmetric relationship between the tribe (the described) and anthropology (the describer) (ibid: 206–209). There are similarities here to the work of Hosono, who counters (one set of) American views on Japan, the Japanese and the exotic in general. In this mirror game of mimicry, the familiar relationship between the subject and the object is transformed in an ironic (if not grotesque) reflection of Other and self. Yet this game only partly resembles the process of "colonial mimicry" (Bhaba, 1994; Young, 1990: 145–48) because it is difficult to apply the term "colonial" to Japan, a country whose political sovereignty was not subordinated to 16th–19th Century western colonialism – a factor which explains why the exceptional dominion of the U.S.A. over Japan and Okinawa since 1945 is of such importance to both Japanese history and Hosono's Trilogy. This history does not mean that Japan has proved impenetrable for U.S. culture but rather that there has been a selective permeability. Japan primarily interacts with the West by means of commodity and informational transactions. Despite the absence of overt western domination, Japanese culture has absorbed many aspects of western culture; and such orientalist attitudes as Said (1978) has criticised are explicit in western discourses on Japan (Milner, 1980: 515f). Without actual domination, Japan has been able to manipulate the image of the West for its own purposes – ie in order to articulate national identity by means of the *imaginary* difference from the West – more freely than most colonised countries. This results in the (essentially) facile Japanisation of all imported items, from Disneyland to the tango (Tobin, 1992).

According to Homi Bhaba, the "difference between being English and being Anglicized" in the British Commonwealth is small but insurmountable (1994: 89–90). It is in this tiny space that colonial mimicry, or the partial repetition of repressed presence, operates. To paraphrase Bhaba's definition of colonial mimicry, Japan is almost westernised, but not quite western. Likewise, Japanese rock is almost

115

Americanised but not quite American. The difference between being Americanised and being American is irreconcilable.

Unlike many critics of colonialism who emphasise the imposition of western power over the colonised, Bhaba stresses the strategic responses of the ruled occasioned by mimetic desire. In this formation, the subordinated are not vacuous subjects. They resist their domination in similar ways to its imposition. From this point on, the domination becomes *indeterminate*:

> [m]imicry emerges as the representation of a difference that is itself a process of disavowal. Mimicry is, thus the sign of a double articulation; a complex strategy of reform, regulation and discipline, which "appropriates" the Other as it visualizes power. Mimicry is also the sign of the inappropriate, however, a difference or recalcitrance, which coheres the dominant strategic function of colonial power, intensifies surveillance, and poses an immanent threat to both "normalized" knowledges and disciplinary powers. (Bhaba, 1994: 86)

In Japan, this *ambiguity* of colonial mimicry – drawing on the play of surveillance and counter-surveillance, and of discipline and mockery under the panoptic authority – depends more on the logic of late consumerism than on the overt and asymmetrical confrontation between master and slaves. It is also concerned with the discrepancy between the 'two Japans' in the global order – the economically and technologically central Japan and the geographically and culturally peripheral one. In other words, it belongs both to the West and "the Rest" (Hall, 1992). The process of mimicry is more ambivalent and complicated than that in the straightforward copying, for example, of the musical style of Led Zeppelin or Albert Collins by Japanese artists. Rather, it is premised on a dislocation of North American aural representations of the extreme-Orient.

What is central to the Trilogy is less the North American approach to exoticising Japan and the Japanese than the Japanese way of exoticising American exoticism. Hence, the subject-object relationship is self-reflective and ambiguous: Hosono is at the same time the viewer and the viewed, the actor and the spectator. His monodrama does not involve the presence of any 'real' U.S.A. Due to the fact that the Soy Sauce Music series was domestically-orientated, addressed exclusively to Japan, Hosono changed direction after its completion, moving to an international focus (and subsequent acclaim) with the Yellow Magic Orchestra. The Trilogy's significance is that it not only used Japanese technology but also *Japaneseness* to problematise or, at least, complicate western paradigms of orientalism. Since the Trilogy is situated in Hosono's career between his involvement with Happii Endo [Happy End] (1969–72) and the Yellow Magic Orchestra (1978–1983), I will open and close the discussions in this chapter with a consideration of these groups, in order to better understand the Trilogy's historical meaning for Hosono's career and Japanese popular music in general.

Happii Endo, Japanese language and rock

In the late 1960s, Japanese rock artists and audiences engaged in an intense debate as to whether the English language was intrinsic to the sound of rock and, indeed, whether rock sung in Japanese was even *possible*. During the 1960s there were two principal categories of imported youth music in Japan, folk [*fôku*] and rock [*rokku*] (see Hosokawa, 1994b). The former came from the New Folk Song Movement of the Brothers Four, Peter, Paul and Mary, and the Kingston Trio, which became popular in Japan around 1965. Their tours in the first half of the decade ignited the Japanese folk boom. As a result, smart-looking singers with full smiles gathered at 'hootenannies' on university campuses, mainly singing Japanese language versions of North American songs such as *Lemon Tree* and *Blowin' in the Wind*. They rarely wrote their songs. Later, in 1967, a group of long-haired singers appeared and sang 'protest songs'. At first they simply translated songs by Woody Guthrie and the like, but then started to write their own compositions. Their political backdrop was the tumult of 1968–70 that culminated in students' (often bloody) protests against the Vietnam War, the construction of the new Tokyo airport at Narita, and the renewal of the Japan-U.S. Security Treaty. Their largest event was a weekly gathering at Shinjuku Station (Tokyo) on Saturday nights from February to July 1969[1]. During this period, singers and audiences alike were interested to see to what extent they could express (and mobilise) their shared feelings and frustrations by using irony, satire and humour in the manner of Bob Dylan and Pete Seeger (Maeda and Hirahara, 1993).

The other strain, *rokku*, paralleled developments in Great Britain and the U.S.A. but, since the initial concern of Japanese rock musicians was simply to copy the original sound, they mostly sang in English. To simplify, *fôku* used the Japanese language and acoustic guitars, while *rokku* used English language and the electric guitar (usually in a hard rock style). This distinction was blurred in 1970 when Nobuyasu Okabayashi, often referred to as 'Japan's Bob Dylan', a long-haired, bearded and overtly political singer, was backed by Happii Endo and participated in the 'Rock Revolt Festival' in Tokyo. At this time Happii Endo consisted of Hosono (bass and vocals), Eiichi Otaki (guitar and vocals), Shigeru Suzuki (guitar and vocals) and Takashi Matsumoto (drums). Matsumoto usually wrote the band's lyrics while the other three provided the melodies and music. The band met each other in college and the festival was the first chance for them to be exposed to a mass audience. Happii Endo's association with Okabayashi was short-lived however, since the band's style tended more towards that of U.S. West Coast groups such as Buffalo Springfield and Moby Grape, rather than message-orientated acts; they therefore preferred playing their own songs to Okabayashi's.

From the inception of Happii Endo, members were preoccupied with how their native language could be used in rock. For many Japanese rock musicians and

117

enthusiasts at this time, singing in English seemed 'natural', since rock music had developed within English language cultures and its language had therefore become internationalised. In the early 1970s several of the emerging rock bands perceived – like many other groups from different non-English language cultures – that the international spread of English language rock music offered them a point of access to a global market (provided that they sang in English; imitated the costume, hair style and stage actions of western performers; mastered the appropriate guitar techniques; and simulated the 'feel' of the western canon). They did not call into question their perception of the (fundamental) authenticity of rock music made in the U.S.A. and U.K., nor question the meaning of being 'foreigners' while perform- ing. Rock in Japanese was an odd and parochial concept for them. They shrieked as hard as Led Zeppelin or Grand Funk Railroad so that the words – and their meanings – were mostly unintelligible for audiences. What was important was success in achieving the appropriate 'grain of voice'; and the particular style of shouted vocals itself symbolised their anti-establishment – or better still, exclusively youthful – orientation. The sonority of vocally-strained rock music (in the western style once referred to as 'cock-rock') was therefore essential for rock audiences and musicians in non-English speaking countries. This might be understood as a form of phonetic consumption of others' tongues without commitment to semantics or syntax.

Curiously enough, the internationalism was transformed into orientalism when the bands travelled overseas. Yûya Uchida, one of the leaders of the English language cohort, toured Canada and the U.S.A. with his Flower Travellin' Band in 1971 and released an album entitled *Satori*. Mickey Curtis, a veteran rockabilly singer who covered Presley and Paul Anka in the 1950s, also named his new band Samurai when they played in Europe in 1969. Despite both groups' rejection of singing in Japanese, they used the names 'Satori' and 'Samurai' since they conformed to western orientalist clichés. They were – and felt they had to be – Japanese in the way the West imagined. Therefore, their internationalism consolidated existing west- ern/eastern dichotomies. Paradoxically, they were 'international' in Japan and 'oriental' in the West.

Happii Endo was unique not only in its West Coast-derived rock sound and Japanese language vocals but also in the complex awareness of its own cultural identity. Writing in 1970, at the time their first album was released, Matsumoto commented that:

> [we sing in Japanese] *[n]ot because we are Japanese and we are in Japan. In the same way that Japan is 'trompe-l'oeil' for us, the framework of rock itself is the Copernican turn of place that forces us to sing in* distorted Japanese. (cited in Hagiwara, 1992: 43, my emphasis)

Matsumoto emphasised that he did not take singing in Japanese for granted since he was firmly convinced of both the foreignness of rock and the opacity of Japan (which

118

he describes as a "trompe-l'oeil"). His emphasis differs from that of folk singers who argued that they sang in Japanese because they *were* Japanese. Matsumoto was too aware of the rapid transformation of urban life through Americanisation (especially after the 1964 Tokyo Olympic Games) to believe in the 'natural' tie between his language and his nationality. For Matsumoto, English language singing did not resolve the inauthenticity of Japanese as a rock language. His criticisms were directed at rock musicians who used the English language, who he, and other critics, saw as 'fake hippies' producing 'Black Ship Worshipper Rock'[2].

Americanism has always been an ambivalent aspect of post-war Japanese culture. While it is opposed to traditionalism it is simultaneously conformist, in that U.S.-Japanese collaborations are central to Japanese politics. For example, the right-wing usually supports Japan's relationship with the U.S.A. (especially the Security Treaty) but rejects the 1946 Constitution imposed upon them, in their version, by U.S. Forces. On the other side of the coin, the communist and the socialist parties support the constitution but oppose the Security Treaty. The literary critic Norihiro Katô calls this ambivalence the "shadow of America" (1985: 87ff, 301–302). This consists of a double process of domination: that of Japan as nation-state by the U.S.A. (the inter-national dimension) and that of the interiorisation of Japanese individuals by Japan as nation-state (the intra-national aspect). Katô poses the question of why the Japanese did not lose their individual and national identity following their defeat during World War Two and the subsequent U.S. occupation. He answers by arguing that the state of Japan is both "dependent upon and parasitic to 'America' " (ibid: 88). Hence the U.S.A. rules the Japanese 'mind' only indirectly. It is Japan as nation-state that mediates this rule. The more one looks up to Japan as nation-state, the more one is forced to be subordinate to the order posed by the U.S.A. This is why the postwar right-wing has constantly had a complex about the U.S.A. (as somehow its 'shadow') while the left-wing behaves more like a conventional nationalist group.

For Matsumoto and others it was important to go beyond the faddish surface of rock music and youth culture and to grasp the undercurrent beneath the monotonous urbanisation and Americanisation of substantial parts of Japan (which resulted in many Japanese effectively becoming strangers in their home country), in order to raise fundamental questions about national identity. In this regard, singing in Japanese was not simply automatic but rather a deliberate choice in order to experiment with how the language could express new feelings, sentiments and meanings (albeit over a North American-derived beat). By singing in Japanese, Matsumoto aimed to overturn the American hegemony of rock music (which he perceived as simultaneously repressive *and* gratifying). This ambivalence to U.S. culture was best articulated in the track *Sayonara America, Sayonara Nippon* (1973) (discussed below).

Happii Endo's lyrics, mostly written by Matsumoto, were accompanied by West Coast-style rock melodies and arrangements. They were, however, presented in such

119

an unusual (and arguably awkward) manner that some listeners were initially irritated by what they perceived as their unintelligibility. The group's unconventional choice of words, mixing neologisms, colloquialisms and archaisms, may also have frustrated audiences. However, the alchemy of Happii Endo transmuted its 'distorted' Japanese into a key aspect of the band's appeal. Instead of imitating imported style(s), Happii Endo measured the distance between Japan and the U.S. in order to locate itself somewhere in the middle. The musical and commercial success of their second and most acclaimed album, *Wind City Roman* [*Kaze Machi Roman*] (1971), clearly widened the horizon of rock in Japan[3].

In 1973 Happii Endo recorded their third and final studio album, entitled *Happy End*, in Los Angeles with producer Van Dyke Parks. Although Hosono recalls his relationship with Parks, as productive, the overall experience was far from a happy one. The atmosphere in the studio was often tense and the band were disillusioned by the gap between the America they had imagined and anticipated and the America they were actually experiencing. One of the main problems concerned communication difficulties between them and the various Los Angeles musicians and studio personnel who assisted on the recording sessions. The experience made them understand that Japanese rock was/is quintessentially Japanese despite its American facade. Nothing conveyed their disappointment better than the closing track, *Sayonara America, Sayonara Nippon* – a song which simply repeats its title, its vocal lines, dubbed, dispersed and distorted through a phase shifter, for more than four minutes. The band felt that they had been betrayed by the American reality but could not abandon the music born from it because rock had penetrated too deeply into their own interiority.

The album's final, experimental track shifted the frame of reference of their music-making. With *Sayonara America, Sayonara Nippon*, it was neither American music, nor its Japanese simulacra, which provided their model. It was only the difference between the cultures that interested them. After the break-up of Happii Endo each of the four musicians developed their own independent styles, thereby contributing to the creation of a sophisticated pop genre, *Nyû Myûjikku* (New Music), in the 1970s. This genre broke away from the traditional music industry separation of the duties of the composer, lyricist, arranger, sound engineer and singer, since the musicians involved could take on all of these roles. Otaki introduced Phil Spector's 'wall of sound' to Japanese pop, while Suzuki has developed his guitar-playing and arranging skills to become one of the busiest studio musicians in Japan. Matsumoto has also gone on to write lyrics for hundreds of hit tunes. The most radical departure however was the one Hosono subsequently explored: the deconstruction of orientalism by mimicry.

Island and archipelago

After saying "Sayonara" to both sides of the Pacific, Hosono identified Okinawa and the Caribbean as new foci of attention. In sleeve notes for *Tropical Dandy*

(1975), entitled 'On The Islands', he described his imaginary cultural circumnavigation in the following terms:

From the beginning of this year I have been less interested in North America than in the landscape of the Caribbean islands, the sea surrounding them, the hazy continents and harbours – as we see them far away. The Caribbean Islands consist of Cuba, Dominica, Haiti, the Virgin Islands, Jamaica and Trinidad and Tobago. Among these, Trinidad and Tobago particularly interest me and may best fit my aspirations. Columbus crossed the Atlantic in the sea around these islands. The Caribbean islands have a French, Spanish and British influence and flavour and have access to the harbour of New Orleans and to the country of Brazil.

Japan is insular as well as continental. It is ambiguous. As for music, there is little continental element. The only music that interests me in Japan is that of the Ryukyu Islands [Okinawa]. *Ryukyan music is no less interesting than that of the West Indian Islands. It is a mixture of the influence of surrounding continents and the pristineness of the autochthon. The prototypes of Japanese* kayokyoku[4] *may have something to do with Korea, as is shown by* enka[5] *which comes from* naniwabushi[6] *and* derorenbushi[7]. *The other strain comes from the western continent. As its route passes through China and along the Silk Road[8], the music is given European melody, mixed up with French Chinoiserie. This music is carried to the American continent by Columbus, then finally to Japan. Therefore, Japanese popular song is different from the genres like* gagaku[9] *that were directly influenced by China. Japan is also insular, it closed itself almost completely for three hundred years due to the isolationist policy of the Edo Period* [1630s–1850s]. *As a result, the country has created original forms of music. However, it has not developed any exciting music that shows the influence and mixture of various countries. It is this type of island music that interests me. The really interesting music, I believe, is a melange* [gottani][10], *a music made of heterogeneous elements, blended by local people within a local milieu.* (author's translation)

Its naive geographical and historical description aside, the first significant aspect of this text is that it identifies Japan's status as an island-nation as both fundamental and ambiguous, as both closed *and* open. The isolation of islands, surrounded by seas, can facilitate degrees of cultural autonomy but, at the same time, their very accessibility allows them to act as cultural crossroads where hybridisation frequently occurs. Hosono indicates his interest in the latter model, that is to say, the island as an alchemical place of cultural plurality – akin to the Caribbean model, as he presents it. The first of the Trilogy's albums addresses the manner in which Japan can be 'Caribbeanised'. With *Tropical Dandy* (1975), Hosono ceases to regard rock simply as a recent fashion imported into Japan from the U.S.A. but as a historical and

121

geographical consequence of Japan's intercourse with the outside world. The issue of whether it is sung in Japanese or English, or whether it is presented in hard rock or folk rock form, became secondary to his music.

The second notable element of Hosono's text is his critique of the contemporary Japanese way of living and thinking as adopting the worst aspect of island culture, sectionalism and isolationism, despite the volume of new information and stimuli in circulation. As he elaborates in the sleeve notes:

> [t]oday Tokyo is like an island. Although few cities in the world have more abundant information than Tokyo, the customs of the age of isolationism in the Edo period are still latent and persist.

In other words, the information serves no communicative function between Japan and the outside. Even inside Tokyo the communication is restricted:

> [i]nside the isolated island of Tokyo, there are lots of isolated islands. Yes, isolated islands. The Caribbean islands are not isolated but form an archipelago.

Hosono's concept of the archipelago allows for an easy communication and mixture with outside cultures. In his view, the Ryukyu Islands (Okinawa) are the only archipelago in Japan. The "archipelago" here is more than a geographic (and musical) model: it is a strategic site for criticising the isolation and closure of Japan.

It is uncertain how the crucial concept/metaphor of the archipelago occurred to Hosono but it may have come from insightful composer-arranger Van Dyke Parks whose album *Discover America* (1972) was released immediately prior to his producing Happii Endo's final album. As Hosono disclosed in an interview published in 1997, *Discover America*:

> ...led me to a sensation I had never before encountered in this existence... [the album] was a hodgepodge of very Hollywoodesque exoticism and nostalgia, and Caribbean gaiety, and it was the sound which inspired my own musical chronicles. (cited in Bell, 1997: 33)[11]

Discover America (discussed in detail in the following chapter) shows how 'America' is ethnically and musically intertwined by focusing on musical genres undervalued by the Anglo-American industry, such as calypso and steel band music, and by reworking quintessential U.S. icons with a Caribbean influence (for example, the tracks *Jack Palance*, *Bing Crosby*, and *The Four Mills Brothers*). The final track, *Stars and Stripes Forever*, with up-tempo steel drums is, above all, evidence of Van Dyke Park's project to dislocate the United States of America. The cover, showing two buses, identifies the concept of the album, the possibility of a two-way traffic between Hollywood and Trinidad.

The discovery of (various) 'Americas' appears to have encouraged Hosono to search for the heterogeneous Japan; and he transposes Van Dyke Parks' ideas of relativism to his own homeland. This leads to the third implication of 'On The Islands', the idea of Japanese popular music as globally hybridised. This reflects an idealistic image of Japan as archipelago. Hosono imagines two-way routes in the making of Japanese music. One is China-Japan, the direct route represented by *gagaku*. The other route passes the opposite way, through China, Eurasia, Europe via America and back to Japan. He opts for the second route because of its more multi-layered blend. As the sleeve notes recount:

> *...I said I liked the continent, the sea and the island. Now I am going to write about the harbour. My favorite harbours are Shanghai, Hong Kong, Yoko-hama, New Orleans. I especially long for Shanghai and New Orleans. My route must not be from Shanghai to Tokyo. It must pass, if I want to be content with it, from Shanghai to France, then to Spain, to the West Indies, then disembark at the harbour of New Orleans. Then, finally, it reaches Tokyo. The music that has experienced such a long journey includes every kind of essence and it therefore tastes excellent.*

> *The flavour of the [Eurasian] continent which the Silk Road transverses, sophisticated Parisian elegance, Spanish passion, African energy, the ma-rine flavor of the Caribbean, all of them are cooked up in a stew. Then this stew gets taken to America, the inclusive, all-embracing continent, where the final spices are added. Then, after, I wonder "What will happen if I add one more spice?" This is what I have to do. I am almost obsessed by this conviction. In short, I let the music travel across the Pacific to add a drop of soy sauce to it. This is what I want to do. I name this form "Soy Sauce Music".*

In Hosono's olfactory and culinary map, "soy sauce" symbolises the Japaneseness in the exotic. It belongs both to the vernacular and the transplanted and is an indispensable ingredient for his conceptual melange. For the West, he states, this cuisine is complete when American spices are added. He is not a traditionalist (of the kind represented by the direct exchange between China and Japan) nor a simulationist but rather a relativist; in the sense that he exoticises the Japanese and the American simultaneously. Soy Sauce Music does not attempt to approximate the centre from the periphery by means of straight copying but by vacillating this bi-polar (centre/periphery) model and establishing an interplay of the simulation and dissimulation of America (or zigzagging between what America means to the Other and what the otherness inflects in America)[12]. We will return to this self-occiden-talisation and self-orientalisation later.

Music concerned with globe-trotting is usually imbued with local colour. In Japan also, popular songs which use exotic instruments, rhythms or lyrics for (referential)

123

local colour have been common since the 1930s. Hawai'i, the Pacific, Paris, China, India, The Americas... all these destinations have been possible and evoked in popular music. Hosono's Trilogy is, however, completely different from those exotic songs for several reasons. First, it is presented in the form of 'concept albums', a type of popular musical expression relatively new to Japanese music. Second, it is based on rock – and associated – idioms. Third, and most importantly, it posits Japan not only on the side of the exoticising but of the exoticised. The Trilogy, far from repeating pre-existent ideas of exotic places and local colours, reveals the political relationship implied in exoticism.

The occupied memory

Tropical Dandy commences with *Chattanooga Choo Choo*, the Glenn Miller standard, but sung here in Portuguese. This would appear to be the first song recorded in Portuguese by a Japanese vocalist (the last verse alone is in Japanese). Hosono, adopting the arrangement of Carmen Miranda's 1942 Decca recording, pays homage to the first Brazilian singer to become successful in Hollywood. Thus *Chattanooga Choo Choo* is doubly exoticised, once by a Brazilian, twice by a Japanese. As noted below, the strategy of 'doubled' or 'detoured' exoticisation is brought in play throughout the Trilogy. But Hosono's counter-position is not a simple remake. From Miranda's rendition he subtracts most of the Brazilian percussion and swinging horn section, and adds drums, electric bass and (Lowell George-style) slide guitar. The superficial appropriation of a Brazilian flavour and (pseudo-)Portuguese vocals reduces the vivid orchestration and dynamic vocal of the original. The South American detour is significant for its navigation because what is at stake is not the reproduction of Miranda's exoticism for North American audiences but the trans-position of an exotic relationship between North and South America in the 1940s to that between Japan and the U.S.A. in the 1970s. Hosono, avoiding the antithetic counter-position of the two countries, draws on a dialogic triangle between Japan, the U.S.A.(/West) and the Rest; in which the three points continuously rotate and transform each other without ceding control to the other two. It is relevant for the Soy Sauce project to show how the exotic gaze of the West covers not only Japan but also the 'Rest' of the globe.

In the West, Glenn Miller is closely associated with the wartime years. In Japan however, his music evokes a slightly later period, the immediate post-War occupation era (and the Japanese ambivalence towards G.I.s)[13]. For Hosono himself, the Miller classic is associated with his childhood. He was raised in uptown Tokyo in the 1950s, hearing Miller and *Chattanooga Choo Choo* on the radio and on record. In this respect, to paraphrase Wim Wenders' aphorism, North American music has colonised the unconscious of post-War Japan.

This reminiscence of a childhood both overwhelmed and enlivened by Americanism is repeated in the following tune, *Hurricane Dorothy*, inspired by Dorothy Lamour, the principal actress of John Ford's *Hurricane* (1937)[14]. The atmospheric use of

124

marimba and piano recalls the work of Martin Denny but the 'tropical' melody embellished by them is more reminiscent of Dr Buzzard's Original Savannah Band in the 1970s. In this regard, it is not merely a copy of nostalgic exotica but its actualised form. The lyrics refer as much to the film as to the occupation period – recalling the manner in which the U.S. Forces gave typhoons female names (such as Typhoon Catherine [1947] and Typhoon Kitty [1949])[15]. "Hurricane Dorothy" thus does not only imply Hollywood-associated nostalgia but also the American way of naming (and thereby taming) the Japanese nature.

The reference to the film is found only in the first verse ("Your eyes are the Caribbean wind/ Your hot gaze/ Blows through palm trees"). The following verses evoke a glossy, exotic femininity ("Her lips are Arabic darkness/Her gloom is [a] Slavic song"). As her language is incomprehensible ("She murmurs enigmatic words/ Abulaka Dabla"), her bewitching appearance and "hot gaze" manifest themselves as the only meaningful sign for the lyrics to represent. "Dorothy" is more than a Hollywood beauty, she embodies an essential convergence of exoticism and femininity (see Kabbani, 1986; Brainowski, 1992) – akin to the covers of Denny's albums[16] – whereby she can become Arabic or Slavic simply by making up as such. The overt stereotyping shows Hosono's concern with the *representation* of exotic femininity rather than the exotic women themselves (this is also the case in *Femme Fatale*, dealing with a vamp in the desert, a Dietrich prototype).

G.I. songs

By the end of the 1940s, around 100,000 U.S. soldiers were stationed in Japan. During the early stages of the Korean War this number rose to between 210,000 and 260, 000[17]. In addition, many civilian members of military-related organisations stayed temporarily in Japan during this period; and many troops visited Japan while in transit to and from Korea (and, later, Vietnam) (Johnson, 1988: 76f.). During this period Japan functioned as recreational 'rear front' for military personnel[18]. As a result of this extended occupation, Japan became, for the first time in its history, a standard tourist destination for North Americans.

There were several LPs released in Japan during the period specifically designed for G.I.s, with English language titles, song-words, sleeve notes and, predictably, images of *geishas* on the cover (such as *Best 10 from the Land of the Rising Sun* [1958] which has English language lyrics and transcriptions of Japanese ones printed on the sleeve). The album opens with *China Night*, originally a hit in 1940. Three of the ten tunes (*Soba Song*, *Gomennasai* and *Japanese Rumba*) are so-called 'G.I. songs' (see below), and four of them are drinking party favourites, *Tonko Bushi*, *Tankô Bushi*, *Sôran Bushi* and *Yatton Bushi*, sung either by Japanese or Japanese-American female singers (two also feature the Okinawan-Hawaiian G.I., George Shimabukuro as a duettist). The album also includes two Korean folk tunes, *Ariran* and *Toraji Flower*, sung in both Japanese and English. The album is nothing more (or less) than a souvenir for returning soldiers.

125

The U.S. occupation gave Japan many musical legacies. These included the FEN (Far East [Radio] Network); bebop jazz; Country and Western music; imported records; and the local rock and soul scenes around U.S. military bases. Another was the so-called 'G.I. songs', compositions addressed to American soldiers stationed in Japan during the 1950s (these include *Gomen Nasai, Rumba Maiko-han, Shimbashi Blues, Geisha Girl, Mambo Musume* and *Pachinko Mambo*)[19]. Hosono's Trilogy includes versions of three G.I. songs: *Sayonara – The Japanese Farewell Song, Japanese Rumba* and *Fujiyama Mama*. Hosono might have become initially acquainted with these curious songs through FEN radio, which was highly influential on the formation of rock in Japan. He was also familiar with a version of *Sayonara* sung by Earl Grant, an Afro-American crooner in the style of Nat King Cole, in the 1950s; but it was Martin Denny's rendition that later reminded him of this type of novelty song[20].

Sayonara depicts an 'ideal', bittersweet separation between an American male and Japanese female:

> *The time has come for us to say "Sayonara"/*
> *My heart will always be yours for eternity/*
> *I knew sometime we'd have to say "Sayonara"/*
> *Please promise that you'll be returning some day to me*[21]

It is no wonder that this song was a success among U.S. soldiers in the Far East in the 1950s (and was also used in the U.S. TV series *M.A.S.H.*) because the song, akin to the final aria of Act 1 of Puccini's *Madame Butterfly*, does not 'speak *for*' its apparent protagonist, a Japanese woman, but rather *to* a specific listener, the American military (the specific addressee of the musical communication). "Sayonara" in the song is not the Japanese woman's own voice; but rather her voice as envisaged in the fantasy of an American who is begged to "promise" to return "some day" to (his) – presumably completely faithful – woman. The song does not refer to *his* sentiment but rather to *her* sorrow as imagined by him. This aspect is foregrounded in Hosono's version, where the song is interpreted by a Japanese male singer whose inflection and delivery suggest his sensitivity to the asymmetric power relationship between the two lovers represented in the song and to the sentimentalisation of Japanese woman.

The second G.I. song, *Fujiyama Mama*, a rock and roll tune originally recorded by Wanda Jackson in 1958, centres on an alternative to the figure of chastity (*musume*) in *Sayonara*:

> *'Cause you're a Fujiyama Mama/*
> *And you're just about to blow your top /*
> *Fujiyama, yama, Fujiyama/*
> *And when you start eruptin'/*
> *Ain't nobody gonna make you stop*

126

You drank a quart of sake, smoked dynamite/
You chased it with tobaccy/
An' then shot out the light[22]

The lyrics suggest that the "dynamite" lady in question may have been the owner of a bar in a restricted area for G.I.s (the proprietress of a night spot was, and usually is, called "Mama-san"). Elaborating the explosive metaphor, the song juxtaposes the eruption of Fujiyama with an atomic bomb explosion in order to express the woman's potential for violent action: "But you can cause destruction/ Just like the atom bomb" and continues:

You've been to Nagasaki, Hiroshima, too/
The thing you did to them/
Baby, you can do to me

These references are muddled, the (Japanese) woman is compared to the (U.S.) bomb and the song's rhetoric does not clarify why the Japanese woman is furious with the American. Significantly, he is neither interested in the reason for her 'eruption' (as the metaphor of volcano shows, it is just her 'nature') nor fearful of her (presumably because he knows that she depends on U.S. patronage). He observes her rage from outside without any kind of affection. Whether faithful or tempered, the two images of Japanese women are totally constructed by and for the American male gaze.

What is specific to the third G.I. song in the Trilogy, *Japanese Rumba* (written and composed by Jack Miller, a G.I. stationed in Japan) is the use of what is commonly referred to as 'Bamboo English', a form of pidgin. According to the linguist Roy Andrew Miller, this form is either:

[a] *jargon of small vocabulary and limited syntactic possibilities... chiefly employed between foreigners in the military establishment and local laborers, servants, or other employees* [or a] *"vocabulary of venery"* [between] *non-Japanese-speaking foreigners and the extensive world of their local lady friends.* (1967: 262–3)[23]

The lyrics of *Japanese Rumba* – reproduced below – conform to the latter category. (NB in the following translations I have translated the Japanese version into English following the order of the words in the original lyrics in order to give an impression of the pidgin used ["Papa-san" means a patron of "mama-san"]):

Doko yukuno koko irasshaine [Where go, here come]
Choto anone ohayogozaimasu [Hey, well, good morning]
Nani mama-san hayaku papa-san [What mama-san, hurry up papa-san]
Ano ojosan choto matekudasai [Hey, fair girl, wait a moment]

127

> *Nani anone sutekine keshou hai* [What, well, nice make-up, yes]
> *Nani yaruno ano konnichiwa* [What do, eh, good afternoon][24]

This language certainly has a markedly "small vocabulary" and "limited syntactic possibilities " (particularly the omission and misuse of the particle, and abuse of phatic interjections such as "anone", "ano", "nani" and "hai") and resembles a digest from an imaginary Berlitz language book (on 'How to court a Japanese woman' perhaps). It provides a snapshot of the haphazard behaviour of an American who flirts with a "mama-san" and "ojosan" (fair girl) by calling to them on the street and complimenting their make-up. The incongruity of the lyrics shows the very limited possibility of developing the conversation. The language serves for the first contact only. What results from this initial contact may be, more precisely, what *Sayonara* eventually laments.

While Bamboo English sounds comic to Japanese, they perceive the 'degenerated' language as a relic of occupation, that is to say, of the forced contact between *real* American people (not American 'culture') and ordinary Japanese without foreign language education[25]. Bamboo English, born from the necessity of communicating with English-speaking people around military bases and night spots, is opposed to what is called 'Japlish', a type of language used in Japanese pop songs full of English loan-words (Hosokawa, 1995); because the latter is a mixed language related to the consumption of western images. As J. Stanlaw rightly notes, "the use of English in Japan is an internal matter" (1992: 74)[26]. In other words, it is used for Japanese purposes among Japanese-speaking people and, significantly, it *domesticates* English words. Bamboo English, on the contrary, perpetuates U.S. (neo-)colonial contact with Japan. The Cuban-styled arrangement of the song sounds exotic to both Japanese and American audiences, and thereby amplifies the humour in the lyrics.

Japanese Rumba was originally recorded by Nobuo Nishimoto and George Shimabukuro in 1951. Both were Japanese-Hawaiian soldiers stationed in Japan at the time. They recorded several sides for the Tropical label, a Honolulu-based company specialising in Japanese music. Although we know little about them[27], the novelty song can be seen to express their ambivalence about Japan; the complexity of their role in conquering the country of their ancestry; and their (gentle) mockery of their fellow soldiers' attempts to seduce Japanese women with odd phrases. Hosono escalates colonial ambivalence by inviting Teave Kamayatsu, a Hawaiian-born veteran singer to sing the track. While Kamayatsu re-located to Japan in the 1930s, and later became naturalised, he never mastered standard Japanese, retaining a style of pidginised Japanese developed by Japanese-Hawaiians, and his accent was part of his trademark. Thus *Japanese Rumba* not only celebrates the happy encounter of Japan with Cuban music but also suggests the unofficial intercourse between Japan (especially Okinawa) and the U.S.A. (especially Hawai'i).

Dis-locating Chinoiserie

Two numbers on *Tropical Dandy* are explicitly addressed to China – *Silk Road* , based on *Magic Monkey*, the classic work of Chinese literature popular with Japanese children, and *Pekin Duck*, a song about Yokohama's Chinatown. The former is concerned with the first point of contact with chinoiserie for most Japanese[28]. The song also refers to the emerging popularity of the 'Silk Road' in the 1970s (partly triggered by the establishment of Japanese-Chinese diplomatic relations in 1972[29]). Hosono, instead of evoking a hackneyed mixture of the desert, caravan and veiled people, sings about the endless fight between the Magic Monkey and the monsters familiar to all Japanese. By doing so, he appeals to the exoticism of the Silk Road in the Japanese collective memory.

Pekin Duck, on the other hand, concerns a major fire in Yokohama's Chinatown (thereby suggesting/alluding to the U.S. bombardment of that area in 1945):

Yokohama, lightening city/
It rains/
Just like an old movie/
"Singing' in the Rain"/
Rain man sings

You put on red shoes [but]*/*
Were taken away by a stranger/
And you got lost/
In this Chinatown/
[There's] *fire all over the place*

(refrain)
Ducks are startled and flee/
Fire keeps on burning/
Sirens and bells ring out/
Red burning town, fleeing away/
That must be Pekin Duck

Yokohama's Chinatown, founded around the 1870s, immediately after the internationalisation of Yokohama harbour, is one of few places that provide archetypal chinoiserie for the Japanese imagination. Surrounded by four commanding gates, it offers peculiar sights such as dragons, arabesques, strange talismans, restaurants and souvenir shops. The figure of a "rain man" (suggestive of Gene Kelly in *Singin' in the Rain*[1952]) leads to an – implicitly white – "stranger" who leads away a girl with red shoes. This scenario alludes to one of the most famous juvenile songs of the 1920s, *Akai Kutsu* ('Red Shoes') :

129

A girl with red shoes/
was taken away by a stranger/
From the harbor of Yokohama/
She went far away on board[30]

This song, for all its sentimentalism, depicts the mysterious disappearance of a little girl who was supposed to have been taken away by an "alien" ("*ijin san*"). This cruel fairy tale remains in the collective memory as more than a stigmatic narrative of a Japanese girl and a white man. It has been debated as to whether the story is real or fictional, and if it represents the Japanese fear of the outsider or their aspiration for escape. In Hosono's apocrypha, the girl was supposed to be taken to Chinatown, an ambiguous and indeterminate space between Japan and the outside[31].

What matters about *Pekin Duck* is that it deals less with the *real* China than the China in Japan, in other words, the Japanised China or the Chinified Japan. It is not concerned with exoticism itself but with the making of exoticism. This critical stance is maintained throughout the Trilogy. To make the song more complicated, *Pekin Duck* uses a Brazilian rhythm, *baião*, that was briefly popular in Japan in the 1950s[32]. Similarly to *Chattanooga Choo Choo*, the exoticism is detoured when Brazil intervenes into the Yokohama-China relationship, undermining the ordinary form of chinoiserie.

Rather than simply wishing to evoke and represent stereotypically exotic paradises, Hosono's exoticism is doubled through the deliberate juxtaposition of heterogeneous ingredients in the studio. In this, his blending is not as spontaneous as that of the Caribbean music he admires. He is conscious of his outside position with respect to locality and ethnicity. Instead of making an essentialist claim on Japaneseness, or simulating the western canon, he identifies a disparate patchwork of non-native elements as operating within Japanese culture. If Japan, even in its most official history, admits a thousand years of Chinese influence, then why is Chinatown so exotic ? The Brazilian rhythm applied to a Chinatown song produces an estranging effect: the listeners disorientate and lose themselves in the artificial maze so that they may know how the 'over-there' is constructed from the here, how the exotic draws on the self image.

Western orientalist music does not always sound comfortable to Japanese listeners because of its misrepresentation of Japan and China. In fact, many Japanesque songs, including *Sayonara*, are perceived to be Chinese-like to Japanese ears. Although they are part of a common musical culture (exemplified by pentatonicism), Japanese are sensitive to the difference between their music and Chinese styles. But given that Japanese students, wealthy merchants and intellectuals once played Chinese music on Chinese instruments, from the 18th Century up to the end of the last century (ie approximately until the outbreak of the Sino-Japan War); the Japanese way of stereotyping China is different from that of the West (where Chinese music has been exposed much more sporadically). It is true that Japan has had a more substantial and consistent intercourse with China than the West but questions as to which type of chinoiserie – Japanese-made or western-made – is more accurate are irrelevant, since both are concerned with representations/discursive fabrications of Chinese-ness by Others.

In the process of occidentalisation since the Meiji Restoration (1868), Japanese have learned not only western techniques but also a western order of world perception and sensibility. In the end what is exotic for the West is also recognised as such by Japanese. The only exception is obviously the exoticism of Japan. Japanese usually perceive the inauthenticity of western chinoiserie/japonaiserie but often miss that of Japanese-made images of China. The Trilogy, making a contrast between the western orientalism of *Hong Kong Blues* and *Sayonara – Japanese Farewell Song* on the one hand, and the Japanese image of China in *Silk Road* and *Pekin Duck* on the other, distances itself from the pitfall of Japanese-made exoticism.

In *Tropical Dandy*, the happy feeling of the sleeve notes quoted above is best represented in *Tropical Night*. Hosono became familiar with Denny's work while preparing the *Tropical Dandy* album and, in affectionate homage, the track opens with Denny's unmistakable aural hallmarks – the sound of bird calls and waves quietly breaking on the beach. The song's mellow and moody melody also conjures up Denny's 'tropicalism'. Its lyrical address is more complex however:

> *Sinking sea, floating island/*
> *The moon completes the quietness/*
> *Now, in Tokyo, the asphalt may be melting/*
> *A river in the city/*
> *Now, in Shanghai, the fishes may be cooking/*
> *[In] the breeze around the marketplace*
>
> *Aromatic water, sleeping ferns/*
> *Here is paradise, heat hell/*
> *Now, in Minnesota, it is hot enough to boil eggs/*
> *I spend a sleepless night/*
> *Dreaming of Trinidad, 'round the world/*
> *Tonight it's a wonderful night*

On first listening, the vocal protagonist appears to be relaxing on a tropical island, under the moonlight, while imagining the experience of heatwaves in Tokyo, Shanghai, Minnesota and Trinidad[33]. But a second listening reveals a different situation. The subject is in fact in the heat and humidity of a hot Tokyo night[34] (a scenario familiar to Hosono and many other Japanese listeners) and the singer is imagining how Tokyo and other places might be imagined if he/she was on a tropical island. The concern here is not simply the image of earthly paradise but the exoticisation of where the author is (Tokyo) by means of an imaginary trip to another exotic place. Through this displacement, he makes the ordinary landscape and

131

weather of Tokyo as strange and exotic as that of Shanghai or Trinidad (to a Japanese). Hosono often quotes the Brechtian aphorism "hold the eyes of a stranger" in his interviews, as a key perspective on the Soy Sauce Trilogy's approach; and the displacement of self to everywhere/nowhere here may be related to such an estrangement – to making the ordinary strange.

In Japan, however, this 'becoming-exotic' does not always perform a Brechtian social critique. Rather, it often functions as a defence mechanism, taming and effacing alterity. Discussing the 'Exotic Japan' campaign run by Japanese National Railways in the 1980s, for instance, Marilyn Ivy uncovers a doubled vision of the non-Japanese as seen through Japanese eyes and the Japan seen through western eyes. Reflecting on this, she sums up the complexity of the Japanese notion and construction of identity as follows:

> [a]t issue here is the notion of an "Other" itself in relation to what might be imagined as a "Self" within a dialectic of identity and difference. Any claim to radical self-identity turns into a claim for radial alterity. For what is radically self-identical is set apart, imagined as non-comparable – and thereby different, "other." All ethnocentrisms operate by this logic: an encapsulation of identity that thereupon guarantees its difference, its otherness from others. (1988: 26)

Self-orientalisation, or mimicry to become "the objects of Western desire and imagination" (Tobin, 1992: 30), may camouflage the unitary identity "encapsulated" behind the ethnocentrism. If this projection of Self onto Other lays down operation of "all ethnocentrisms", then what is the specificity of Japanese ethnocentrism? From where does this free-floating self-identification come? It is the *style* of consumption, Ivy answers, that produces the (alleged) extreme malleability of the Japanese to "become Other." The sociologist Koichi Iwabushi discusses further aspects of Japanese pleasure in becoming exotic:

> [w]hile Orientalism enjoys the mysterious exoticism of the Other, self-Orientalism exploits the Orientalist gaze to turn itself into an Other. It is something like declaring that Japanese possesses "the secret and ability to read the stereotype." "Japan" is not an inferior Orient any more and, no less importantly, has become "pleasurably exotic" to the Japanese themselves. (1994: 70)

Although the Trilogy overtly engages with the pleasure of orientalism and self-orientalism, it has a further dimension which distances itself from the consumer-orientated use of elsewhere of the 'Exotic Japan' campaign. Its self-reflective play between 'here', 'there' and 'everywhere' subtly deploys an exoticism of exoticism, a mimicry of mimicry. In other words, it displaces the epistemological condition of both exotic and mimetic Japan by way of a critical appropriation of Japanese exoticism and mimicry – and then recycles the morbidly convex Self/Other images so produced. By doing so, it unleashes the complicit relationship between exoticism and mimicry in Japan.

Therefore *Tropical Dandy* is more than simply electronic exotica. It successfully explores Japanese post-war identity in relation to the social memory and effect of the years of U.S. occupation. But compared to the last two albums of the Trilogy, it places less emphasis on Japan's historical role in atlases of the exotic. The Martin Denny sound alone is not sufficient to dis-locate and subvert the exotic order. The key place is the Okinawan archipelago, geographically situated between Japan, Taiwan and China, and occupied by U.S. forces until 1972. Although Hosono noted his interest in Okinawa in his statement 'On the Islands', he did not fully explore it in *Tropical Dandy*. It is symptomatic that he 'discovered' Okinawa in Hawai'i. Out-of-place-ness is crucial to the Trilogy.

The voyage from Hawai'i to Okinawa

In Hosono's navigation, Hawai'i and Okinawa offer two important harbours in which to anchor. Both archipelagos were (and are) politically subject to larger neighbouring states but maintain their cultural identity due to their enormous capacity for hybridisation (Buck, 1994). Nothing crystallises the Hawai'i-Okinawa route better than the particular instrument used in the opening of *Bon Voyage Co.*, a *sanshin* (a tenor-ukulele-sized, guitar-shaped, snake-skin resonator covered, three-stringed instrument), Hosono bought in Honolulu's Chinatown in 1975 while producing Makoto Kubota's *Hawaii Champroo*[35], a sister-album to *Bon Voyage Co.*[36]. Despite its Okinawan origin, the *sanshin* also has affinities with Portuguese string instruments (the unexpected mixture reminding us of the history of two peoples working together in sugar cane plantations during the early 1900s[37]). This unusual – what might be termed 'pidgin Okinawan' – instrument suggests the receptive aspect of Okinawan music essential to Hosono's notion of the "archipelago".

What is significant to Hosono about Okinawa is the predisposition of its people not to simulate but to interact with visiting cultures. This may owe more to the history of the Islands' subordination to Japan, China and the U.S.A. than to any simple, essentialist idea of ethnic 'character'. Okinawan people have different approaches to notions of self and Other to those of the Japanese (see Ueda, 1994: 305f); and it is this process of multiple and fluid identification, rather than the Okinawan sound itself, that inspired Hosono. The issue of negotiating this Okinawan syncretism was key for Hosono's attempts to go beyond exotica, and, in this, Okinawa is to Hosono what Hawai'i was to Denny. Hosono's perceptions and responses were more complex however, since his own infancy was also colonised by the country of rock, hapa haole music and Denny[38], sensitising him to the underlying political relationships involved.

The close intertexuality with Denny begins with *Bon Voyage Co.*[39]. *Hong Kong*

133

Blues and *Sayonara – the Japanese Farewell Song* are, for instance, versions of songs from Denny's repertoire (from *Exotica* and *Exotica II,* respectively), while *Tokyo Rush*, the opening song of *Paraiso*, is an obvious remake of *Rush Hour in Hong Kong* from *Exotica II*. Hosono does not only 'electrify' the Denny sound but emphasises the orientalism by adding percussion, marimba, vocals in 'Bamboo English' and chinoiserie introductions and counter-melodies. Unlike *Tropical Dandy*, a mixture of chinoiserie and Latin American fantasy, *Bon Voyage Co.* represents a departure by exoticising Japan through appropriating and reversing styles associated with Denny.

Hosono does not simply revive outdated fantasies but rather recombines elements of Denny's approach and oeuvre in an ironic and humorous way. His strategy is not to assert any kind of 'authenticity' (for his music) in contrast to Denny's (manifestly 'false') exoticism but rather to produce inventive pastiches of the latter. The strategic self-exoticisation is immediately evident in the first track of *Bon Voyage Co.*, *Cho-Cho-San*. Led by the sanshin, a New Orleans-style piano part features prominently behind the vocalist, who intones:

> *Cho-Cho-San, show me how to fly/*
> [I've] *fled away from Tokyo/*
> *That girl was* Ocean Liner Girl/
> *Hey Captain,* Sail away/
> Just-a *"chotomate"*[40] moment please/
> *I'm sailing away from Tokyo to go and get that girl*
>
> *Cho-Cho-San, captain/*
> Show me how to fly away with you/
> *If I can see that girl/*
> *Good-by bye bye Cho-Cho-San/*
> *Captain, Cho-Cho-San*
>
> *Cho-Cho-San, show me how to fly/*
> *From Tokyo, faraway sea/*
> *Rapid* Ocean Liner Ship/
> *Captain, you wanna try/*
> Just-a *"chotomate"*[40] *moment please/*
> *Cho-Cho-San flies, the end of sea is paradise*

(NB Lyrics in roman font are in English in the original version.)

Here Cho-Cho-San is not an obedient Nagasaki *musume* but rather a liberated Tokyo girl who "sails away" to the end of the seas. The lyrics are so cryptic that it is difficult to unravel a specific story beyond that of a girl's desire to "fly away" like a butterfly. She is more of an 'independent' woman than an exotically 'fixed' Japanese one. The song undermines the listeners' expectation and displaces its orientalism by an odd mimicry on the part of the exoticised. Japanese songwriters wrote a series of popular songs which reproduced the Puccinian sentimentalism of *Cho-Cho-San* between the 1930s and 1960s. What is perhaps most striking about this output is that none of them questioned the racial and gender implications of their stereotypes. Japanese audiences usually accept western stereotypes of Japanese women (precisely because they are accepted by the West). Hosono twists this Japanese propensity for self-exoticisation since he, conscious that rock was born in the country of Lieutenant Pinkerton, is faced with the cultural (and political) hegemony of the U.S.A. But, unlike Puccini's heroine, he is not forced to be subject to it. What he proposes is less a nationalistic counter-plot than an oblique transposition of the Japan-U.S. relationship because, in that he plays rock, he cannot disapprove of the American influence. Curiously, the language used in *Cho-Cho-San* is neither Bamboo English (except "chotomate") nor does it use loan-words, but rather comprises a combination of Japanese and English.

Another twist in *Cho-Cho-San* is the participation of an Okinawan female group as backing vocalists. The mixture of New Orleans-style piano and Okinawan folk song style is developed further in *Loochoo Gumbo*[41]. The sound comprises a marimba part, a repeated Okinawan vocal phrase, sanshin lines and a Dr John-style funky piano part[42]. Hosono sings over the powerful beat of *kachashi*, a cheerful Okinawan festive dance genre, while the female vocalists sing in Okinawan (syntactically compatible with Japanese but lexically and phonetically different from it), alluding to the discrepancy between two peoples and the superiority of Okinawan language:

> *This is not Japanese language/*
> *My inner heart is secret/*
> *The scent of the wind from the South, Loochoo Gumbo/*
> *Somehow it burns my heart, Loochoo Gumbo*
> *Yamato* [main island] *people will be blown away/*
> *They can't beat the Southern wind/*
> *Feeling happy with kachashi groove, coming over the sea/*
> *Okinawan guts are here/*
> *Let me hear the song of island, let me smell the scent of island*

The "wind from the South" is an obvious metaphor for Okinawa; and *Loochoo Gumbo* fades out with a brief quote of *Haisai Ojisan*, the first attempt to blend rock and *kachashi* rhythm, produced by Shoukichi Kina and a major hit in Okinawa in 1972–3 and later, in 1977, on main-island Japan[43]. The popularity of *Haisai Ojisan*, and the Okinawan culture it represented and popularised, was a contributory factor in the campaign to scale-down the U.S. presence in Okinawa, and subsequently restore Japanese control, which achieved partial success in 1972. Following this, Okinawa started to receive Japanese mass media and tourist attention. *Haisai Ojisan* secured access to the music industry of main-island Japan and represented a new era for the archipelago.

135

Another important reference to Okinawa in the Trilogy is *Asatoya Yunta*, the best known Okinawan folk song in Japan. Hosono's version not only combines an electric sound with an Okinawan vocal, in the manner of the pieces discussed above, but also contrasts the verses popularised in Japan (in Japanese) with those orally transmitted in Okinawa (in Okinawan). The Japanese verses, which are concerned with flirting, appear to have been transported to main-island Japan by officials, soldiers, policemen and merchants who had been entertained by Okinawan women in drinking parties during their stay (and presumably heard the song in this context). The Okinawan verses, by contrast, deal with the epic suffering of a local woman. Throughout four verses, the Okinawan refrain is common to both. In the Japanese version it functions solely as a hook, however, in the vernacular original, the refrain, as in many genres of folk narrative, is a recurrent motif which propels the woman's story as well as producing a rhythmic frame by its cyclic recurrence.

The bilingualism is more than a straight juxtaposition: it unleashes the linguistic conflict inherent in the centuries-old Japanese rule over the Archipelago. By switching gender and ethnic roles in the song (with an Okinawan woman singing the part of Japanese man in Japanese, and a Japanese man singing the part of an Okinawan woman in Okinawan), *Asatoya Yunta* clearly evokes (and maintains) the cultural and historical intercourse between Japan and Okinawa[44]. It is not, however, Hosono's concern to condemn the Japanese 'counterfeit' and to glorify the original version but rather to focus upon the inter-dependence of two cultures. He mimics both the 'real' Okinawan music and its Japanese appropriation. He goes beyond his inspiration, Martin Denny, to reach a point of cultural critique of the exotic.

Paradise in the mind

Along with the engagement with Okinawa as a strategic site, there is another dividing line between *Tropical Dandy* and the last two albums of the Trilogy. The latter are also marked by a religious sensibility and awareness of paradise. This transition of accent from the exotic to the sacred merits discussion. Although exoticism and the representation of earthly paradise are inseparable, the 'far-away' in *Tropical Dandy* essentially recombines and augments the euphoric ingredients of the Martin Denny sound and has no association with the sacred. But *Bon Voyage Co.* is different. The lyrics of *Chow Chow Dog*, for example, delivered over a ska-reggae beat, concern a dog escaping from a hut (a metaphor of *this* world). The refrain states:

> *Thou, Chow chow dog, wake up/*
> *If* [you] *want to know the way to the heaven/*
> *Thou, Chow chow dog, chant* hannya haramita/
> *Then,* [your] *heart* [will reach] nirvana/

> [*Hannya haramita* in Japanese, or *prajnaparamita* in Sanskrit, is the opening word of the sutra most known in Japan]

136

The second person "thou" (*nanji*) is now archaic in Japanese and survives almost solely in its Biblical/Christian context. The song also refers to the "end of China" as the dog's homeland ("chow chow dog" is a type of puppy used in some Chinese cuisines)[45]. The use of Buddhist terms such as "Hannya haramita" and "nirvana" signal the development of a religious consciousness connected with exoticism (chinoiserie) in Hosono's work. Though a sense of homelessness pervades *Tropical Dandy,* as is clearly perceived in *On Drifting* ("Underneath drifts [my] illusory homeland/ No destination at all/ I am on a raft"), it is in *Bon Voyage Co.* that Hosono alludes to the sacred destination (and destiny) of his journey (and *Paraiso* furthers this allusion).

Paraiso was recorded at a critical moment in the development of Hosono's sense of a spiritual identity. He has mentioned on various occasions how he became interested in the supernatural, eschatology and mysticism (in the form of the writings of Carlos Castaneda, yoga etc.) in the mid-1970s, when his life and musical activity seemed to have no purpose.

Paraiso, or *Haraiso* if one uses the Japanese translation, is a Portuguese word for 'paradise'. This was a term used by Japanese Christians who were converted by Jesuit missionaries in the 16th–17th centuries but were subsequently forced to conceal their religious identity and to live on a remote island between Nagasaki and the Korean Peninsula after fierce persecution in the 1630s. They disguised the cult of the Virgin Mary in that of Amaterasu, the supreme goddess of Shintoism, the vernacular religion of Japan, and chanted in a version of Latin so 'Japanised' that it was incomprehensible (even to congregations)[46]. It was not until the 1870s, when the Meiji government permitted Christianity for Japanese, that the group publicly re-emerged. The significance of this reference in Hosono's work is that it implies that the sacred does not belong (solely) to the western universal religion nor to the Japanese autochthon one. The reference to syncretism camouflaging the foreign deity (like the cult of Maria de Guadalupe in Mexico and that of Oxun-Maria in Afro-Brazilian religion) suggests that Hosono's search for the 'far-away' does not simply involve the evocation of exotic women and/or nature but rather implies a pilgrimage to the imaginary sacrarium suggested in the cover design of *Paraiso* – a collage of a Buddhist statue and the Taj Mahal along with hula dancers, tropical birds and flowers, coconut trees, a colonial hotel, an ocean liner and the Manhattan skyline[47].

Paraiso includes three tracks which refer to Buddhism: *Crossroads Song*, *Shambhala Correspondence* and *Worry Beads*. *Crossroads Song*, superbly using the synthesiser in harmony with Trinidadian steel drums, relates one person's quest for the four principal tropes of Japan's traditional aesthetics (flower, bird, wind and moon), in mythical places in four directions over four seasons. The four imaginary destinations include "Caribia" in the south, "Cardia" in the east, the north island where the Phoenix lives, and India in the west. The four verses are called 'Spring Flower', 'Summer Wind', 'Autumn Moon' and 'North Bird' (the latter referring to

137

Winter). Such a quadruple frame successfully combines exoticism with the time-honoured poetics of Japanese nature writing and drawing. The lyrics of the first verse describe a journey west to meet God. This is related to the Japanese Buddhist belief that Elysium exists faraway in this direction:

> *When the morning comes, I am going to leave/*
> *From the west door/*
> *To* [go to] *India, where the lotus flowers are/*
> *In order to see the kami* [God]

Instead of referring to the Buddha (*hotoke* in Japanese), as might be expected, the song refers to the "kami", the Shinto deity. This slippage is inherent to Shinto-Buddhist syncretism in Japan. As the historian Akio Yoshie (1996) has explained, the universal religion of Buddhism (which salvages the spirit of individuals-in-general) has constructed an abstract – and therefore 'universal' – system of belief. By contrast, Japan's local animistic religion, from which the nationally- (and politi-cally-) orientated Shintoism has developed, has, since its inception in the 6th Century, been based on the concept of impurity and the practice of purification. The form of syncretism involved has seen the two (seemingly incompatible) religions linked in an "open system" (ibid: 213), resulting in a tolerant coexistence of the vernacular and the transplanted cultures. For example, a Shinto shrine can be a Buddhist temple without dissimulating itself and people can pray for the two different deities in the same place. The universal Buddhism does not give way to the pre-existent animism and vice versa. This form of syncretism, in Yoshie's charac-terisation, contrasts to the 'closed system' of European religious history where Christianity attempted to suppress local belief systems, casting them as heresies, and often forcing them into oppositional and resistant stances. The Shinto-Christian syncretism of the Edo period is unusual in Japanese religious history since Christi-anity was banned (unlike Buddhism) and could survive only as a form of 'assimilated heresy'.

Like *Crossroads Song*, *Worry Beads*, recorded with a light reggae arrangement, combines an exoticism with a Buddhist form of prayer:

> *Let's go and return to the desert under the moonlight/*
> *Plant in* [your]*breast* [heart] *the seeds of the moon*
>
> *The seeds of one hundred and eight worries/*
> *Just count one, two/*
> *Look,* [your]*body becomes so light/*
> [That you] *can go wherever you wish right now*
>
> *Under the moonlight,* [you] *count the beads and breathe deeply/*
> *Look, the desert under the moon is penetrating your breast* [heart]/
> *And right now*

138

(Refrain, in Sanskrit)
Om Nama Chandraya
Shanti Shanti Chandraya

The reference to "seeds of one hundred and eight worries" derives from the Buddhist conviction that every human is deemed to have committed one hundred and eight sins ("worries"). Each of the "worry beads" represents one "worry" and the prayer involves touching and counting beads while asking pardon from Buddha for each of the sins. Hosono draws on and cross-associates this traditional form of redemption with levitation. The refrain in Sanskrit reinforces the religious/spiritual address.

The "desert" in this song is a place to which one should "go and return". It is both destination and home, over there and right here, exotic and familiar. The cyclic journey to and from the desert is associated with nostalgia because the "desert under the moon" is from a title of a well-known juvenile song (*Tsuki no Sabaku*). The "return to the desert" suggests a return to a familiar place. In this regard, the meaning of the desert goes beyond the mere exotic (as is found in *Femme Fatale* on the same album) and may imply that the desert is actually a conceptual place – in Tokyo itself.

Shambhala Signal ("Shambhala" is a Sanskrit word for paradise) is an instrumental which marries melodies performed on gamelans with an electronically produced rhythm track – creating a style which might be described as 'techno-orientalist'. In accordance with Hosono's tendency to increase the technological component of his music, this interlocking of primitivism and technology is more complex than Denny's exotica. The track also provides an excellent pre-figuration of the Yellow Magic Orchestra's work[48]. The approach to the sacred in *Paraiso's* exoticism is as much an engagement with the (so-called) 'New Age' movement as a belated echo of the hippy dream of community and India (since Hosono does not refuse technology or urban comfort but sees the computer, for example, as a vehicle to transcend the material world). His approach to Eastern philosophies/religions is distinct from that of the (diffuse) New Age movement. After questioning the dichotomy between Japan and the U.S.A. in Happii Endo, he discovers the potential of exoticism to dislocate world power relationships (*Tropical Dandy*) and encounters the 'anamorphosis' of his native country via Okinawa (*Bon Voyage Co.*). Finally in *Paraiso*, inspired by dissimulated Japanese Catholicism, he casts light on the forgotten sacredness and the symbiotic syncretism of Japan.

The Trilogy ends with a song called *Haraiso*, whose lyrics include the revealing lines:

That fantasy I once dreamt of/
[I] have chased it and reached a pier/
Here is the big, comfortable city we live in/
An insular country one cannot escape from, even tomorrow

139

and:

> *Paradise, Haraiso/*
> *Enrich* [your] *fantasy/*
> *Mirage, Haraiso/*
> *Dissolve the reality*

After a long journey around the world chasing his exotic fantasy, Hosono returns home and realises that he cannot escape from it (hence the song's dedication to Tokyo City on the album sleeve). The Trilogy thereby concludes with a certain sense of fatigue and resignation. Yet, Hosono continues to say "Adios, Farewell". But to whom? To the clear-cut boundary between reality and fantasy, mirage and paradise. It is no accident that this finale coincides with the development of Japanese technologies which are, according to the architect Arata Isozaki, "blurring the line between the real and the simulated" (cited in Morley and Robins, 1992: 153). This description may serve to explain Hosono's shift away from exoticism and towards (advanced) technology in the late 1970s. Disillusioned by exoticism, he moved on to the ironic technological address of the Yellow Magic Orchestra (YMO), which operated between 1978–83.

Although YMO recorded a version of Denny's *Firecracker*, and alluded to Okinawan music on its early albums, the ensemble was more engaged in the material here-and-now than any spiritual or geographical elsewhere. The trio seemed more interested in playing with the new stereotype of hi-tech Japan and gradually moved to experiment with state-of-art equipment (made mostly in Japan) challenging the technological limit of pop music[49]. The ambiguity and humour characteristic to Hosono's Trilogy was replaced by a more serious, controlled techno-orientalism. YMO were timely and well-calculated as a group designed to succeed in overseas markets. As a result of their international popularity, YMO concealed aspects of their Japaneseness by recording a greater proportion of instrumental numbers and by using English language lyrics more than Japanese[50].

The mid-1970s marked the beginning of global attention to 'yen power', as characterised by Ezra Vogel's tract, *Japan as Number One* (original and Japanese translation in 1979). Subsequent books by western revisionists on Japanese culture and technology fortified a Japanese self-confidence that had been lost since 1945. (Western endorsement is, paradoxically, absolutely necessary for Japan's self-image.) Encouraged by western commentators, Japanese nationalism and internationalism rose simultaneously. The YMO, for instance, became a symbol of the internationalisation of Japan's incomparable techno-culture, Japanese journalists reacted patriotically to their success; as exemplified in the following headlines: "The ambition of Yellow Magic Orchestra to conquer the world from Japan", "Directly exported to Paris! Attention to Yellow Magic Orchestra!" and "Chasing the 'YMO phenomenon'. Even the Western bands imitate them" (cited in Hagiwara, 1992: 99).

140

Although the Trilogy neither enjoyed, nor intended to enjoy, the overseas success of the YMO, its deliberate play of out-of-place-ness and belatedness disrupted the spatio-temporal order that necessarily perpetuates asymmetrical cultural relationships between Japan and the U.S.A. more radically than any of YMO's albums.

Belated exoticism

According to Chris Bongie (1991), the loss of the 'elsewhere' from western reality is not simply an accompanying fact but rather a constitutive element of exoticism. It is the paradox of exoticism, he continues, that it can never recover the loss of an authentic past and of a primitive world that the modernity originating from the 18th–19th Century Europe expelled – precisely because the project of exoticism involves the process of *creating* such a loss; it searches in vain for what it banishes. Thus exoticism seeks for the trace of what modernity has effaced. In this sense, exoticism, like 'allegory' in the historical philosophy of Benjamin, "is a posthumous project and thus precluded from ever truly realizing what it sets out to achieve" (Bongie, 1991: 17). By the end of the 19th Century optimistic exoticism gave way to a pessimistic – or, if one uses the Benjaminian figure, *melancholic* – exoticism, one in which the authors were aware of the impossibility of reaching somewhere intact, an earthly paradise where modernity had not come to hold sway. Such authors were, in the words of Ali Behdad (1994) "belated travellers". Their disillusion was historically synchronised with the gradual but postponed dissolution of colonialism. Broadly, the belated reading of exoticism is not "an orthodox reiteration or reapplication of a previous theory" but "an interventionary articulation of a new problematic through the detour – or, perhaps more accurately, re-tour – of an earlier practice" (Behdad, 1994: 3). The oppositional potential of belatedness is relevant to the Trilogy because when the albums were released, the Martin Denny sound had sunk into oblivion (especially for the rock generation) and Hosono's fascination for exotica was thereby marked by its own belatedness. His work intervenes in the strategic recovery of colonial memory of the American occupation and in the re-writing (re-sounding?) of chinoiserie and Japanesque music by means of global detouring and re-touring (as imaginatively delineated in 'On the Islands').

As noted in the Introduction to this chapter, Japanese rock audiences and musicians are habitually preoccupied with catching up with the latest (imported) sounds and thereby neglect the colonial history latent in the formation of Americanism that affects them so deeply. This amnesia, in turn, produces the discursive space for western and Japanese rock in Japan – in which one listens to and performs any sound one wants without reflecting on the distance (in terms of ethnicity and locality) between the sound and the listener/performer. Most Japanese rock fans and artists believe in the universal aspect of western popular music so naively that they tend to erase the difference between western and Japanese cultural conditions in order to assimilate themselves within the universal-western point of view. Hosono's imaginary circumnavigation employs the detour or re-tour in order to disjoint and subvert

141

this type of universalist *credo* – vacillating between the U.S. image of Japan and the world and Japanese counter-images (which are, in turn, heavily modelled by western perceptions).

Notes

1. These were finally prohibited after a series of brutal confrontations with armed police, since the site was technically a 'passageway' (to walk through) rather than a 'plaza' (to congregate in).
2. The "Black Ship" allusion refers to the U.S. battleships that menaced and undermined Japan's isolationism in 1853.
3. The sparkling debut of Carol, a working-class, leather-clad, rock and roll band, ended the debate in 1973, demonstrating the Japanese language's capacity to articulate simple and effective rock music.
4. A form of mainstream popular song.
5. A romantic form of ballad.
6. A narrative song genre popular before World War Two.
7. A narrative genre popular in the 18th–19th centuries.
8. The ancient caravan route between Japan and Persia transversing Central Asia.
9. Imperial court music.
10. Gottani has no clear English equivalent, 'melange' is one interpretation, 'hotchpotch' (with its connotations of a 'lumpy' unblendedness) is another.
11. Later in this interview Hosono stated that his *Tropical Dandy* album "might well have been called *Discover Japan*" (Bell, 1997: 34).
12. His blatant stereotyping ("Parisian elegance", "Spanish passion", "African energy" etc.) does not simply represent a formulaic exoticism but rather arises from his perception of Japan as exotic in a similar manner to that of the U.S. perception of Africa and Spain. In his exotic atlas, Japan is equidistant from China and Trinidad, as much as the U.S.A. is as far from Japan and Central Asia.
13. And it is for this reason that Japanese documentary films often use Miller's *In the Mood* to evoke the period. (NB all U.S. music was banned from Japan during the War – see Hosokawa, 1994: 62–63 for further discussion.)
14. References to infancy are also found in *Three O'Clock Lullaby* and *Exotica Lullaby*.
15. With Japan's recovery of sovereignty in 1952, the previous practice of naming typhoons with an ordinal number, or the toponymy of the area it most seriously damaged, was revived.
16. See Chapter Three for further discussion.
17. In the years immediately following the War, the figure fell to below 100,000.
18. This aspect is represented in Robert Altman's film *M.A.S.H.* (1969), which uses Japanese songs popular during the Korean War to evoke the period.
19. All these songs are compiled on the CD *Exotic Japan – Orientalism in Occupied Japan*, compiled by Tôyô Nakamura. There were also many G.I. films made in the U.S.A. in the 1950s, *Teahouse of the August Moon* (1956) being one of the best known examples. Gina Marchetti's remark on the film *Sayonara*:

    Sayonara *seems to be saying that just as it is natural for men to love and dominate passive women, it is natural for America to take a similarly dominant posture toward Japan.* (1993: 135)

    has strong resonances with *Sayonara – Japanese Farewell Song*:
20. The composer credited, Hasegawa Yoshida, is supposedly a Japanese-American but the credit may be a pseudonym of an American because both Hasegawa and Yoshida are last names (unless it was *they* who composed the song?).

21. Lyrics by Freddie Morgan.

22. Music and lyrics by Earl Burrows.

23. Also see also Stanlaw (1992: 61).

24. This Pidgin Japanese is also used in *My Ichiban Tomodachi* sung by Nancy Umeki: "...'Cause this handsome lad/ Is just my ichiban tomodachi [best friend]".

25. According to Peter Mühlhäuser, the contribution of 'foreigner talk' to the formation of pidgins is "restricted to relatively early stages of [their] development" (1986: 106). Bamboo English is a language that almost completely disappeared after its "relatively early stages of development" owing to the gradual diffusion of English language education in Japanese primary schools. Thus the lyrics of *Japanese Rumba* are associated with a specific period in Japanese history.

26. Also see Miller (1967), Chapter 6.

27. George Shimabukuro, an Okinawan-Hawaiian G.I., later worked in show business in Honolulu and made a few albums for a local label. He also personally escorted Arthur Lyman on his tour of Japan in 1964.

28. Just as Kipling's *Jungle Book* (once) provided the first images of India for British children.

29. On the cultural context of the Silk Road boom, see Ivy (1988: 24).

30. Lyrics by Ujô Noguchi.

31. Here, perhaps, Hosono is also alluding to Roman Polanski's film *Chinatown* (1974).

32. The same rhythm is twice used in *Black Peanuts* on *Bon Voyage Co.* This calypso-baião song is the only political satire in the Trilogy. The title refers to a key word in the Lockheed scandal that resulted in the dismissal of the (then) Japanese prime minister in 1974 ("one peanut" referred to a unit of illicit money among the accomplices). The song also parodies a rumba classic, *Manicero* [*The Peanut Vendor*]. Another reference to actual events is found in *Tokyo Rush*, whose words, "From Moscow, from Dacca", alludes to the Dacca aeroplane highjacking by the Japanese Red Army in 1977.

33. This second verse refers to *Minnesota no Tamago Uri* ('The Egg Vendor of Minnesota') a boogie woogie hit in 1951 sung by Teruko Akatsuki. This singer also recorded *Tokyo Shoe Shine Boy* in the same year, referred to in *Tokyo Shyness Boy* from *Bon Voyage Co. Tokyo Shoe Shine Boy* seems, in turn, to be a local remake of *Chattanoogie Shoe Shine Boy*, recorded by Frank Sinatra in 1950. In Hosono's words, "Tokyo shyness" is a G.I. idiom that designates the "un-open attitude of Japanese" (1992: 116). The track is, by Hosono's admission, a "copy" (ibid: 115) of Professor Longhair's style of piano boogie. (Hosono's affinity with non-mainstream popular music is also apparent in the blend of slack-key guitar with a swing rhythm on *Pon Pon Jôki* which is, according to Hosono, influenced by Texas [Western] Swing and Jerry Lee Lewis [1992: 134]).

34. In Japanese meteorological terminology, the term tropical night' is used when the minimum night temperature does not fall below 30 °C.

35. Champroo is an Okinawan dish, a sort of 'hotpot'.

36. During the same trip they also bought many Denny albums in second-hand shops.

37. Okinawan migration to Hawai'i started in 1885, some twenty years after Portuguese workers arrived.

38. During the Soy Sauce Music period, Hosono produced and collaborated on numerous albums. *Super Generation* (1974), a collection of Ryôichi Hattori's songs performed by a female jazz singer of the 1950s, Izumi Yukimura, is of particular importance. This album uses rock and soul styles to update the pre-War exoticism of Hattori – who prematurely blended various popular styles in the 1930s and 1940s and featured ukulele, castanets, accordion, rumba, tango, swing, foxtrot, boogie woogie etc. (See Hosokawa, 1994). One of the songs on that album is *Soshu Night Serenade*, a Chinoiserie hit in 1940, re-recorded by Martin Denny on *Exotica II*.

143

39. A title which derives from an actual trading company in Nagasaki.

40. *Chotomate* means "just a moment" in Bamboo English.

41. *Loochoo* is a heteronym of Okinawa .

42. Hosono has declared his enthusiasm for Dr. John's music (1985: 92–95)

43. Subsequently, Makoto Kubota, Ry Cooder, Fred Frith and Henry Kaiser, among others, have covered it. (Also see Mitsui, 1998 and my sleeve notes for the Shoukichi Kina and Champloose album *The Music Power from Okinawa,* Globe Style, 1991 for further discussion).

44. This dimension, somehow compatible with the Mexican and Hawaiian tunes performed by Ry Cooder, is absent in Ryuichi Sakamoto's aestheticist rendition of the same folk song on his album *Beauty* (1993).

45. Hosono has cited a previous dog song, *Won Tan Tan* by the Coasters (date unknown), as an influence on *Chow Chow Dog* (Hosono, 1992: 132).

46. See Miyazaki (1996) for further discussion of the sect.

47. The cover of *Paraiso* was designed by Tadanori Yokoo, who had previously provided the sleeve designs for albums such as Miles Davis' *Agharta* and Santana's *Amigos.* Hosono's acquaintance with Yokoo, who had previously published an essay on meditation, yoga and transcendental psychology, inspired him so deeply that, since their meeting, he notes, "my orientation has been turning from dazzling ethno-like images and fake exoticism to heavy India" (1979: 19). Their short visit to India, immediately after the recording of *Paraiso,* resulted in the production of their electro-instrumental collage *Cochin Moon,* released in September 1978, five months later than *Paraiso* and two months prior to the release of the YMO's debut album. *Cochin Moon,* inspired by Kraftwerk and Brian Eno, anticipates not only YMO's instrumental tracks but also Hosono's later ambient works such as *Sightseeing Music* (1984) and *Endless Talk* (1985).

48. The CD cover credits this release to 'Harry Hosono and The Yellow Magic Band'.

49. For YMO the Japanese music industry coined the term *tekuno-poppu* ('techno-pop').

50. But at the same time, the band avoided the ambiguous riddle about who are exotic to whom, a dialogical question ceaselessly asked – but never answered – in the Trilogy. In this regard, at least, YMO offered a clear, one-dimensional answer to one of the questions Hosono was attempting to address (however colourfully and dynamically) in the Soy Sauce Music series.

51. Both are complicit in post-War Japan, see Iwabushi (1994: 64ff); Sugimoto and Mauer (1986); and Yoshimoto (1989: 22f).

Discography

Happii Endo	*Kazemachi Roman,* URC, 1971
———	*Happy End,* King, 1973
Haruomi Hosono	*Tropical Dandy,* Crown, 1975
———	*Taian Yôkô,* Crown, 1976
———	*Haraiso,* Alfa, 1978[51]
——— and Tadanori Yokoo	*Cochin Moon,* King, 1978
Shoukichi Kina and Champloose	*The Music Power from Okinawa,* Globe Style, 1991
Makoto Kubota and the Sunset Gang	*Hawaii Champroo,* Showboat, 1975
Izumi Yukimura	*Super Generation,* Columbia, 1974
Various	*Exotic Japan,* Audibook, 1996

Chapter Six

MUSICAL TRANSPORT

Van Dyke Parks, Americana and the Applied Orientalism of *Tokyo Rose*

JON FITZGERALD AND PHILIP HAYWARD

Introduction

Since the late 1960s, Van Dyke Parks (VDP) has explored various facets of Americana (understood as the elaborated cultural expression of aspects of the socio-cultural history of the U.S.A.) in a range of solo and collaborative projects. In the early-mid 1970s he complemented and inter-related this with a series of engagements with the music of the Southern Caribbean. In 1989 his work took a further turn with the release of an album entitled *Tokyo Rose*. This project deployed a range of musical orientalisms to produce a complex representation of aspects of U.S.-Japanese relations in the mid-late 20th Century[1] and also drew together a number of elements present in his previous oeuvre, particularly in his engagements with Americana *through* a Caribbean 'tropicalism' in the 1970s.

The chapter opens with an introduction to VDP's career, comprising a discussion of his various explorations of Americana, his approach to composition and orchestration, and of similarities between his musical approach and the post-war musical exoticism discussed in Chapters 1–4. Following a lengthy analysis of *Tokyo Rose*, the chapter concludes with a characterisation of the geo-cultural context of VDP's 'applied orientalism' and the manner in which this informs the production of *Tokyo Rose* and other elements of VDP's oeuvre.

145

I. Americana – routes and reflections

Quotation – call it plagiarism if you will – is my beck and call. It figures in a lot of my works, either in the construct of a song, or in the ornaments of its arrangement. I try to keep a light hand in the process, and brush the unsuspecting unconscious with what matters most. (VDP – e-mail to the authors, 19.4.98)

VDP was born in 1943, in Hattiesburg, Mississippi. He showed early musical talent on the clarinet and went on to become a boarding pupil at the American Boychoir School in Princeton, New Jersey, studying voice and piano. During his early teens he performed in live opera, stage musicals, television and cinema[2]. He then went on to study piano and composition at the Carnegie Institute of Technology, Pittsburg before returning to California in 1962. From 1962–64 he participated in various musical projects: working as a studio clarinettist for CBS TV[3]; performing with his brother Carson in two groups, as a duo called the Steeltown Two (playing a repertoire of [mostly] Mexican songs from the 1930s–40s), and in a larger folk music ensemble, The Greenwood County singers. During this period he also collaborated informally with other musicians working on the local folk club circuit, jamming with instrumentalists such as Taj Mahal[4]. In 1963 he began working as a session keyboard player in the film industry, an activity he continued through to 1966, performing on the soundtracks of films such as Disney's *The Jungle Book* (released in 1967). He also worked as a session musician on rock and pop recordings, contributing to albums by bands such as Paul Revere and the Raiders, The Byrds and The Grateful Dead; and producing pop bands such as Harpers Bizarre and the Mojo Men.

In 1966 he began an association with Brian Wilson, writing lyrics for songs such as *Heroes and Villains* (1967) and contributing ideas to the arrangements of seminal Beach Boys' tracks such as *Good Vibrations* (1966)[5]. Indeed, his input appears to have been an important stimulus for Wilson to move to the lavishly arranged musical complexity which has been regarded as a high-point of his and the Beach Boys' careers. Influenced by working with Wilson[6], VDP's first solo album, *Song Cycle*, was released in-mid 1968. The album contains a variety of musical approaches, including rich, evocative orchestrations on tracks such as *Palm Desert* and *Widow's Walk;* and a highly complex 'modernist' arrangement of the Randy Newman song *Vine Street*[7]. The sophistication (and manifest ambition) of the album's music and lyrics prompted a number of laudatory reviews, one of the most notable being penned by *New York Times'* reviewer Richard Goldstein:

Not since Gershwin has someone ... emerged with such a transcendent concept of what American music really means. Song Cycle *is that album we have all been waiting for; an auspicious debut, a stunning work of pop art, a vital piece of Americana* (cited in Tomasulo, 1996: npd)

Writing some thirty years later, Timothy White produced an astute complement to this evaluation, describing the album in terms of an expanded characterisation of Americana – "an awesomely melodic pastiche, its liquid music a moving, gently surreal homage to the mythic American experience" – and emphasising the album's debt to a tradition of "great film and show scores from Rodgers and Hammerstein and Alfred Newman ... to Elmer Bernstein and Ennio Morricone" which, he argues, have been seminal in the 20th Century's "codification" and "celebration" of Americana (White, 1998: npd)[8].

VDP's address to Americana has been one element of a complex oeuvre which has developed over a thirty year period. Since *Song Cycle*, he has released five solo albums (*Discover America* [1972], *Clang of the Yankee Reaper* [1975], *Jump* [1984], *Tokyo Rose* [1989] and *Moonlighting: Live at the Ash Grove* [1997]); a compilation album, *Idiosyncratic Path* (1994); an album jointly credited to Brian Wilson, *Orange Crate Art* (1995); and written a number of film scores. During this period, he has also worked extensively as arranger, producer and/or performer on other artists' recordings[9].

Following the release of *Song Cycle*, VDP became interested in Southern Caribbean calypso and steelband music, visited Trinidad and Tobago and went on to produce a single for the Andre de la Bastide Steelband in 1969 and an (eponymous) album for the Esso Trinidad Tripoli Steelband in 1971[10]. In 1971 he drew on this experience to blend Trinidadian music styles and cultural themes with his previous interest in Mexican, New Orleans and (earlier styles of) U.S. popular music on an album entitled *Discover America* (released in 1972), produced in close collaboration with orchestrator Kirby Johnson and musicians such as Lowell George[11]. Eleven of the compositions are calypso songs from the 1930s–1950s and the four other tracks are cover versions of contemporary U.S. compositions (Allen Toussaint's *Occapella* and *Riverboat* and Lowell George's *Sailing Shoes*) and a version of John Philip Sousa's *The Stars and Stripes Forever*.

Despite its pronounced Southern Caribbean flavour, the album reflects cultural and musical flows around the Gulf of Mexico, linking U.S., Mexican-Hispanic and Caribbean histories. Befitting this conceptual location, *Discover America* is a multi-perspectival work. It includes songs with lyrics addressed to Trinidad and Tobago (*Ode to Tobago*, *Your Own Comes First*); to U.S.-Trinidadian history and cultural relations (*FDR in Trinidad*, *Sweet Trinidad*); and to U.S. cultural history (*Bing Crosby*, *G-Man Hoover*). The album overlaps the musical traditions of the Southern Caribbean and the U.S.A. with blends of calypso, mariachi, New Orleans funk and Rhythm and Blues (on tracks such as *Occapella*, *Riverboat*, *Sailing Shoes* and *Your Own Comes First*), and with arrangements of calypso tunes 'crooned' to light orchestral accompaniments (*Bing Crosby*, *The Four Mills Brothers* and *John Jones*).

Fittingly, for an album which is informed by a sense of the history of U.S.-Trinidadian relations, *Discover America* ends with a short, extemporised rendition of *The*

147

Stars and Stripes Forever, performed by the Esso Trinidad Steel Band, where the pomp and rhythmic squareness of Sousa's march is replaced by a joyful, loose-limbed, up-tempo calypso feel[12]. This re-signification of a U.S. anthem represents what might be termed an 'applied' exoticisation of its referent. The exoticism here is not so much 'detoured', to use Hosokawa's phrase, as *détourned*. As Sadie Plant has discussed, this term describes a particular textual strategy:

> *[t]he closest English translation of* détournement *lies somewhere between 'diversion' and 'subversion'. It is a turning around and a reclamation of lost meaning ... it is plagiaristic, because its materials are those which already appear... and subversive, since its tactics are those of the 'reversal of perspective'.* (1992: 86)[13]

After producing the Mighty Sparrow's *Hot and Sweet* album in 1974, VDP went on to release a second Trinidadian influenced album, *Clang of the Yankee Reaper*, in 1975. In contrast to the variety of arrangements and production sounds on *Discover America* (and its sonic 'under-statedness' and subdued flashes of colour), *Clang...* , produced and co-arranged by Trevor Lawrence, has a uniformly brighter production quality. Up-tempo tracks predominate and the rhythm section and horns are featured prominently throughout, while steel drums and high-set strings provide extra emphasis to the upper register in a number of tracks. VDP himself sings in a higher vocal range than on *Discover America*.

The album opens with its title track – the only VDP composition on the album – celebrating the U.S. invention of a new mechanised harvesting technology (the "yankee reaper" referred to in its title) , with lyrics which use this to point to the decline of the British Empire. With typical VDP quirkiness, the album presents this as a full-on epic, employing a wide range of instrumental and vocal colours (from high-set backing vocals to assorted percussion sounds and the human whistle); together with chromaticism and surprising harmonic twists. This 'filmic' arrangement highlights the song's satirical lyrics, in a way which might be seen to provide a foretaste of many of the later *Tokyo Rose* arrangements. Standing out from the calypso-style tracks which predominate on the album, the title track has its counterpoint in the album's finale, where VDP manipulates the theme from Pachelbel's *Canon in D* in what might be described as a playful fashion[14]; transposed to A-flat major and employing a funky sixteenth rhythm with a 'skank'-style guitar (in place of the original square eighth feel of the original melody); and using short stabbing bass motifs in a manner reminiscent of [then] contemporary film music such as Isaac Hayes' *Theme from 'Shaft'* (1971)[15].

Bracketed by the scale (and ambition) of the title track and the concluding instrumental, the remainder of album comprises up-tempo versions of calypso standards such as *Iron Man* and *City on the Hill* (together with a gentle piano and vocal version of New Orleans' songwriter Jack Nocentelli's song *You're a Real Sweetheart*). As in the opening and concluding tracks, the arrangements of the calypso compositions utilise big-band orchestrations, comprising horns, strings, a rock ensemble and steel drums behind VDP's vocals. If *Discover America* resembles a quirky B-movie, notable for its ingenious use of dynamics of light and shade; then *Clang...* can be compared to a wide-screen, technicolour epic. Despite the differences, *Clang...* also followed *Discover America* in making minimal impact on a U.S. music market with little interest in either calypso music or arrangements of the degree of sophistication present on both albums.

At this point, within the focus of this book, it is pertinent to consider to what extent VDP can be considered to make musical exotica (within the same framework as Chapters Two-Four outline for the prototypical approaches of Baxter, Denny, Lyman and Sumac). Essentially, the key links between VDP's work and classic post-War exotica resides in his choice of a diverse range of musical instruments (and combinations) in arrangements and his inventive use of timbre, texture and aural dynamics. These are manifest in the layering of instrumental sounds in the ensembles he has recorded with; the mixing and spatial alignment of these in the stereo mix; and the interplay and thematic association of these with particularly complex and allusive lyrics[16] (and often highly stylised vocal performances).

While VDP has directly aligned himself with aspects of classic exotica with state-ments such as: "I don't think of any instrument as a primary cultural attachment ... I like them to perform in novel combinations" (Dart, 1996: 14); his work eschews the deliberate 'strangeness' of classic post-War exotica[17]. Instead, his uses of particular instruments derive from his sophisticated musical palate and his desire to fully explore and deploy musical colour in his arrangements. He has explained his unusual approach to orchestration, production and mixing in terms of his desire "to explore instruments which have been relegated to the darker corners of the orchestra and bring them forward" (cited in Dart: 14). He has also noted the 'plagiaristic' element, included in Plant's characterisation of détournement, stating that he enjoys marrying colourful, eclectic arrangements, his own composition and songwriting and his "undefeated impulses" to continually allude to and rework seminal pieces of (public domain) music (ibid).

Clang... marked the conclusion of VDP's engagement with Southern Caribbean musics (to date). Following a period in which he concentrated primarily on collabo-rating with other artists, VDP returned to a more direct engagement with Americana in the 1980s and produced a group of texts which revived and re-told a seminal piece of (multi-cultural) U.S. folklore – Joel Chandler Harris's famous adaptation of the Afro-American Brer Fox and Brer Rabbit folk tales. These appeared in the form of an album, *Jump* (1984), and a trilogy of children's books illustrated by Barry Moser, 'Jump' (1986), 'Jump Again' (1987) and 'Jump On Over' (1988)[18].

Both the books and record were well-received[19]. Several critics perceived the album as a renewed engagement with the strain of Americana VDP had explored on his

149

debut LP in 1968. This was aspect was highlighted by the album's lyrical themes and the prominence of brass band instrumentation, VDP's honky-tonk piano and Fred Tackett's banjo and mandocello parts, giving the music an 'old-time' flavour, offset and complicated by the inclusion of occasional steel drum and marimba features. The album's originality and accomplishment led Timothy White to characterise *Jump!* as a:

> *... masterpiece, gaining momentum from all that went before but giving voice to a dramatic new strength of purpose. Rarely had a pop-rock framework been expanded to such stunning effect, with eleven song setpieces, daubed in subtle shades of Aaron Copeland, Gilbert & Sullivan, Jacques Brel and Stephen Sondheim, but brimming with a crisply original foreground ... that described America's unfinished quest for racial and social concord.* (1998: npd)

Following the partial 'interruption' of his 1989 *Tokyo Rose* album (discussed in detail in the following section), VDP continued to explore similar musical territory, producing a series of evocative film soundtracks (most notably for *Wild Bill* [1995][20]) before releasing the work which (arguably) represents the apogee of his Americana orientation to date, his collaboration with Brian Wilson on the *Orange Crate Art* album. This marked the reunion of the two musicians some thirty years after their first collaboration, writing songs such as *Heroes and Villains*[21] for Wilson's band The Beach Boys. *Orange Crate Art* (1995) was produced as an affectionate homage to the recent history of California, and is richly nostalgic[22]. Perceptions of California as a state – or, to be prosaic, a state-of-mind – have informed much of VDP's work. However, for VDP, California is a state with a history, a complexity, existing in flux.

Orange Crate Art's title and inspiration derives from a particular form of American vernacular art, the visual designs that adorned orange crates from the late 1800s on. VDP has characterised these images as "propagandist", in that their exotic imagery[23] served an ideological purpose, "romanticizing California" as "an inducement to immigration" and thereby facilitating "a frenzy of land speculation through boom and bust periods" (VDP, 1997: npd)[24]. While aware of this aspect, the album approaches its topic through layers of personal reminiscence. As VDP has recalled:

> *... when I first heard of California [as a child] it must have been a Christmas ... California was a very far away and exotic place and a romanticised ideal and I wanted to capture that impression where everything was possible, larger than life ... just perfect.* (1995, *Words + Music* CD)

On *Orange Crate Art* VDP draws on the dynamic between memory, myth-making and more objective histories to produce a reflective complexity in the series of lushly orchestrated and sentimental ballads featured on the album. These are redolent of the pre-rock, pre- "age of anxiety" music that VDP has declared as an inspiration and model:

> *... a lot of the music of this age of anxiety doesn't excite me, and I don't listen to a lot of music which expresses the urban pathology of the developed nations. I like music to transport me either beyond my place or beyond my time, and most of that is written by guys who have stepped off the planet* [ie deceased]. (cited in Dart, 1996: 14)

Despite this emphasis, VDP's music, and particularly the orchestrations on his solo recordings, is not primarily concerned with musical pastiche – with the creation of a high-gloss aural *pastness* – but rather constitutes a contemporary form of complex aural commentary which has more in common with modernism, at least in terms of its critical and referential address. Indeed, VDP has explicitly sought to distance his work from simple retro/nostalgia, arguing that:

> *[n]ostalgia suggests a resignation of sorts. It's a static thing. It's non-dynamic, and I would like my work to serve some purpose.* (ibid)

In this manner, VDP aspires to what might be termed a 'retro-activatory' mode – 'retro' in its address to past cultural forms and histories; and 'activatory' in the sense of not simply reviving and/or revisiting previous forms but also re-activating and redeploying them. There is, of course, an unlimited potential for slippage between aspiration and achievement here. Similarly there is no guarantee that audiences might not respond actively and interrogatively to music intended as purely nostalgic; nor the opposite.

II. *Tokyo Rose*

> *I'm fascinated by songwriting. Songs are the most portable cultural baggage available. They combine thoughts, through words, and feelings, through music.* (VDP – e-mail to the authors, 19.4.98)

Tokyo Rose resulted from VDP's long-term interest in Japanese culture, his desire to explore the U.S.A.'s "ever-changing dynamic with the Japanese" (cited in Infusino, 1989: 87) and his deep sense of ambiguity about Japan – a simultaneous fascination with Japanese culture and an anxiety concerning its (once) military and (current) economic power, and the threats to U.S. stability constituted by both. More specifically, VDP's interests were heightened through a series of particular encounters and perceptions.

In terms of VDP's anxieties, these were stimulated and sustained by two factors – his continuing historical interest in World War Two and his unease over Japanese economic ascendancy. In particular, he has cited his reading of letters from U.S. General Wainwright, written to his family while a Japanese prisoner-of-war (from

151

a "vanquished point-of-view"), detailing the cruel, harsh nature of his imprisonment, as making a particularly vivid impression upon him (e-mail to the authors 6/4/98). During the album's promotion, VDP made a number of essentially similar characterisations of the principal motivation behind the album's production. One typical statement was that:

> [t]he record explored my own sensations about the emerging Japanese economic animal and the impact it had on me. I decided to do it with some degree of humour, but also with a great many fears. (cited in Dart, 1996: 14)

In another, more recent, characterisation, VDP characterised the album as having "externalized my own bête noire" (e-mail to the authors 6/4/98)[25].

In the 'politically correct' 1990s such comments are startlingly honest, the complete opposite of the forgive-and-forget (ie displace) mentality of post-1960s liberal counter-cultures; awkwardly frank in the context of the revival in western racism, its anti-racist opposition and the consequent polarisation of debate and perceived attitudes on such issues. As VDP found out upon delivering the album to Warner Brothers Records, such attitudes and, more pointedly, a sensitivity to American-Japanese industrial associations, affected the company's view of the product, with one vice president asking VDP to "rethink" some of the lyrics fearing that they would "offend" Warners "sister company" in Japan (cited by VDP, e-mail to the authors 6/4/98).

Coverage of the album in U.S. magazines included substantial reference to VDP's explanation of the anxieties which prompted him to produce the record[26]. In the main, however, writers were careful to distinguish this aspect from that of any simple anti-Japanese sentiment, citing VDP's inclusion of the song *Manzanar* on the album (a critique of U.S. WW2 internment policies – discussed in detail below), and the contribution of various Japanese musicians, as 'balancing' factors.

Whatever the anxieties of Warners' executives, the album was well-received by a niche audience on Japan and garnered several positive reviews. Writing in *Music Magazine*, for instance, Masakazu Kitanaka began by noting that "this new album is well timed in its appearance because of the [current] trade frictions between Japan and the U.S.A."; and went on to discuss VDP's sensitivity in exploring such issues, commenting that:

> ... there are several factors which, if approached superficially, might prove sufficiently grating for Japanese listeners to make them label the album "mistaken", "racist" or "discriminatory". However, the album is far from a superficial, indirect attack or misunderstanding [of Japan] ... there is a deep psychological entanglement in the relationship between Japan and the U.S.A.. Van Dyke Parks is trying to go back to the root of the entanglement.

Before concluding that:

> *[a]though material produced by a many other English and American musicians has drawn upon Japan or Tokyo, it is impossible to find anything like this album in terms of its conceptual/intellectual sophistication.* (1989: 24 – translation by Rika Saegusa and Philip Hayward)

Musically, VDP's sense of Japanese culture was stimulated by various factors. These included his production of the Japanese band Happii Endo's final album (*Happy End*) in 1973, and his acquaintance with the work of band member Haruomi Hosono, who he acknowledged on *Tokyo Rose's* sleeve notes[27]; and a well-received tour of Japan he undertook in 1988. As he has recounted, the idea for the album arose from a press interview in which he stated "that I was going to do a record called 'Discover Japan' ... I came back to Los Angeles realizing that I better keep that deal" (cited in Infusino, 1989: 87).

More significantly however, the orientalism of the album was enhanced – in terms of sophistication and accomplishment – through VDP's employment of two virtuoso Japanese musicians in leading instrumental roles, Osamu Kitajima on the koto and biwa (Japanese string instruments) and Masakuza Yoshizawa on bass and treble shakuhachi (Japanese flutes)[28]. VDP became acquainted with Kitajima, a Californian-resident since the 1980s, while working with him on Ry Cooder's score for the film *Paris Texas* (1984)[29]. He has characterised Kitajima's work as "respected in his homeland for his fluency with traditional instruments and vernaculars" and identified him as an exemplary collaborator since his work "fuses these influences easily with jazz and other 20th Century idioms" (e-mail to the authors 20.4.98). Kitajima's own evaluation of working with VDP has a similar emphasis to Kitanka's assessment of the cultural collaborations and dialogues offered on *Tokyo Rose*:

> *... the music he and I create together is very unusual, unique and interesting. I can not explain what it is in writing, but I think it is almost like a balance of ying and yang – such as simplicity and complexity, East and West, and the sun & the moon (etc.)...* [Regarding] *Japan-U.S. relations, I think that both countries need to appreciate and learn eachother – like Van Dyke and me. Heaven and Earth make love, and a sweet dew-rain falls. The people do not know why, but they are gathered together like music. We had better not fly in the face of Providence.* (e-mail to the authors 7.5.98)

The album's title has complex resonances. The name 'Tokyo Rose' has (at least) three sets of (inter-connected) associations within immediate post-War U.S. discourse. The first, most obvious use is as a common term of reference for a Japanese woman desirable and/or available to American males on military service in Japan. The second, associated meaning, from which the first appears to derive, is that of the mythologised/demonised figures of the (various) sensuous-voiced, female Japanese-American radio announcers who broadcast Japanese propaganda messages to American soldiers during World War Two[30]. The third level of association, deriving from, and inadequately represented by, the second, is the single person usually characterised as *the* ('mythical') 'Tokyo Rose' – Iva Ikuko Toguri. Toguri was a Japanese-American (*nisei*) typist working for the NHK broadcasting organisation who was coerced into serving as a DJ and announcer in the period 1943–45 (*after* the myth of – a single -'Tokyo Rose' had been established). After the war she was tried and imprisoned by U.S. authorities (despite her clear subversion of her on-air role in broadcasts), and later pardoned by U.S. President Gerald Ford. The levels of complexity and shifting perceptions of political allegiance (and cultural connotations) of the term make 'Tokyo Rose' a fitting title for an album concerned with the intricacies of Japanese-U.S. inter-cultural relations and disjunctures.

Tokyo Rose opens with a prelude – an instrumental version of *America (My Country 'tis of thee)*. This serves two purposes. Firstly, it establishes the patriotic thread which runs through the album. Despite being present on the album in a solely instrumental version, the sleeve notes include a reproduction of the first five lines of the anthem:

> *My country 'tis of thee/*
> *Sweet land of liberty, of thee I sing,*
> *Land where my fathers died/*
> *Land of the Pilgrims' pride/*
> *From every mountainside let freedom ring*

Almost uniquely in contemporary popular music, these lyrics are reproduced unashamedly and un-ironically. They serve to flag VDP's pride in being a U.S. citizen. Immediately setting the tenor of the album, the arrangement of the song shifts and problematises its patriotic association and introduces the "anxiety" which its music and lyrics negotiate. Paul Zollo (1996) has provided a succinct characterisation of the manner in which the track foreshadows the subsequent album. Using a cinematic model, he argues that VDP "[sets] the stage without words, like the great cinematographers of the silent era, he allows the orchestra to tell the whole story in the opening" (1996: npd[31]).

America is characterised by a juxtaposition of standard western and orientalist musical elements, harmonic ambiguity, a wide range of instrumental colour, distortions of the traditional melody, and marked rhythmic changes. The first two of the above-mentioned elements are clearly in evidence from the very opening of the track. The introduction first presents the opening two notes (Bb, C) of the melody on the piano (a western instrument) as though the theme is to be presented in the key of Bb. This impression is immediately challenged, as oriental-sounding pentatonic figures are introduced on flutes and string sounds – but now in the key of C. Harmonic ambiguity is subsequently maintained throughout the introduction, until the tonality finally settles on F major at the end of the introduction. In this way VDP signals from the outset of the arrangement that his intention is to manipulate and mutate the anthem. This is confirmed by the subsequent developments.

The track presents the theme (or at least parts of the theme) in four contrasting versions. The first of these (introduced by a harp glissando) bears a strong resemblance to film music associated with Hollywood Westerns – with a clichéd up tempo 3/4 rhythmic ostinato, and accompaniment provided by acoustic piano and staccato strings. The track also introduces a typical harmonic twist before presenting the final phrase of the tune. The second version continues the rhythm pattern of the first, but the melody now features a distinctive koto sound throughout; while the third version combines a shakuhachi part with strings. The third section (which omits the first section of the melody and begins with the second section) also features a repeated pedal idea in the bass, as well as frequent and often surprising (even disturbing) shifts between a sense of F major and F minor tonality in the melody. The fourth section introduces a distinctive military feel by employing a prominent accented 'square' rhythmic figure, a prominent snare drum, a strong bass line, and a range of contrapuntal counter-themes typical of a military band arrangement – all while still continuing to provide surprising chord progressions and moments of tonal ambiguity. The coda sees a return to a freely- articulated rhythm (as in the introduction), and the mood is primarily orientalist – with shakuhachi melodies, a drone and the major pentatonic mode. By making regular deviations from the standard melody and/or chord progression, and presenting the theme in with various instrumental colours and rhythms, VDP deliberately disrupts the normally serious, reverential tone of the American anthem – inviting comparison to the (more straightforward) Caribbeanisation of *The Stars and Stripes Forever* that concludes *Discover America*. In addition, the anthem is orientalised in a manner which, given the U.S. sensitivity to the status of cultural icons, has threatening and disturbing implications (despite the appeal provided by the lush and sophisticated sound of the arrangement).

Following this prelude, the album moves into its title track, which produces a rich evocation of the glamour of Japan for the U.S. and, specifically, GIs stationed there. Sung by VDP, the track opens in a manner which parallels the introduction to *America*, with the presentation of a repeated two-note melodic motif. This time, however (in a manner typical of film music composition) the motif is varied slightly, and consists of a descending semi-tone step as opposed to the ascending tone step of the opening track. Other elements which parallel the introduction to *America* include the free rhythmic feel, the wide range of contrasting instrumental colours (koto, strings, harp, percussion etc), and the harp glissando which leads into the establishment of a regular rhythm.

VDP goes on to combine a range of typical Hollywood film music devices with numerous elements which are employed for their oriental association. The main melody is itself an interesting stylistic hybrid – based for the most part on the (oriental-sounding) major pentatonic scale, but also employing rising chromatic

155

movement more typical of a song from a Hollywood musical. Other elements typical of the film genre include string doubling of the vocal melody and chromatic counter themes; and the subsequent chorus further reinforces the filmic nature of the instrumental/vocal scoring by featuring female vocal harmonies and *divisi* string passages[32]. As in *America*, VDP ends the arrangement with a strongly oriental-sounding section, featuring pentatonic scales, parallel fourth intervals and instruments such as the koto and gong – although his use of a distinctive rising chromatic theme helps to maintain a sense of stylistic duality.

Significantly, VDP's lyrics avoid any simplistic Japonaiserie and instead view the experience of Japan through a collage of exotic referents, evoked by slick word plays. The opening lines begin this by introducing a mid-Pacific reference into its Oriental scenario:

> *In sight of the lights of Roppongi... the night life of To ki yo goes/*
> *And out on the streets with a beat from Tahiti a neon moon lollipop glows*

But, used allusively, these lyric do not detract from the scenario established in its lyrics and music. This aspect is delayed to the final verse, where the theme is reprised – and implicitly reconnected to VDP's 1970s' Caribbean emphasis – through the final verse's referential cocktail:

> *Down on a Cajun veranda... a Barbajian band in a stew/*
> *Were playing a soca when I reawoke we were back at her penthouse us two*

The effect of this disjunction of scenarios, a collage of exotic referents and images, constitutes a sense of an exotic 'magic realism' rather than any actual (quasi-documentary) address. Similarly the geisha/bar girl who is the ostensible subject of the song is rendered in a more complex allusive manner than the female subjects of the G.I. genre of songs detailed by Shuhei Hosokawa in Chapter Five. In VDP's version, the vocal protagonist of his song introduces "The girl I call To ki yo Rose" in the following terms :

> *A women in silken pajamas is seen on the screen of a door/*
> *She slips on a rice paper dress by Dior less the price of the ice on her clothes*

and goes on to describe how:

> *She trips through a door for hot sake/*
> *Unzips as her hips hit the floor*

The latter, at least, offers a classic, easily recognisable scenario. The song however, ends ambiguously, on a wittily succinct instant of communicative disjuncture. The protagonist speaks to his Japanese paramour of his "love for [General] MacArthur – the man not the park in LA". Unimpressed by this line of conversation, the song's female subject covers herself and comments coolly on the vocal protagonist's advanced age...

The album provides a direct counterpoint to its title track in the form of the composition *Calypso*, sung by Japanese vocalist Mari Iijima, in a ('cutely' stilted accent[33]), in the persona of a (gentle, respectful) 'good time girl'[34]. The song itself is premised on a set of *double entendres*. The first of these concerns its title, which alludes to both the song's conceptual theme and its underlying calypso-derived beat (of the sort featured prominently on *Discover America* and *Clang...*).

The song and its title set its specific scenario against a wider mythic context, that of Homer's epic poem *The Odyssey*. This is signalled, in a typically cryptic, seemingly 'throwaway' Parksian manner, in the female chorus line which proclaims "[h]e is speaking Greek to me...". *The Odyssey*'s opening scenario has its hero, Odysseus, in the ninth year of his stay on the seductive, exotic island of Ogygia. Here he resides with his (immortal) lover Calypso, a woman with several captivating attributes. One of these is her ability to grant him immortality, so long as he remains with her. Yet this is not enough for Odysseus. He longs to return to his (mainland) home, even though he will lose his lover's charms and her gift of eternal love. He is out-of-place and even paradise does not feel right for him. Ever the ideal lover, Calypso eventually accepts his decision to leave[35].

This myth has strong resonances with the projection of such values upon the (patient, devoted, ever-understanding) 'Tokyo Roses' celebrated in G.I. songs. *Calypso's* lyrics, the speaking position of the vocalist, and her address to a (single) serviceman, identify the song's female protagonist as (young) woman willing to form relationships, of whatever duration or nature, with American service personnel. This is made blatant in the double entendre of the song's chorus:

Take a missionary position/
Yes the missionary position/
For a man who is on a mission/
Other things should come to mind

In this, the acquiescent, understanding stance of the song's latterday Calypso conforms to the clichés of the G.I. song genre. Yet the final sequence, where a chorus, representing a (collective, non-specific) GI viewpoint, returns to a Caribbean referent as an exemplar of *un*-complicated exoticism:

If my heart could only speak/
We'd take a week in Martinique and just go crazy neh?

To which the Iijima's protagonist responds, coolly and realistically, in an aside:

He is speaking Greek to me/
It is hide and seek you see/
this can be our fantasy today

While tracks such as *America* and *Tokyo Rose* begin with a focus on melodic, harmonic and textural/timbral elements, *Calypso* begins with a prominent rhythmic pattern and immediately establishes a solid beat – which features a bass figure, as well as a number of complementary rhythmic syncopations. The drum kit is prominent throughout the arrangement, while instrumental call-response ideas add to the rhythmic orientation of the track, and the horn section regularly punctuates the music with rhythmic stabs. The main melodic theme is also highly syncopated in places.

Other elements enhance the sense of contrast between this track and those tracks which feature more regular and obvious orientalist musical references. Saxophones in close harmony (utilising techniques such as trills) provide a type of 'sour horn' flavour which is often associated with Caribbean (and Mexican) music. VDP employs the complete major scale and distinctive rising melodic sequences, rather than using more oriental-sounding pentatonic melodic ideas; and he avoids the oriental-sounding outros of tracks such as *America* and *Tokyo Rose*. Equally, he avoids the juxtaposition of oriental and non-oriental instrumental sounds which characterises many of the tracks on the album. It appears likely that, for VDP (and the listener), the youthful, oriental-sounding female lead voice provides a sufficiently striking contrast with the Caribbean elements to obviate the need for additional oriental musical suggestions.

The use of scenarios of (heterosexual) relationships to demonstrate and illustrate broader political situations is continued on the album on *Manzanar* and *Cowboy*. *Manzanar*, sung by VDP, and set in Los Angeles, offers a fairly straightforward scenario of the love affair between an (implicitly W.A.S.P.) male and a Japanese-American female disturbed by the outbreak of U.S.-Japan conflict; and, more specifically, by her forcible re-location to the (now infamous) Manzanar detention centre in Southern California[36]. VDP has described the song as "a homage to the Nisei... [addressing] a regional bête noir" (e-mail to the authors, 19.4.98). Unlike many of the songs on the album, the vocal protagonist's position is relatively unambiguous, characterised as a mixture of shame and impotence and a refusal to renounce his feelings. Similarly, the song's conclusion is unusually direct and overtly polemical (for VDP's oeuvre) identifying the Manzanar detention centre as "a camp of concentration/With a stamp of degradation and shame".

As well as incorporating a range of elements common to many of the tracks on the album (pentatonic melodies and motifs, harp glissandi, chromatic passages, bell sounds etc); the use of Mexican musical elements in the recorded arrangement of the song contributes another dimension to its lyrics, evoking and inscribing the Southern Californian location of the detention centre. VDP has emphasised his deliberate use of Mexican musical elements as complicating factors in the (otherwise binary) scenario – representing California as "a stolen piece of Mexican real estate if there ever was one" (e-mail to the authors, 19.4.98). While the repeated use of mariachi-style horns on the dominant note of the key is a clear Mexican-influence, this aspect is most marked by rhythmic elements, specifically triplets and irregular and syncopated rhythms, which derive from the Mexican *huapango* rhythm[37]. Commenting on this element, VDP has remarked that:

> ... *huapango rhythm, with its 2-against–3 sense of tense excitement, served the pathos of this piece. The bass notes, placed as they are, as a rule push into the 3rd beat ... There are rules in these rhythms and scansions, and* Manzanar *is a faithful redux of this fabulous Mexican rhythm.* (ibid)[38]

While retaining a Mexican theme, *Cowboy* switches the geographical focus, settling on a mid-point between Japan and California – Hawai'i. The song sketches a scenario of the love affair between an indigenous Hawaiian girl – referred to in the lyrics as "Wandering Wahini" – and a *paniolo*. The original paniolos were Mexican cowboys brought to Hawai'i in the 1830s by King Kamehameha III to help control and manage introduced herds of cattle threatening the local environment[39]. Paniolos subsequently became romanticised in Hawaiian folklore, with a number of songs being written about them (such as *Hawaiian Cowboy* and *Pili Me 'Oe*). Since the early 1800s many of their successors have continued to work in the cattle business, and some continue in this occupation to the present. *Cowboy* concerns one such paniolo whose idyllic life is suddenly complicated – as the song's narrator interrupts his narration to recall:

> *I forgot to mention, it was nineteen forty one/*
> *Zeros kept a-comin' like to blanket out the sun*[40]

Framed within this context, of the idyllic love affair between an indigenous Hawaiian girl and an Mexican-descended cowboy, the song presents a vivid cameo of the invidious perfidy of the Japanese military in attacking Hawai'i unannounced[41]; and, what's more, one where the U.S. fleet in Pearl Harbour, the principal target of the attack, is sidelined as a consideration.

Somewhat surprisingly perhaps, in the context of the album, there is no attempt to infuse the arrangement of the song with obvious musical Hawaiianisms nor with any devices designed to allude to Mexican music[42]. The music employs a light shuffle rhythm, a pentatonic melody, a melodic ostinato accompaniment, a simple harmonic scheme and backing vocals supporting the main lyric hook – all typical elements of Hollywood Western music. However, as might be expected, given VDP's inclination towards quirky musical hybrids which support the cultural juxtapositions inherent in his lyrics, other elements are added to create a less predictable stylistic mix. These elements include more complex harmony, chromatic melodic passages, linking harp glissandi, and the album's signature inclusion of oriental-sounding instruments.

159

Once again, the outro section employs a free, flexible rhythmic sense and a distinctively oriental flavour – with koto and shakuhachi sounds, pentatonic scales and high-set muted strings.

In combination with these four songs, with their specific wartime address, the remainder of tracks on the album provide scenarios of other facets of Japanese-American cultural relations. *Yankee Go Home* provides something of a historical preface to the album's main themes. Its lyrics are (loosely) based on U.S. Commodore Matthew Perry's isolation-breaking naval incursion into Tokyo Bay in 1853, which led to the establishment of trade and diplomatic relations between the countries following the signing of Treaty of Edo in 1856. The song employs a number of elements which have close stylistic links to Mexican *ranchera* music. Most notable is the repeated "Ay ay ay ay ay" phrase which culminates melodically in a sustained dominant note[43]. Farquharson has noted that, despite its elements of joyful expression, *ranchera* music is "essentially nostalgic and pessimistic – the lament of a people who have left their land and are lost in a strange city or in a different country" (1994: 543). The associations and mood of the music thereby enhances one strain of the song's lyrics, describing the simultaneously assertive and uncertain demeanour and predicament of the American naval personnel concerned, with the local response to their arrival neatly summed up in the song's refrain – "Yankee go home".

Together with the romantic ballad *Out of Love*, the three remaining songs on the album address post-War topics. *White Chrysanthemum*, identified by VDP as his favourite song on the album[44], is a quirkily humorous account of the funeral of a WW2 veteran (who had been "better than the best in forty one/ When blue Hawai'i glistened like a diamond lights the sun") who had subsequently come to terms with his dislike for Japanese "when the Nissan plant was built down by the run". Like *Trade War*, *White Chrysanthemum* employs a regular drum kit rhythm and an uncomplicated musical form, and is strongly focused upon lyric content. The *Ave Maria* theme recurs throughout the arrangement, and the vocal style resembles a priest intoning a funeral sermon[45]. Typical VDP arranging techniques include high-set female backing vocals, chromatic melodic passages, surprising harmonic shifts and the hint of oriental instrumentation occurring at the end of the track.

The reference to the initial phase of Japanese economic incursion into the U.S., contained in *White Chrysanthemum's* lyrical mention of Nissan plants, is developed and brought up to date (ie the late 1980s) in the following track, *Trade War*. This song is sung by VDP with a similar narrative-orientated delivery to that employed in *Yankee Go Home*, albeit less assertive than Hutton's spirited rendition, and employs a strong 4/4 rock rhythm, harmonic pedals in the bass part, typical VDP major-minor ambiguity, and a sequential-type chorus melody. The arrangement lacks the variety of colours, rhythms and textures of many of the other tracks – facilitating a focus upon the lyric content. Although musically unrelated, the lyrics, and particularly the topical theme (and pace of delivery) reflect VDP's knowledge of the traditions of cultural-political polemic in calypso songs. *Trade War*, for instance has much in common with *Your Own Comes First*, the protectionist rallying call for Trinidadian advancement included on *Discover America*. As its explicit title suggests, *Trade War*, above all other songs on the album, provides the most concerted (and unapologetic) statement of the economic anxieties discussed earlier. While almost any line of its lyrics serves to illustrate this contention, its closing lines provide perhaps its clearest rallying cry:

> *May our nation not surrender, oh no !/*
> *For just one race to rule the world/*
> *Keep that battle flag unfurled !*

In contrast to *Trade War's* powerful and highly specific polemic, the following track, *Out of Love* – a delicate, moody, romantic ballad whose lyrics have little apparent connection to the album's predominant lyrical-conceptual theme – provides a gentle contrast. The continuities it offers with the main body of the album are primarily musical. The track employs a number of distinctly oriental-sounding elements (pentatonic melody, shimmering pentatonic accompanying motifs on strings and flutes; high bell sounds) together with a basic 4/4 rock rhythm and characteristic features such as female backing vocals and harmonic twists. Typically, VDP also introduces a musical contrast at the end of the arrangement, with the prominent and (unexpected) sound of the sharpened fourth note.

The album concludes with *One Home Run*, recorded with a simple, country-style arrangement incorporating a 4/4 feel, slide guitar, a major scale and simple major chord sequences. The song comprises a richly nostalgic ode to baseball, the quintessentially American game which took off in Japan in a major way during the post-War occupation years, sung by a father – of indeterminate cultural status – recalling his and his son's enjoyment of playing the game. The track (and album) end with a melodic and linguistic surprise, a detour into a section which employs female voices singing a Japanese language verse (written by Amy Furumoto) utilising the sweet sound of third-based vocal harmony. While un-translated in the CD sleeve booklet (and thereby enigmatic, for English-language audiences)[46], the final lines of these translate as:

> *Let's go to the field where the blue sky is above us/*
> *Today is a day for baseball/*
> *My only wish is to hit just one home run/*
> *Just to face the ball and play with all my ability*
> (translation by Rika Saegusa and Philip Hayward)

This switch to Japanese language at the album's conclusion, within the context of a song on the shared (U.S.-Japanese) joy of a quintessentially U.S. sport, offers a point of social-cultural contact, communication and affinity between the antagonistic scenarios and personas presented on the album – a conclusion as harmonious as its musical realisation in the song's final verse[47].

III. Conclusion: beyond the final ocean

Six years after *Tokyo Rose*, VDP re-united with Brian Wilson to record *Orange Crate Art* . The album featured a significant addition – or, perhaps, afterthought – to the orientalist discourse around California/the U.S.A. and Japan/The Orient developed on *Tokyo Rose*. The composition in question was entitled *Palm Tree and Moon*. The track, which stands out from others on the album by dint of its use of musical orientalisms, is premised on a cameo of a Chinese migrant staring out across the Pacific, recalling a distant homeland. VDP has explained that the song was inspired by his viewing of a painting of a Chinese fishing community near Monterey (Southern California) in the 1880s and his desire to both "rhapsodise on an immigrant's impressions of a new land" (cited in Dart, 1996: 14) and communicate the manner in which California "might have been an exotic rude awakening" to such migrants (*Words + Music* CD, 1995). This marks a significant perception, inscribed within a particular geo-historical location; one where VDP juxtaposes his own exotic imagination of California, as the far west coast of the American pioneer dream, with the very different geo-spatial orientation of an Asian migrant.

There are significant parallels here to the themes developed in James Clifford's essay 'Fort Ross Meditation' (1997). In this, Clifford considers various aspects of Californian and U.S. history, inspired by a visit to the old pear orchard above the former Russian settlement of Fort Ross, established some 150 kilometres to the north of the city of Carmel in the early 1800s. As Clifford elaborates:

> [s]tanding at the reconstructed Russian fort, one finds it odd to recognize that when its builders gazed at the Pacific horizon they were looking back, not out. Odd that is, for someone conditioned to think that the direction of historical development in the "New World" was from east to west. The national space of the United States has long been conceived as an expansion west ... This westward-looking dream topography had its origin along the Asiatic and African edges of Europe, over centuries of violent and creative contacts. The dream – productive, expansive, violent – had a destination: the Pacific. Here the "West" culminated. Beyond the final ocean lay the East. (1997: 302–303) (my emphases)

Musically speaking, the orientalist inflection of the melodies and arrangement of *Palm Tree and Moon* creates an unusual and highly effective musical hybrid by juxtaposing elements of post-1960s Californiana (such as a basic 4/4 rock beat allied to complex vocal harmonies [with falsetto passages], melodic sequences and chromaticism reminiscent of The Beach Boys) with orientalist elements (such as major pentatonic vocal melodies and instrumental ostinatos, and a range of distinctive instrumental sounds – koto, bells etc). The smooth integration of these suggests a

162

stability – and manifest *lack of* 'anxiety' – to the cultural history and hybrid it represents; a contemporary reflection on a cultural past, produced (in 1995) at a cultural moment at some distance from the specific anxieties of the late 1980s which striated *Tokyo Rose*.

As this chapter has demonstrated, VDP's work – or, at least, that strand analysed here – offers a set of complex articulations of musical, lyrical and thematic elements. The level of accomplishment of these is all the more surprising given the 'gloss' and 'ease' of listening to his sumptuously produced albums, with their clarity of mixing, warm, soft-edged sounds and highly melodic focus. Indeed, it could be argued that these attributes actively serve to discourage complex and/or analytical readings, given that most 'serious', 'progressive' and/or avant garde rock practitioners – of the kind usually afforded in-depth studies – deliberately eschew, and even oppose, such approaches.

What is notable about VDP's work, particularly on *Tokyo Rose*, is the manner in which he uses his trademark eclectic, complex and highly colourful orchestrations to facilitate intricate negotiations of cultural difference, anxiety and fascination. In this manner, we can characterise the musical lustre of *Tokyo Rose* as resulting from a creative process akin to that of the aggregation of a pearl around an irritant. The irritant in question here is, as discussed, Japan's relationship with the U.S.A. (and, more specifically, California). In this manner, while there is something politically indelicate about VDP's preoccupation with the threat of Japan and the chequered 20th Century history of U.S.-Japanese relations, his production of a jewelled musical artefact in response to perceptions of cultural-economic rivalry should be seen as a singularly rich and productive enterprise, one that transcends 'mere' orientalism and exotica and utilises these practices in an applied, détourned and dialogic form.

Thanks to Van Dyke Parks for co-operating with our research on this chapter; also to Rob Bowman, Rebecca Coyle, Lee Dempsey, Shuhei Hosokawa, Nicholas Kent, Bob Merlis, Tony Mitchell, Toru Mitsui, Don Richardson and Rika Saegusa for various other assistances.

Notes

1. In this regard, the album might be understood as something of a mirror-image of Haruomi Hosono's similar explorations of Japanese-U.S. relations in his 'Soy Sauce Music' trilogy, analysed in detail in the preceding chapter.

2. Appearing with Grace Kelly and Alec Guinness in *The Swan* (1955), and in *Heidi* (1957).

3. On the variety show *Art Linklatter's Party*.

4. "[D]epending on [his] extemporaneous skills to toss things off" (cited in Tomasulo: npd).

5. For an account of VDP's contribution to arranging *Good Vibrations* see VDP (1996).

6. Referring to the aborted *Smile* album project, VDP has recalled that he:

   ... gleaned a great deal from Brian Wilson: about dignity in defeat; about the potential of the human spirit. I also collected a few observations about studio technique, and tried to apply them to my more modest ends. (e-mail to the authors 1.6.98)

7. Including a series of key changes and complex transitions and a one minute-long introduction lifted whole from another recording.

8. And also added, more prosaically:

   [i]ndeed, Parks' work evoked all those post-war movie music sensibilities that honor the innocence which balances our society's often-ravenous nature: the articulate strings that tutor our hearts, the stark keyboards that name our reflex fears, and the clipped French horns that somehow heighten our generosity of spirit when the lights go down in the cinema. (ibid)

9. Since the 1960s, VDP has worked as songwriter, keyboard player, composer, producer and arranger for a variety of musical clients. One of his most distinctive attributes has been his ability to write arrangements, which open up relatively simple pop-rock songs into miniature epics – a characteristic of 1960s pop producers such as Phil Spector but an increasingly rare ability in the western music industry. In this regard, his work can be seen to have an almost cinematic aspect, a panoramic, 'widescreen' approach, in his use of the 'depth' and 'breath' of the sound mix and the variety and complexity of musical timbres and textures he deploys within it.

10. The Andre De La Bastide Steelband's single *Proud Mary/Mas in Brooklyn* was released on Reprise Records; VDP's productions of the Esso Trinidad Tripoli Steelband appeared on the Warner Brothers label.

11. The album was notable as a precursor of a number of contemporary musical syncretisms of the kind later characterised as 'world beat', and thereby merits a more detailed study in its own right than this chapter permits.

12. VDP has recalled that he "thought the piece had great emotive value for the record, and urged the engineer to roll the tape ... I caught them [the band] at the apogee of their collective skills" (e-mail to the authors 8/6/98).

13. While the concept of *détournement* has its roots in a series of early 20th Century avant garde art practices, its contemporary usage appears to derive from the work of the Belgian surrealist Marcel Marien in the 1950s and was popularised – as perhaps their *key* textual strategy – by the Situationists in the 1960s.

14. The canon is a form of polyphonic composition, dating back to the 13th Century (at least), which is based on strict thematic imitation.

15. The cinematic feel of the track is appropriate to the album's dedication to Fred Wainwright, a film director with whom VDP worked at Warner Brothers before his death in a car accident, and the director of a short film *Ry Cooder*, which VDP has characterised as "the first promotional film subsidised by any record company [in Los Angeles]" (e-mail to the authors 8/6/98).

16. Brian Wilson has characterised VDP's style of lyric writing as akin to "the way a mosaicist chooses stones for color and shape and relation to each other and magical resonance and then puts them together and they make a story, a picture" (cited in Tomasulo: npd).

17. The very reason the form was profiled by Re/Search publications within volumes entitled *Incredibly Strange Music.*

18. Published by Harcourt Brace Jovanovich (with a principal author credited to Joel Chandler Harris).

19. The books were, for instance, described by a *New York Times* reviewer as "racially irreproachable" with a "combination of elegance and humor perfectly suited to the diction and tone of the text" (cited in Tomasulo, 1996: npd).

20. One review of the film commented that "Van Dyke Parks' arrangements of nineteenth century songs would have excited John Ford's admiration" (cited in Tomasulo, 1996: npd).

21. A celebration of Californian pioneer life in the late 1800s.

22. In this regard, it is also significant that VDP also recorded instrumental versions of George Gershwin's *Rhapsody in Blue* and Robert Thiele and George Weiss's *What a Wonderful World* –

arranged by VDP and Fred Myrow – for intended inclusion on *Orange Crate Art*. (At present both of these remain un-released.)

23. This 'romanticisation' of California was not simply accomplished through romanticised representations of (an actual) California – it was also accomplished through a range of exotic stereotypes. One notable example was provided by the Yorba Orange Growers' Association. Inspired by the vogue for 'Araby' following the success of Edith Hull's novel *The Sheik* (1919), and the subsequent film starring Rudolph Valentino in the title role (1921), they marketed their 'Rebecca' label product with an image of a veiled exotic woman, camels and palm trees in a desert. (See Starr, 1985: 158–166 for further discussion of orange crate art.)

24. Roman Polanski's film *Chinatown* (1974) provides a fictional account of the fall-out from one such 'frenzied' land speculation. VDP went on to write the score for its follow-up, *The Two Jakes* (1989) – in which he also made a cameo appearance as an attorney.

25. As accurate as characterisations of VDP's conscious motivations as the quotations cited above may be, the album, and impetus behind it, also need to be situated in a more complex, historically and geographically determined, context. One important aspect is VDP's perspective as a *Californian* reflecting on Japan. This is a significant element. California, on the U.S.A.'s West Coast, is directly opposite Japan, across the Pacific, and part of a triangular maritime (and now air-) link between Japan-Hawaii-California, with its own cultural histories.

26. Including interview statements from him such as:

     Japanese money owns 40 percent of downtown Los Angeles real estate ... are we going to relinquish our land to our landlords in absentia ? ... Americans should stand up for themselves. There needs to be a political sensibility that develops a strategy toward land use while inviting multinational participation. (cited in Infusino, 1989: 87)

27. As Shuhei Hosokawa argued in Chapter Five, Hosono's initial contact with VDP, and Hosono's exposure to the *Discover America* album, released in the previous year, provided a significant influence on Hosono's development of notions of cross-cultural 'archipelagic' music-making. The connection between the two was re-established in the late 1980s when Hosono played bass in VDP's ensemble which toured Japan in 1989 to promote *Tokyo Rose*.

28. Regarding his selection of Yoshizawa as the shakuhachi player on the album, VDP has noted that while "the instrument is played with some facility by occidental musicians", his perception that accomplished performance on the instrument is (necessarily) "filled with nuance" led him to employ a recognised Japanese virtuoso (ibid).

29. Kitajima has recalled that when VDP contacted him he was already familiar with *Discover America* and was happy to work on *Tokyo Rose* after discussing the concept behind the album (e-mail to the authors 7.5.98).

30. Since there is no evidence that this name was ever used in any Japanese radio broadcast, it appears that this was a U.S. nickname. Iva Ikuko Toguri actually used the radio name 'Orphan Ann'.

31. Item on the Van Dyke Parks web site.

32. Where the separate string sections (eg first violins, second violins, violas etc) themselves divide into two or more parts.

33. Describing her vocal delivery, Kitanaka commented that "Mari Iijima seduces in her lisping sweet English" (1989: 19) (translation by Rika Saegusa).

34. Iijima met VDP shortly before the recording of *Tokyo Rose*, on a visit to California to record her debut album. As he subsequently recalled, (at the time) her English was "remedial, at best", making her voice ideal for its narrative role in the song. She has since become a resident of California (VDP, e-mail to the authors 20.4.98). (Information about her subsequent career can be obtained at http://home.earthlink.net/~maricircus/)

35. Thanks to Marie-Louise Claflin for her comments on Homeric mythology.

165

36. As a result of Roosevelt's Executive Order 9066, over 10,000 Japanese Americans were relocated to Manzanar, most of whom were Californians, although a number of residents of Washington, Oregon and Hawai'i were also detained there.

37. VDP has recalled that "I learned how to play this rhythm on nylon string guitar in 1962 when I [first] arrived in California. (e-mail to the authors, 19.4.98)

38. He has also added "having studied this rhythm for years, I'm thoroughly satisfied with its insinuation into this song." (ibid).

39. Fancifully alluded to in VDP's lyrical couplet: "King Kamehameha met with Captain Cook upon the shore/ Looking at all the cattle asked him 'What the hell are these for ?'".

40. The allusion here is to Japanese Mitsubishi Zero combat planes attacking Pearl Harbor and the surrounding area.

41. The work of 1970s' paniolo songwriter Marcus Schutte offers an interesting alternative – and complicating – angle on this, given that one of his compositions, *Jiro and Ichiro* relates the story of two Japanese-Hawaiian cowboys.

42. The song is appropriate in this regard since Kanahele (1979: 292–294) states that none of the (extant) paniolo repertoire has any obvious Mexican musical elements.

43. Farquharson has described *ranchera* music as characterised "by joyful exclamations that come from singer and audience alike" (1994: 543), and also notes that "singers stretch out the final note of a line" (ibid: 544).

44. In an interview with Paul Zollo, VDP commented:

    It starts with plainsong ... The nice thing about plainsong is that you can put any number of notes on to it. It stays on one chord. I stayed on one chord and said, "Somewhat overwhelmed by the dimension of her lovely breast" and on the word "breast" I changed the chord. And I had to make sense so I said, "The rector turns his face from Mother Nature back to God." I wanted to make the priest human, so he's paying attention to Mother Nature's breast, [laughs] and then I reminded myself that I wanted to do something serious so I used the word "God". And then I decided he would say something, and that was "Therefore in the valley of the shadow we are truly, truly blessed," that rhymed – "now we return our brother to the sod." Okay, so that all rhymed. I took that as a successful effort, probably taking me five days of rigorous work to repeat that on the next couplet where it gets harder ... So I did the funeral scene. I got the man in the ground. that's why I say it's my most favourite song; its the most successful song on this album. Because it took effort. (cited in Zollo: npd).

45. VDP has remarked that "Schubert's *Ave Maria* was chosen to Catholicize the blue-collar dilemma in *White Chrysanthemum* ... it played into my love for anecdote in my songs." (e-mail to the authors, 19.4.98)

46. These are transcribed in the album booklet in individual phonic syllables – rather than in orthodox English language spellings of Japanese words – so as to be readable/singable for an English language audience.

47. Fittingly this track was rated as one of the most successful by Japanese reviewers, such as Kitanaka (1989), and also by Eiji Ogura, who bridled against what he saw as various "misunderstandings of Japan" on the CD (ibid: 24) but nevertheless characterised the track as "the only masterpiece helping the whole album" (ibid).

World Wide Web Resources

Van Dyke Parks' Web Site: www.brerwabbit.com/parks/vdparks.htm

Discography

Van Dyke Parks	*Song Cycle*, Warner Brothers, 1968
———	*Discover America*, Warner Brothers, 1972
———	*Clang of the Yankee Reaper*, Warner Brothers, 1975
———	*Jump*, Warner Brothers, 1984
———	*Tokyo Rose*, Warner Brothers, 1989
———	*Idiosyncratic Path: the Best of Van Dyke Parks*, Diablo Records, 1994
———	*Moonlighting – Live at the Ash Grove*, Warner Brothers, 1998
Brain Wilson and Van Dyke Parks	*Orange Crate Art*, Warner Brothers, 1995
———	*Words + Music*, Warner Brothers (limited edition promotional release), 1995

Chapter Seven

THE YANNI PHENOMENON

Musical Exotica, Memories and Multi-Media Marketing

KARL NEUENFELDT

Introduction

"W ondrous", "romantic", "foreign", "fascinating". These synonyms appear when I check the word "exotic" in the thesaurus of my word processing program; an antonym is "ordinary". The musician-composer Yanni – and the phenomenon of his fame (and fortune) – is describable as all of the above. This chapter examines how he and the industry which has sprung up around him personify and epitomise a particular kind of musical exotica. In both guises (as phenomenon and musician-composer), Yanni, the icon, has strong brand name identification. Consumers know what they are buying beforehand and are willing to pay for a product which is predictable and consistent[1]. There are no surprises in the Yanni phenomenon; only variations on a single theme. Whether consumed live in concert, 'semi-live' on video[2], or on albums and the Internet, the theme is that of combining musical exotica, memories and multi-media marketing. The music is supposedly at the heart of the phenomenon but arguably functions more as an incidental soundtrack for the making of memories and the subsequent marketing of these. As this chapter discusses, the Yanni phenomenon circulates in the global cultural economy of sound, sight and sentiment.

The commercial phenomenon

Born in Kalamata, Greece in 1954, Yanni Chryssomallis emigrated to the U.S.A. in 1972 and went on to study at the University of Minnesota, receiving a Bachelor of Arts degree in Psychology in 1976. After the common pop music career trajectory of playing in bands and submitting demo tapes, he signed his first recording contract in 1986 (with Private Music), moving to Hollywood in 1987 to write and record his own compositions and work on film scores. Yanni went on to tour extensively in North America, and internationally, playing numerous concerts with his band and with local symphony orchestras[3]. In 1993 he recorded *Yanni Live at the Acropolis* with London's Royal Philharmonic Orchestra, documented in a video directed by George Veras[4]. Shown on PBS (Public Broadcasting Service) in the U.S.A., the video attracted over fifteen million viewers and was a successful fund raiser for the publicly funded network. He has now performed for millions of consumers in North and Central America, Asia, Europe and Australia. Recent high profile 'mega-events' include concerts at the Taj Majal in Agra, India and the Forbidden City in Beijing, China. Both were recorded and videoed for the latest video *Tribute* (1997), a how-it-was-done documentary *No Borders, No Boundaries* (1997), and a television special on PBS. He signed with Virgin Records in 1996[5].

Yanni's album, video and concert sales are noteworthy. His ten albums have sold in excess of fifteen million units worldwide. At the beginning of 1998, *Billboard* magazine (3/1 and 10/1) ranked Yanni as the top New Age artist in the entertainment industry and five of his albums featured in *Billboard's* list of the top twenty five best-selling New Age albums, including the just-released *Tribute* album with six weeks at number 1 (ibid). The videos have also sold well, *Live at the Acropolis* is the third highest selling music video ever. Live-to-air television broadcasts of mega-events (later edited into videos) are estimated to have reached over half a billion people worldwide[6]. Concert tours have consistently sold out, grossing US$ 10.7 million in 1995 and US$12.3 million in 1996. Individual compositions have been used for signature or segment music for major televised sporting events (such as the Olympics [Summer and Winter Games], CBS Television's coverage of the U.S. Open Tennis championship and NBC Television's coverage of U.S. Open golf tournament); the Imax large screen format film *Whales*; award winning TV commercials (such as British Airway's *Aria* commercial); and live sporting galas[7].

Phenomenal exotica

Commodification and technologisation have been crucial to the successes (and excesses) of the Yanni phenomenon. Commodification has included the production, distribution and marketing of albums, videos, television specials, and live performances to millions of people. Technologisation has included staging and chronicling pageant-like mega-events in exotic locales, spectacles which have come to characterise the Yanni phenomenon and are part of a deliberate strategy[8]. Physical places and metaphorical spaces consumed thus far include the Acropolis in Greece (the

169

citadel of ancient Athens), the Taj Majal in India (the mausoleum built by a Mughal emperor in memory of his wife), and the Forbidden City in China (the former home of the imperial court and family). Proposed mega-events were cancelled for The Pyramids of the Sun and Moon in Mexico and Table Rock Mountain in South Africa, but smaller scale events have also taken place at the Royal Albert Hall in Great Britain and the Toji Temple in Japan.

In the context of musical exotica, the Yanni phenomenon is unlike the lower-profile activity of earlier exoticists such as Les Baxter, Martin Denny and Arthur Lyman. While their style(s) antedated today's globalised mass market for musical exotica – variously marketed as New Age, world beat/music, easy listening and/or adult contemporary (all labels which have been applied to Yanni's music) – these artists epitomised musical exotica at an earlier and less grandiose stage. None were iconised to the extent which Yanni has. However, iconisation has a flip-side: demonisation. While 1950s' musical exotica may have been disparaged by the rock generation, critics and DJs during the 1960s and 1970s, it has scarcely been demonised and (even had the Internet existed during this period) it is doubtful whether Baxter, Denny, Lyman or Sumac would be the focus of the kinds of hate-groups and loyal fan-groups accessible by typing "Yanni" into the 'Find' window of any major Internet search-engine[9].

The Yanni phenomenon is noteworthy because of what it says about its time and place. It is also of interest due to the manner in which music is circulating at the end of the millennium. The main issues informing this analysis concern the mercantile, performative and cultural logics underlying the phenomenon; questions as to whether the phenomenon is more about marketing than music or memories; and why it polarises opinions. The reader may have noticed that Yanni himself is absent from the issues I have raised; he (as-a-person) is, in a sense, incidental to his own phenomenon. I argue Yanni, or more importantly the concept of *a* Yanni, is a socio-cultural and commercial phenomenon as much as it is a musical one, based on artistic or aesthetic factors. The Yanni phenomenon is the logical conclusion for a certain kind of use (and some would contend abuse) of musical exotica.

The music

Yanni's most recent musical ensemble (as featured on the recent *Tribute* album and video) consists of Yanni on keyboards and a core septet (drums, bass, percussion, keyboards, guitar, violin, woodwinds) augmented by four female vocalists. The orchestra consists of a conductor, concert master, twelve violins, four violas, four celli, one contra bass, one oboe, two trumpets, four French horns, two trombones, one didjeridu, and one harp. Although there is a conductor, Yanni also cues the whole ensemble and responds to the music and the performances with a repertoire of hand gestures, facial expressions and dramatic poses which have been labelled by a fan as "expressive moments" (http://www.teleport.com/ncelinec/yanni.html). In performance, Yanni is stage-centre and the rest of the musicians and vocalists are spread out across a large stage area. However, they are linked by headphones and monitors which provide a 'click-track' to help keep the ensemble rhythmically in synch with each other. Elaborate and dramatic lighting further enhances the presentation of the music, as do state-of-the-art sound systems and sound-shaping devices.

In recording and performance, the all-around quality of the musicianship is high. Along with the trained and experienced orchestra members, the core septet and vocalists are talented musicians, many with solo careers outside of their involvement with the Yanni phenomenon. For example, violinist Karen Briggs has recorded several CDs, as has bassist Danny Fierabracci. Woodwindist Pedro Eustache has a flourishing career as a performer and composer, as does didjeriduist David Hudson as a recording artist, painter and actor. Vocalists Alfreda Gerald and Vann Johnson have successful careers as session and back-up singers with major pop artists[10]. Some core musicians and vocalists have been involved with the Yanni phenomenon for years while others remain for shorter periods. The rehearsal and travel schedules are demanding: six weeks of rehearsal preceded the *Tribute* World Tour (1997), which featured daily sound-checks. Tours have lasted eighteen months with, for example, the U.S./Canadian part of the *Tribute* world tour including one hundred performances in over ninety cities.

In general terms, Yanni's music can be characterised as a pastiche of late 19th Century Romantic music mediated through Hollywood film music[11], then re-mediated again by Yanni. There is a nod to world music, through the (primarily ornamental) inclusion of 'ethnic' instruments, sounds and musicians. The music is firmly located within long-standing western musical traditions and extra-musical attitudes and practices. The orchestral voicings, instrumentation, pitch ranges, and timbres fit within the customary boundaries of a conventional (small size) Romantic orchestra, with standard arrangements for the strings, horns and woodwinds. As various contributors to Bellman (ed) (1998) have detailed, various 18th and 19th Century composers drew on stereotypical aural images of the Orient (ie the Middle and Far East), which were also visually enhanced in Orientalist opera. They also employed musical elements which they variously identified and/or constructed as typical of, for example, Gipsy (Rom), Turkish or Slavonic traditions; transforming them in the process of appropriation. The results lacked the element of 'authenticity'[12], present in the work of more methodical musical nationalists such as Bartok or Kodály. Such composers often worked from transcriptions of national indigenous music forms and attempted to develop these in ways they themselves identified and asserted as 'faithful' (in a usually undefined manner) to aspects of their original cultural contexts. The shift between this approach and Yanni's is as significant in epochal terms as it is stylistic. Yanni's work is paradigmatically representative of a world seen in terms of globalism, where cultural 'fusion' is valorised – an opposite of the moment of European 19th Century nationalism which attempted to re-assert national cultures seen to be threatened by effacement during a previous period of European cultural homogenisation.

The flavour of Yanni's individual compositions are often provided by melodic lines which evoke aspects of musical/cultural 'otherness' by some degree of allusion/adherence to particular (non-western) intervals and scalic patterns. However, the arrangements repeatedly use standard harmonic progressions and rhythmic patterns and often utilise stereotypical orchestral notions of a 'Latin' or 'Indian' sound. The overall orchestral sound is an amalgamation of a range of influences which together identify the music as being both different from western art music and rock and roll but *not too different* from either to be discordant or confrontational. There is an absence of musical gestures which would interrupt the standardisation; it is seamlessly linked together sonically and orchestrally.

The core septet also operates within well established musical boundaries. The drums, bass and percussion function as would any mainstream pop, jazz or country rhythm section, providing the basic rhythmic pulse. The acoustic and electronic keyboards provide the uncomplicated arpeggios which underlay many of the compositions, while synthesisers provide keyboard colourations. The soloists in the band and the orchestra operate similarly within strict boundaries. For example, violinist Karen Briggs, guitarist Ramon Stagnaro and woodwindist Pedro Eustache all display virtuosity on their instruments. However, they play dynamically and structurally predictable solos which move, jazz-like, from the simple to the more complex. The solos, whether played alone or in duets with other instruments, are used repeatedly to add dynamics to the standardised arrangements, although over the course of several compositions they engender a feeling of 'pre-programmed spontaneity'. They also allow the introduction not only of the 'exotic' instruments and sounds but also the personalities of the musicians, which are, understandably, usually overshadowed by Yanni's. The vocalists range across pop and operatic styles and can shift between rhythm and blues-ish and aria-like passages within the same song. The 'grain of the voice' varies from smooth to rawer and, in the general absence of lyrics, the ensemble singing often uses the voice as another colouring instrument in the orchestra, via vocables and obbligatos. The minimal lyric-based vocal style is decidedly pop orientated, which is understandable given that the vocalists themselves perform with pop singers.

In combination, the vocalists, core septet and the orchestra create a generic, homogenised sound which is unobtrusive. It is designed to induce a state of relaxation and comfort, with dynamic levels only approaching significant intensity at the end of a composition. The formula consists of alternating between building-up textures and building-up styles in order to assemble the structure of a particular composition, always moving from the simple to the complex and back again. This horizontal and vertical building up of textures (using voicings) and styles (using instrumental references) eventually becomes the style *per se*. The styles become another kind of soloist, the instrumental soloists in turn then become the mediators of that style.

Powers (1998) provides an overview of the genealogical context of Yanni's music, along with the kind of pointed criticisms which will be noted in more detail later. Power identifies Yanni's music as generically comparable to:

> ... the likes of John Barry and Bill Conti; the early New Age experiments of the French composer Jean Michel Jarre and the Japanese artist Tomita; hits from the classical string catalog like Barber's 'Adagio for Strings'; [and] contemporary theatrical pieces like Bill Whelan's music for 'Riverdance'. (E–28)

And goes on to assert that :

> Yanni is a composer in the tradition of easy-listening 'exotica' artists like Martin Denny and Yma Sumac, although the hipsters who seek out their vintage recordings disdain him. Exotica sought out diverse cultural influences in the name of urbane sophistication: Yanni goes cosmopolitan seeking higher goals. Yanni structures his pieces to carry the message that every culture is noble, and difference matters little in the light of individual excellence. The excellent individual here is Yanni himself, of course. (ibid)

Commenting specifically on one of Yanni's live performances, Powers argues that Yanni's image predominates, over and above the music:

> [p]resenting himself as a cross between the romance-novel cover boy Fabio and the New Age soul doctor Deepak Chopra, Yanni rode his music's crescendos (and it contains few dynamics besides crescendos) in a show of personal expansiveness ... Yanni does mine a worldwide tradition – a modern and urban one. (ibid)

While Powers' observations help position where the Yanni phenomenon fits genealogically, the musicians who perform with Yanni have their own perceptions of the music and their role in its production. For example, David Hudson, the Aboriginal Australian didjeridu player who was a featured performer at both the Taj Majal and the Forbidden City concerts, reports having enjoyed the experiences personally and professionally (interview with the author 12/5/98). As a musician he recalls the concerts were interesting because:

> You're working with a large contingent like an orchestra and it's different than playing solo or with a small band [as per usual]. It's showing the depth of the didjeridu and how you can have an orchestra, and all these so-called 'western' instruments, like trumpets and French horns, and all of a sudden there is one of the world's oldest wind instruments being played with them and it works fine. (ibid)

Hudson also recalls that the experience was interesting, as a performer, because of his desire to promote Aboriginal culture:

173

[f]rom what I could gather from the audiences' reactions [at the Taj Majal and the Forbidden City concerts], *when I came out dressed in traditional costume and playing the didjeridu it was very, very positive. They were absolutely intrigued.* (ibid)

Overall, Hudson suggests combining the orchestra, core septet and vocalists in the context of the mega-events is:

... a great way of uniting different cultures from different parts of the world through music and dance ... [Outside the First World] *they don't get many western bands and orchestras* [and with Yanni's orchestra] *they're seeing the best of the best.* (ibid)

The "best of the best" is a phrase which can be validly applied to the musicality of the performers working within the Yanni phenomenon, if not always to the individual compositions or the overall music. Regardless of Yanni's individual talents as a musician and composer, the standardised orchestral arrangements, and the predictable dynamics of the septet's and the vocalists' performances; when the music of the Yanni phenomenon is offered to consumers it is competently and attractively arranged, performed and recorded. However, the title of the behind-the-scenes documentary of the Taj Mahal and Forbidden City mega-events, *No Borders, No Boundaries* (1997), is a misnomer in the sense that although the Yanni phenomenon may move across geographic borders, the music always remains within well-defined (and well-rehearsed) western musical boundaries.

Yanni – live and semi live at mega-events

The multi-media mega-events now synonymous with the Yanni phenomenon can be appreciated as highly sophisticated but substantially domesticated large-scale cultural productions, an essential element in a very successful business equation: "Yanni plus international monument equals event programming" (Andersen, 1998: 13). They also seem to be as much about grand architecture and lofty aspirations as music. For example, the Acropolis is typified as "one of the central icons of human history", and the Taj Mahal and Forbidden City are typified as "two of the greatest manmade structures on earth" (Baker, Winokur and Ryde, 1998: 1). The performances at sites such as the Taj Mahal and the Forbidden City are rationalised by Yanni in the *Tribute* album liner-notes (1997) as:

... essential because they remind us all of our own potential for greatness. The spirit of their builders remains incredibly vibrant. For the members of my band and my orchestra, the nights spent in the shadows of these monuments provoked inspired work and often, tears. I hope, in a small way, we have been able to pay tribute to those many souls, many years ago, the nameless artisans and laborers, who erected these incredible structures.

The mega-events were all recorded simultaneously in multi-media formats in exotic locales and all make an unstated but obvious connection between the grandeur of the architecture, the lofty aspirations, and the magnificence (and munificence) of the Yanni phenomenon.

There are two premises underlying the use of exotic locales as backdrops for the mega-events. First, that something transcendent, or at least something memorable, will happen just by being there, even vicariously, wherever 'there' may be. Second, the essence of the place and the atmosphere of the space can be and will be captured by the technology, transported trophy-like back to where it can be commodified and consumed at leisure. It is almost as if the full splendour of the Yanni phenomenon and the majesty of the music can only be fully appreciated, and thus fully memorialised, in the presence of other manifestations of excellence. There is an inescapable underlying assumption that big is not only better, it is essential; and bigness combined with grandiloquence is even better.

The exoticism of the music is in many ways irrelevant. The process of spectacularising and then domesticating the cultural production is what is significant. Whereas in the past musical exotica's natural habitat was often indoors in a suburban living room or a hotel/tiki lounge, Yanni has literally moved it outdoors – pursuing a philosophy that the more exotic the locale (in the sense of being culturally, historically or symbolically loaded) the more effective the spectacle. The venues, or more accurately the destinations, in both touristic and metaphysical terms, are a major part of the mystique and marketing of the Yanni phenomenon; that is, 'where to next?', 'what will be discovered?', and 'how will the music and the man survive the expedition and the experience?'. Mega-events are ubiquitous in the international entertainment industry but in the quest for ever more sensational spectacles, the Yanni phenomenon has currently cornered the upper-end market in musical exotica which combines at least the illusion of on-location recordings, environmental sights and sounds, and 'traditional' music cultures.

The sheer size of the mega-events is impressive. A crew of 140 people staged, recorded and filmed the Taj Majal and the Forbidden City concert performances and many more market them. The scale of the cultural production is always acknowledged in advertisements, promotional materials and cover-notes; it is an integral part of the spectacle. The hardships experienced are also recounted. The film documentary about the cultural production of the Taj Mahal and Forbidden City mega-events, *No Borders, No Boundaries* (1997), contains numerous "travellers' tales"[13]. It is described as: "a film journal describing the extraordinary effort, purpose and achievement of Yanni's groundbreaking performances [in India and China]" (http://www.pbs.org); and summarised as: "a dishy serve of the trials leading to the *Tribute* events" (Gerakiteys, 1998: 9). The travellers' tales have an underlying ethos embracing, and implicitly celebrating, a sense of 'civilising' encountered locales and cultures through First World mediated music. The journey out into the 'wilderness' (even amidst the billions of people in India and China) is

175

made safe by returning, once there, back to the familiarity of the Yanni formula. It is possible to perceive a strong undercurrent of imperialist nostalgia here[14]; that is, a mourning over what one's (First World) culture has helped to destroy by visiting places and peoples which have survived western colonisation and are not yet totally McDonald-ised. Somewhat paradoxically, the live-to-air television broadcasts may also have been the first opportunity for some people in India and China to actually 'experience' their own national monuments, albeit in a idiosyncratic context (Gerakiteys, 1998: 9). Also somewhat paradoxically, the mega-events may actually exacerbate the stress of mass tourism on the destinations. There are potentially millions of Yanni fans who may want to make a pilgrimage to the newly anointed 'sacred sites' of the Yanni phenomenon to experience live what they had only experienced semi-live on video or vicariously via the Internet.

As would be expected, the publicity machine behind the Yanni phenomenon downplays the sometimes painful, confusing and conflictual politics underlying the mega-events. For example, a local citizen's group filed a lawsuit to stop the Taj Majal mega-event because of fears the sound coming from the large orchestra and amplification system would damage the fragile exterior of the mausoleum, already weakened by pollution. As well, five Indian farmers threatened to immolate themselves because they had not received what they considered adequate compensation when their watermelon fields were commandeered to erect concert seating. These conflicts were dismissed as minor annoyances by the production companies[15]. According to *People* magazine, Yanni shrugged off the citizen group's concerns as "absolute baloney" because he had "donated all US$2.7 million in ticket sales to the landmark's preservation". As to the farmers' concerns, *People* reported that "the growers, who earn about US$300 a year, wanted a bit more [money] but relented after meeting with Yanni" (cited on http://pathfinder.com/people/971208 /picksnpans/tube/tube3.htm).

Significantly, there was also substantial support for Yanni amongst particular – affluent and influential – sections of the Indian population. An on-line poll conducted by *India Pulse* in response to the question "Should Yanni's concert be allowed to be held near the Taj Majal?", found 43% said Yes, 29% No, and 29% undecided. Sample comments on http://pulse.webindia.com/op230102.htm included:

> *Yanni is a very good, very romantic musician. Taj Mahal will be a beautiful place to resound his music. India should participate in the global events.*

> *He is one of the Best Musicians in the world and besides all proceeds are going to the Betterment of the Taj Majal, which is turning black due to the pollution.*

> *The Taj is more important than Yanni, it should maintain its image as a historical monument, not anything else.*

A review in *The Hindu* newspaper described the mega-event in the following terms:

> [The Taj Mahal is] *a rather sorry sight during the day, what with the marble having lost its sparkling white colour to pollution, the Taj this evening basked in the indirect light of the illumination and appeared to have regained some of its pristine glory ... the showstopper of the evening was the lighting which was breathtaking, varying as it did in colour and intensity with the music ...* [The composition] Aria *evoked the best response as people recognised* [it] *immediately as the British Airways commercial's jingle.* (http://webpage.com/hindu/daily/970321/02/02210005.htm)

Given the multi-media formats and the success of the videos and television broadcasts, the mega-events of the Yanni phenomenon can be readily re-lived semi-live at home. Given the reification of performances and arrangements by means of the videos and broadcasts, they can also be re-lived live in concerts, minus the exotic locales but still with highly technologised performances. The videos of the mega-events have become a – if not *the* – main means of artistic communication; with the result that live performances, to an appreciable extent, have to adhere to the conventions established in the videos. To be successfully commodified, the live performance has to mimic the video, and not vice versa, as is more usual. The video cannot be the mimic of the performance, the performance actually has to be the video[16].

The live performances must exactly mimic each other to facilitate inter-splicing and cross-fading between different performances of the same song in different locales in post-produced product – as occurs at the end of the *Tribute* video, which cuts between the Taj Mahal and Forbidden City performances. The multi-media feed off of and back into each other. There may be the addition of new material to live concerts but the older material has been repackaged many times and the musical style and performative dynamics are rehearsed and formulaic. Regardless of the technologisation used however, the Yanni Phenomenon live at the local entertainment centre or gambling casino simply does not equate to Yanni performing semi-live via video at the Acropolis, Taj Majal or The Forbidden City. On the exotic locale scale, the Taj Majal in Agra, India (March 1997) rates highly; Donald Trump's Taj Majal Casino in Atlantic City, New Jersey (May 1998) hardly rates at all; except perhaps as a certain kind of kitsch[17].

Perhaps the most perceptive (and brutally parodic) depiction of the international entertainment industry's engagement with exotic locales (and by extension the Yanni phenomenon's mega-events which celebrate them), is found in Rob Reiner's spoof 'rockumentary' *This is Spinal Tap* (1983). It happens in a scene where an 18 *inch* (rather than the expected 18 *foot*) foam replica of Stonehenge is brought on stage by dancing dwarfs as the band Spinal Tap performs a quasi-Celtic Heavy Metal song while wearing Druidic garb. The absurdity of the (barely visible) 18 inch model monument is only increased by the absurdity of the band's pretentiousness in mounting the 'spectacle' in the first place. There is a fine line between homage and parody. Some critics suggest the Yanni phenomenon steps over it with great regularity (although many consumers obviously disagree). While the status of the Yanni phenomenon remains open to debate, the discursive places and spaces of the Internet provide a unique media site for sustained discussion of the phenomenon.

The Yanni phenomenon on the Internet

The Internet is a rich source for accessing information on the Yanni phenomenon. There are a range of advertising, fan-group, hate-group, and newspaper and com-mentary review sites (some seemingly amateur and relatively spontaneous, others more calculated), but in total they constitute an instructive discourse on the global cultural economy in operation. Because the Yanni phenomenon is global, I can be in Australia and access, for example, information about where to get tickets if I want to go to a live concert in Seattle, Washington. On the same site there is advertising about where to stay and eat, and how to find a plastic surgeon or a crematorium should I feel the need (http://seattle.sidewalk.com/detail/4370). The Internet dis-course says a lot about the confluence of the mercantile, performative and cultural logics underlying the Yanni phenomenon. It also says a lot about how musical exotica, and information about it, now circulates in the global cultural economy. Economy is the operative word. Over the last five years, the Internet has been rapidly and thoroughly – though not exclusively – colonised by commerce; which means much of what is extracted from the Internet has to be judged in the context of its underlying commercial agenda. Most sites are not economically 'innocent'. Regard-less of this, such sites contain useful information because they often touch on vital behind-the-scenes facets of cultural production.

Advertising sites

The advertising sites drawn on here include those connected to various facets of the Yanni phenomenon – such as retailing and recording, broadcasting, lighting design, and video and audio production services. There are also more peripheral sites associated with band members, travel and ticket agencies, and even a marble retailer.

With regard to the retail facet, Internet-based retailers such as Indigo Records (http://indigo-records.com/artists/cp/special.htm) and IMUSIC (http://imusic.in-terserv.com/showcase/contemporary/yanni.htm) offer Yanni products along with those of related artists. Retailers are keen to offer Yanni products because they appeal across several marketing genres, have sought-after sales demographics, and have a sizeable back catalogue. With regard to the recording industry facet, there is information on the Windham Hill site, which contains lists of recordings and their contents, biographical data, and how to order products. The Windham Hill site summarises Yanni's appeal as providing "his audience something more than enter-tainment; he helps them get in touch with their own emotions and inspires them to explore their potential as individuals" (http://www.windham.com/art-ists/yanni.htm). The Virgin Records' site states:

> *Welcome to the official Yanni Website! We are delighted to share the 'World of Yanni' with you. As you travel through the site, you'll be able to learn about Yanni's recent projects and his tremendous accomplishments and successes.* (http://www.virginrecords.com/yanni/html/index2.html)

The Windham Hill and Virgin sites also link up with other sites which serve as gathering places for news from the international entertainment industry. One such example is the Dot Music site (http://www.dotmusic.co.uk/MWtalentyanni97.htm) which ran a feature on the marketing challenges in Britain faced by Yanni's latest label, Virgin Records. It is instructive in revealing how a concept such as a 'Yanni' is translated into marketing practice. Under the heading 'Selling an Unconventional Artist', the feature states:

> *Yanni is five letters that add up to an unique challenge in music marketing ... His image has helped deliver a massive worldwide audience that is 75% female. But despite 10 albums in as many years with Private Music through BMG, Britain has thus far remained immune to Yanni's charms, leaving him best known for his well-publicised tryst with Linda Evans of* Dynasty *fame.*

While there is acknowledgement of his "medallion man image", the site also notes:

> *... a major stumbling block for Virgin is* [his] *lengthy, orchestral-based music which fits no accepted format in the U.K. But EMI Recorded Music president Ken Barry who signed Yanni and is still* [CEO] *of Virgin Music Group treats the artist as a wake-up call for the label. "Dealing with an artist like Yanni forces you back to first principles on how to sell records to the public – not just Top Of The Pops and Radio One".*

The broadcast facet is emphasised in other sites. For example, an upcoming showing of the *Yanni: No Borders, No Boundaries* documentary is advertised on PBS's site as part of its "commitment to present universally available programs that appeal to viewers of all ages" (http://www.pbs.org/whatson/1997/12/press/yannino97pr.htm). Similarly, a local PBS affiliate (KTEH San Jose California), under the headline of "Mystical and Magical Yanni Plays the Taj Mahal", advertises a broadcast of *Yanni: No Borders, No Boundaries* as an encore to *Yanni: The Tribute Concert at the Taj Majal and the Forbidden City* (http://www.kteh.org/news/media/yannita-jmahal.htm).

On a lighting design site, the company involved with the *Live at the Acropolis* and *Tribute* mega-events, Ocean Rose and Associates, advertises its pivotal role in cultural production. Under a headline 'Postcards from Yanni', it states:

179

> *... if his modus operandi for choosing venues to showcase his live perform-ances is any indication, Greek New Age musician Yanni is not affected by the petty insecurities that plague mere mortals. In fact, the opposite seems true – the grander the scale and the more exotic the location, the better ... Because his music is not controversial in any way, lyric-wise or stylistically, he can travel anywhere and be welcome to play in these fantastic places.*[18]
> (http://ocean-rose.com/yanni2.htm)

The video and audio production services company involved in the *Tribute Concert Tour* (1997), PMTV, advertises its role in the mega-events on its site (http://pmtv.com/yanni.htm) and provides brief 'travellers' tales' on the challenges of producing their facets of the mega-events. For example:

> *[t]o say the very least,* [the Taj Mahal concert in Agra, India] *was an extremely challenging effort for all the companies and personnel involved. Yanni's staff and associated companies basically created a small production city on a sandy river bank in a very remote city.*

Regardless of law suits and threats of disruption (described as "localised situations"), the site contends that:

> *... the end result were some of the most compelling and beautiful concert performances ever seen. Yanni and his orchestra performed superbly, and with the Taj Majal as a gorgeous visual element, excellent lighting and sound production, we captured 3 nights of musical magic!*

The travellers' tale ends with a postscript which parodies disclaimers at the end of films using live animals: "no Sacred Cows were harmed during this production".

Band members, present and past, also exploit the Internet to tap into the Yanni phenomenon. There are sites for drummer Charlie Adams, violinist Karen Briggs, bassist Ricc Fierabracci, didjeriduist David Hudson and percussionist Kalani[19]. Tranquillity Travel in Delaware U.S.A. advertised a trip to New York City for one of the ten sold out concerts at Radio City Music Hall in January 1997. The US$199 fee included a concert ticket, transportation, accommodation, food, sight seeing and shopping time (http://www.tranquility-travel.com). And finally, Macedonia Marble & Granite in the U.S.A. ("Suppliers of the Finest Greek Marbles and Stones") has on-site links to excerpts of Yanni's music when site visitors click on samples of marbles such as "Olympic White", "Crete Grey", and "Thassos Select".

As these advertising sites demonstrate, the Yanni phenomenon is predominantly about delivering markets and demographic groups and only marginally about making music. It is also about how the global cultural economy privileges commodification and technologisation over concerns for artistic and aesthetic content. Apparently, hawking services for plastic surgeons and crematoriums or selling

180

chunks of marble does not strike the Internet advertisers as an illogical or incongruous use of musical exotica.

Fan-group sites

The fan-group sites vary as to quality of presentation and whether they are initiated and maintained by individuals or collectives. Predictably, they are sometimes syrupy and very often sycophantic.

They include the Official Yanni Website[20], whose table of contents ends with the command, "Enjoy!" (http://www.yannitribute.com/yanni/html/index2.htm); and The Unofficial Yanni Fans Web Page (http://www.teleport.com/~celinec/yanni.htm), which provides information, numerous merchandising links, and a guestbook. The guestbook declares:

> *Read the Dreambook! Sign the Dreambook! Note: Yanni himself doesn't see the entries. This guestbook is meant to leave your thoughts and comments to other fans, and to the site owner, Celine. Please don't ask Yanni questions, etc., as he won't see what you write.*

The Unofficial Yanni site was started in June 1995 and when I visited in May 1998, I was visitor number 100,535 since March 9, 1997.

A major fan-group on the Internet is Listeners of Yanni On-line (LOYOL) which identifies itself as "The Online Source for the Fans of Pianist-Composer Yanni" and provides this background on its genesis:

> *The roots of LOYOL began in the Spring of '95 on Yanni's bulletin board on AOL [America On Line]. As Yanni's music touched people during his 1995 world tour, many of us chose to share our excitement and concert experiences on the Internet ... LOYOL has been a wonderful place to share questions and answers about Yanni and our feelings about his music. It is a place we can literally network about Yanni. Many friendships have started as a result of the club and several of us have met each other in person (even travelling from coast-to-coast) to share the common bond of Yanni's music ... LOYOL looks forward to Yanni's next release and tour, and to the formation of more online and real life friendships.* (http://members.aol.com/greg17/loyoldir.htm)

The following edited postings to the LOYOL site give a flavour of the fan-group discourse:

> *Yanni, When life seems so full and you feel overwhelmed by what seems relentless monotony, Close your eyes and dream ... Should you ever find your heart yearning, one awaits your presence with love in her heart.* (http://www.i-depth.com/P/j/jc01611.frm.loyol.msg/229.htm)

181

Message to Yanni, see you in Persopolis ... I am an American with persian ancestors. Yanni's music is so universal and pervasive that I hope one day Yanni with his admiration of architecture would perform his music in the Persopolis, where the persian artisans and architects built a city 25 centuries ago. (http://www.i-depth.com/P/j/jc01611.frm.loyol.msg/214.htm)

Hi my name is Aimee and I love Yanni. How do I become a member of the fan club?? I think Yanni's hot!!! I'm only 15 but I listen to him everyday! I even make my friends listen to him too! They gag but after a while they ask me to play it for them. Then I grin. (http://www.idepth.com/P/j/jc01611.frm.loyol.msg/136.htm)

The fan-group sites demonstrate how for many people the Yanni phenomenon is only tangentially about the music. It is much more about how the actual experience of the music is memorialised by domesticating it within the context of consumers' day-to-day lives, and loves.

Hate-group sites

The hate-group sites are a different but not discordant kind of fan-group. Although supposedly oppositional, they too are a symbiotic part of the Yanni phenomenon, feeding off it while disparaging it, albeit usually facetiously and sometimes humorously. The No Yanni Organization (NOYO) unambiguously states its credo:

We the people, being of sound mind and good taste in music, hereby declare war on that evil menace to society know as Yanni. We are establishing [our organization] *to combat this evil force, along with those like him (Kenny G, John Tesh, Kathy Lee Gifford etc.). Yanni is a bad influence on everyone. He encourages people to do things that suck. People see him making a lot of money for making crappy music. They also see him adored by millions of people ... then they think they can become rich and famous by making their own awful audio atrocities. This type of evil must be brought to an end ... Here is a link to Yanni's Homepage. Now you can witness his evil on-line ... Here are a few useful keywords and phrases that will help people find NOYO through search engines[:] Yanni sucks ... Yanni should be shot ... Disembowel Yanni with a spoon.* (http://members.tripod.com/~noyo/index.htm)

The No Yanni Organization guestbook contains entries such as:

Ahh, finally someone who knows the truth about the no-talent Greek whose only reason for fame is his wife, Linda Evans. Hey come on, anybody who knows anything about composing music can see through the bleep-blops Yanni puts together. The quasi-intellectual stuff he backs up his concepts [with] *makes me sick. Really, it does! I can admit he looks good, so why not*

go into modeling so we music lovers can breath in some cleaner air.[21]
(http://www.Lpage.com/wgb.wgbview.dbm?owner=noy)

As is apparent, fandom informs both the pro and anti Yanni groups, who are mostly
amateurs using the Yanni phenomenon as a vector for a whole range of compliments
and complaints about the world and themselves. Descriptions of the music *per se*
are vague, personalised and subjective, when noted at all. The environmental
surroundings or personal responses at the moment of consumption are what is
memorialised. There are, however, professionals whose job it is to offer (supposedly) more objective opinions on artistic and aesthetic concerns.

Newspaper and commentary sites

Reviews of the Yanni phenomenon by professional critics appear on or are indexed
on newspaper and commentary sites. As a counter-pose to how celebrities are
routinely idolised on fan-group sites, there is often a reverse trajectory of demonisation in critical media, especially for commercially successful acts and artists
whose adulation eludes or offends the cognoscenti. In the often either hyper-acerbic
or hyper-sycophantic world of the international entertainment industry, some actions
(commercial success) beget predictable reactions (adverse critical reviews); and
critics have been savage (sometimes hilariously so) in their assessments of the Yanni
phenomenon (which in many ways presents a very easy target for even vaguely elitist
professional reviewers).

A reviewer for *Billboard* (1997), a music industry magazine not noted for putting
potential advertisers offside, has pithy words to say about the *Tribute* album, despite
acknowledging certain high sales for the product:

> *[m]ost musicians feel humble in the presence of ancient wonders, but
> Yanni's 'Tribute' to the Taj Mahal and the Forbidden City is more suitable
> for the* [Donald] *Trump Taj Mahal in Atlantic City, N.J. Like Trump's
> casino, Yanni appropriates the monumental and covers it in glitz and glitter.*

The reviewer maintains:

> *[u]nderneath, it does not come across as genuine. With an orchestra,
> singers, and his septet, Yanni dresses up his bombastic anthems in faux
> exotica, including Middle Eastern reeds and Australian didgeridoos.*
> (http://www.billboard.com/reviews/48/al8yanni.htm)

Outside of industry-orientated publications such as *Billboard*, newspaper review
headlines such as: "Create a concept, *then* find the guy" (Andersen, 1998); "Music
Contrived to Ease the Angst" (Strauss, 1995); "Soothing, Melodious, Risk-Free
Sounds from Yanni" (Sutherland, 1997); and "Mining One Message in a Blur of
World Influences" (Powers, 1998) leave little doubt where the critics are coming
from and where the reviews are going. "Why ask Y? Just give in to the man"

(http://nypostonline.com/entertainment/2716.htm), summarises an almost palpable defeatism repeatedly expressed in reviews about the Yanni phenomenon. It presents a challenge to reviewers in their role as artistic and aesthetic gatekeepers, namely, how to protect the masses from themselves and the 'illogical' and/or 'offensive' choices in the entertainment they choose to consume.

In a review entitled 'The Yanni Files' , Andersen writes about how to "create a concept, *then* find the guy" (1998: A–13). He facetiously takes credit with friends for inventing the concept behind the Yanni phenomenon. He pinpoints and then lampoons and deconstructs some of its main ingredients: the visual image ("we knew the dark shag haircut and the big droopy moustache would work" as would the "billowy shirts" and the "waterbed smile"); the name ("we wanted unique, yet not particular-country-identifiable, and we wanted a word that didn't mean something unsavory in any major language"); and, the music:

> *[o]ne of our wisest choices ... was to create a virtually complete oeuvre before we even had hired a performer ... we went in ... with dozens of eight-track tapes (the* Planet of the Apes *and* 2001 *soundtrack albums, a bootleg of the Wide World of Sports' theme song) and emerged two weeks later with 49 hours of brand-new Yanni music.* (ibid)

In another review, entitled 'Music Contrived to Ease Angst', Strauss (1995) observes how the music of the Yanni phenomenon serves a purpose similar to that of film music: "channel[ing] emotions through lush orchestral landscapes, climactic fanfares and running rhythms" (I–10). However, for Strauss, a filmic approach creates a problem because "without filmic images or any substitute for context, the passion Yanni's music inspired was like a holistic healing center built on air" (ibid). The homily-like introductions to compositions are characterised by Strauss as even more problematic:

> [Yanni] *said one song was about romancing life, another about the power of dreams and a third about the bond that exists among all human beings. These are all healthy and worthwhile ideas, but ... the concert began to seem like a musical medicine show.* (ibid)

Strauss continues by likening Yanni to a snake-oil salesman:

> *It was an exotic oil, filled with extracts from far-off lands, from the low didgeridoo piping of Australia to the hot salsa rhythms of Cuba to the close-knit harmonies of South Africa. Except, like all snake oils and sugar pills, it created only the illusion of healing. What it actually did was distract – and, at its most effective, anesthetize – the listener, blotting out the pain, confusion and conflicts of the world.* (ibid)

Regardless of the spectacle, however, Strauss feels:

184

What actually emerges is the artist's potential for injecting ever-greater bombast into his surging, darkly rhapsodic vamps, thanks to the widescreen orchestral firepower added to Yanni's core septet. Off-center time signature and world music filigree, including didgeridoo, charango and bamboo wind instruments, do conjure a vague Eastern mood, but there's little to suggest a formal invocation of Indian or Chinese musical traditions. And the music, for all its muscles, recedes quickly in memory. (ibid)

Along similar lines, a review by Sutherland (1997), entitled 'Soothing, Melodious, Risk-Free Sounds from Yanni', declares:

New Age's answer to [male model] *Fabio,* [Yanni] *applies considerable sound and fury to his pumped-up passionate music. But while he's prone to citing mystical purposes to his florid soundscapes, it's hard not to suspect that his records are best heard as the aural equivalent to bodice-ripping Harlequin romances, makeout music for moderns who've finally tired of Ravel's* Bolero. (http://seattle.sidewalk.com/detail/4117)

The marketing considerations are also noted:

The new album's scale and concept are even more bombastic than its predecessors, reflecting the deeper pockets of Yanni's new label home, Virgin, and the cross-marketing potential of a companion PBS special ... filmed at the Taj Mahal and China's Forbidden City. (ibid)

In 'Mining One Message in a Blur of World Influences', Powers (1998) also identifies a problematic aspect of the Yanni phenomenon:

He makes world music for the age of the Benetton ad, in which cultural difference dissolves in a commercialized message of good will. The message is a better one than, say, militant separatism, but is hopelessly muddled and essentially imperialistic. (E–28)

Powers describes a scene very similar to one documented on the *Tribute* video:

As the aboriginal musician David Hudson, who displayed great skill on the didgeridoo ... did a primitive jitterbug with [vocalist Vann] *Johnson, a Native American dancer emerged in full feather to join in. There Yanni stood – all in white, surrounded by his black background vocalists, his body-painted didjeridoo player and various tuxedoed members of his orchestra – suggesting nothing so much as Walt Disney, the designer of a fun-filled, boundary smashing ride.* (ibid)

Powers concludes on a cautionary note: "[i]t *is* a small world after all ... [a]nd

185

popularizers like Yanni know how easy it is for certain people to take it over" (ibid)[22].

Some reviews are more positive, at least considering or begrudgingly acknowledging what the appeal might be for consumers. For example, Sullivan (1997) states:

> *Yanni's forte is mixing pop, classical, and world music (all lite) into a bubbly, frothing brew. He dips his toe into exotica – featuring a duduk here (ancient Armenian oboe) and a didjeridu (huge aborigine wind instrument) there and makes a point of noting the country of origin of many of his musicians.* (D-03)

A pragmatic assessment of Yanni as a product designed for a particular market is acknowledged in Sullivan's observation:

> *... yes, Yanni criss-crossed the same lush terrain a lot. But, you know, the same could be said for oblique alt-rock darlings the Cocteau Twins, and in a sense, faulting Yanni for his major-chord marches – his upward spirals – is like slamming Nine Inch Nails for harshness and negativity. They're just doing their job. Yanni's music may not be deep or difficult, but he succeeds in creating a better, Disney-esque world for a few moments.* (ibid)

Taken together as a discourse, the Internet sites and postings discussed above epitomise how the Yanni phenomenon polarises opinion and acts as a vehicle for the projection of personal perspectives and the making of personal memories. As the review sites demonstrate, critics frequently characterise the Yanni phenomenon as buying wholesale into two Romantic conceits: creativity as a form of genius and artistic expression as a form of culture, which both occur in a political vacuum. It pretends all that matters *is* the music. The problem here is that, in many critics' opinions, the music is lacklustre to the point of parody or insignificance. However, the fan-group sites show how the Yanni phenomenon is domesticated and how millions of consumers willingly buy into the Romantic ideal of art as transcendent and the creative artist as a vehicle of genius, similar to how majestic architecture can supposedly embody noble aspirations. Or, in the case of the hate-group sites, the related perspective that while Yanni may be 'false' transcendence personified (and thus worthy of demonisation), nonetheless other artists do possess 'true' transcendence (and it is simply a matter of clicking on a Yanni hate page link to hear 'real music' – as identified by the site designer's favoured/favourite musicians). And, finally, the advertising sites show that regardless of critics' reservations about the artistic and aesthetic merit of the Yanni phenomenon, it is still very successful as a technologised commodity.

Conclusion

This chapter has argued that the Yanni phenomenon is not primarily a musical one (based on artistic or aesthetic factors) but rather a socio-cultural and commercial phenomenon based on the mercantile, performative and cultural logics of late 20th century capitalism. The Yanni phenomenon is partly a triumph of the commodification and technologisation of the exotic within the global cultural economy. It is also partly a triumph of the multi-media marketing of spectacle, privileging the ambience and formula over the music *per se*. The cultural production of exotica is no longer only about sounds. It is also now about sights and sentiments and how they all can be woven together into a seamless web of multi-media consumption so the same basic product can be sold several times in different formats. Yanni, the phenomenon, polarises opinions because it is a vector for extra-musical issues pertinent to its time and place; not only commodification and technologisation but also globalisation and appropriation.

Returning to where I began, what *is* wondrous about the Yanni phenomenon as a particular kind of musical exotica? One answer is that it has an extravagance of performance unmatched by any other musical exoticist artist thus far. And romantic? It has a good looking icon at centre stage who plays keyboards, shares "expressive moments" with his predominantly female fans, and is touted as a genius at expressing universal emotions and uplifting aspirations through music. And foreign? Its icon is a hyphenated *artiste*, a Greek-American/*Americanised* Greek, western but with a touch of otherness enhanced by a multi-national orchestra, multi-cultural instruments, and mega-events in exotic locales. And fascinating? It has a complex and innovative mode of cultural production and an accompanying industry which uses the latest technology to enhance the sense of spectacle. And, finally, what is ordinary? Critics contend that without the multi-media marketing the music is at best a pedestrian appropriation and pastiche of Romanticised film music; and at worst a calculated and mercenary mis-appropriation of 'exotic' peoples, places and things. What the Yanni phenomenon says about its time and place is that, however consumed, musical exotica has moved into yet another era, once again engaging with new mediums for commodifying and technologising consumption (and, ideally, for enjoying the music).

Acknowledgements: The opinions expressed herein are mine alone but thanks to former Yanni orchestra member David Hudson for insights on the cultural production; to music educator Phillippa Roylance for background on the music; and to Yanni's personal manager Danny O' Donovan for providing research materials.

Notes

1. There is a sticker on the front of the 1997 *Tribute* CD which notes: "The first new music from Yanni since *Live at the Acropolis*", which was released in 1993.

2. By which I mean the videos are predominantly chronicles of live performances, which then create expectations for subsequent live concerts.

187

3. The 'Revolution in Sound Tour' (1991), the 'Dare to Dream Tour' (1992), the 'Symphony Concerts Tours' (1993–94), the Pacific Rim and European tours (1995) and the India and China Tours (1997).

4. Previously, an eight-time Emmy Award winner.

5. The fable behind the Yanni Phenomenon is a publicist's dream come true: an emigrant leaves his homeland (Greece), struggles to get his music heard in a new country (U.S.A.), and 20 or so years later returns home in triumph for a concert at the national icon of the Acropolis (1993), performing for his mother and father (Felitsa and Sotiris) and his high-profile paramour Linda Evans (who played Crystal Carrington in the U.S. television soap opera *Dynasty*) – and continues to appear and prosper all over the world.

6. For example, in India one hundred million viewers (the Taj Mahal concert) and in China one hundred and fifty million viewers (the Forbidden City concert).

7. Information provided in this section is taken from Baker, Winokur and Ryde (1998).

8. For a useful discussion of the role of spectacle in contemporary society see Debord (1977).

9. The closest response would be recent controversies surrounding particular world music products. See respectively Meintjes (1990) on Paul Simon's *Graceland*, Feld (1996) on "pygmy pop" and Zemp (1996) on the controversial use of ethnomusicological music recordings.

10. See Adams (http://plainjames.com); Briggs (http://www.digitalrain.net/bowed/briggs.htm); Fierabracci (http://www.swreng.com/swrqaeight.htm); and, Kalani (http://www.iuma.com/IUMA–2.0/ftmp/1vo/IUMA/ftp/music/Kalani/in dex.htm) and Hudson (http://www.cairns.net.au/~didge).

11. NB As Caryl Flinn (1992) has argued, Hollywood music itself is largely predicated upon a nostalgic re-enactment of Romantic music in the first place.

12. Even acknowledging the problematic aspect of this term.

13. Hall (1992) discusses how traveller's tales have contributed to the discourse of the 'West and the Rest'.

14. See Rosaldo (1989) for an examination of "imperialist nostalgia" in the context of popular culture forms such as film.

15. Yanni's concert at the Forbidden City in Beijing, close to Tiananmen Square, provides another example of how the publicity machine behind the Yanni phenomenon downplays the politics underlying the mega-events (although it should be noted that the *No Borders, No Boundaries* video *does* touch on these). The mega-event took place close to the site of the massacre of hundreds of demonstrators by the People's Liberation Army in June of 1989. The following excerpt from one of the production company's traveller's tales chronicles how superior technology helped defeat official Chinese concerns for what was being filmed aside from the mega-event:

    One of the more memorable events was the surprise 'green meanies' [police] visitors to our control room one afternoon ... We had placed a camera on an 80 [foot] scaffolding and were panning around the general area outside the [Forbidden City] compound taping some 'B Roll' of Tienaman Square, a definite NO NO. Our tapes were 'confiscated' but returned several hours later when it was realized there weren't any Digital Beta machines available for viewing in Beijing (other than in our control room). (http://www.pmtv.com/yanni.htm)

16. NB It is noteworthy that no camera ever appears on screen in the *Live at the Acropolis* and *Tribute* videos.

17. Because of the multi-media nature of the Yanni Phenomenon, the audience at the imitation Taj Majal in New Jersey could feasibly go home, put on the *Tribute* video, and commune with the audience at the original Taj Mahal in India, in effect reliving semi-live the live concert they had just attended.

18. On a related site, Ocean Rose and Associates inform visitors Yanni's *Tribute* PBS Special broadcast in 1997 has been ruled ineligible for a Primetime Emmy Award by the Academy of Television Arts & Sciences (ATAS) because it had been released by Virgin Records first in a home video version. It unsubtly provides information and instructions so: "If you'd like to register your feelings on the subject, send email to the Academy" (http://www.ocean-rose.com/Yanni_emmy.htm).

19. There are also some music-based sites from which visitors can down-load MIDI files of Yanni compositions. These include a commercially orientated site (http://midimirror.etter.ch/yanni.htm) and a fan-based site (http://ubl.com/ubl/cards/003/0/77.htm) which states: "[s]everal dedicated Yanni fans have created MIDI files of Yanni's music ... listen to their technical and musical talent, and enjoy Yanni's music via your computer. New ones are added as they become available".

20. With features including *Spotlight*, where visitors "can discover the effort and purpose behind Yanni's long-awaited new album *Tribute*, as well as hear and view clips"; *Events*, up to date concert dates and television broadcasts; *Timeline*, a chronology of achievements and composition lists from the albums; *Fan*, merchandise, links, and a free newsletter; *News*, current Yanni topics and a trip through his "musical village"; and *Sound Clips*, located throughout the site and accessible using Real Audio software.

21. On a different note, another entry states: "I think this site is mean and rude! Yanni is excellent! I saw him in concert and loved it! This is mean to all Yanni's fans, get rid of this site. You jerk!" (ibid)

22. On a lighter but no less pithy or insightful note, Loudon Wainwright the Third's take on the Yanni Phenomenon is:

> ... *what are we to make of the most dominant musical event of the week* [in New York City]*, the New Age Peloponnesian phenom Yanni? He has sold out 10 shows at Radio City Music Hall ... and could have sold out 20 ... Recently I listened to a few tracks from a Yanni CD and found the music to be rather soothing, with a piquant air of expectancy about it. After awhile I found myself mysteriously being lifted, as it were – well, in an elevator.* (1998: A–25)

Discography

Yanni	*Dare to Dream*, BMG/Private, 1992
–––––	*Live at the Acropolis*, BMG/Private Records, 1994
–––––	*Tribute*, EMI/Virgin Records, 1997
–––––	*In The Mirror*, BMG/Private, 1997

Videography

No Borders No Boundaries (1997) directed by George Veras
Tribute (1997) directed by George Veras

INFORMATION ABOUT THE AUTHORS

Philip Hayward is Director of the Centre for Contemporary Music Studies at Macquarie University, Sydney, and an adjunct professor of Southern Cross University, Lismore (attached to the Music Archive for the Pacific). He established the Pacific music research journal *Perfect Beat* in 1992 and edited it until 1998. He has published several previous books on contemporary music, including *From Pop to Punk to Postmodernism* (1992), *Music at The Borders* (1998) and *Sound Alliances* (also 1998).

Jon Fitzgerald is a senior lecturer in Popular Music History and Theory at Southern Cross University, Lismore. He is an experienced performer and composer with research interests in the creative process and has published articles in journals such as *Perfect Beat* and *Popular Music and Society*.

Shuhei Hosokawa is an associate professor at the Tokyo Institute of Technology. He works in the areas of popular music study and Japanese-Brazilian research. His publications include *The Aesthetics of Recorded Sound* (1990) and *Samba in the Country of Enka* (1995) (both in Japanese) and *Karaoke Around the World* (1998, co-edited with Toru Mitsui).

Rebecca Leydon is a professor of music theory at Oberlin College Conservatory. She holds degrees in music from University of Toronto and the Eastman School of Music. In 1996 she completed a PhD at McGill University with her dissertation 'Narrative Strategies in Debussy's Late Style', a project which explores relationships between musical form and the editing techniques of early silent cinema in

France. She has read numerous papers on 'Lounge Music' at conferences around the U.S.A. and Canada.

Karl Neuenfeldt is a lecturer in Media and Communications at Central Queensland University, Bundaberg, and co-editor, since 1998, of the Pacific music research journal *Perfect Beat*. His edited anthology *The Didjeridu – From Arnhem Land to Internet* was published in 1997. He is currently researching and editing an anthology on contemporary Torres Strait Islander music.

Timothy D. Taylor is a musicologist who teaches in the Department of Music at Columbia University. He works on a variety of issues concerning music, identity, postmodernity, postcolonialism and globalisation. He also plays Irish traditional music on several instruments. His book *Global Pop: World Music, World Markets*, was published in 1997 by Routledge.

BIBLIOGRAPHY

AA.VV. (1987) *Iles*, Paris: Gallimard (Centre George Pompidou)

Ames, M (1992) *Cannibal Tours and Glass Boxes – The Anthropology of Museums*, Vancouver: University of British Columbia Press

Andersen, K (1998) 'The Yanni Files', *New York Times* 17/6

Appadurai, A (ed) (1986) *The Social Life of Things: Commodities in Cultural Perspective*, Sydney: Cambridge University Press

———— (1990) ' Disjuncture and Difference in the Global Cultural Economy', *Public Culture* v2n2

Attali, J (1985) *Noise: The Political Economy of Music*, Minneapolis: University of Minnesota Press

Baker, Winokur and Ryde Public Relations (1998) *Promotional Materials* (Yanni Publicity, 6311 Romaine St., Suite 7232A, Los Angeles, California 90038)

Barkan, E and Bush, R (eds) (1995) *Prehistories of the Future -The Primitivist Project and the Project of Postmodernism*, Stanford: Stanford University Press

Barnouw, V (1956) 'Incense in the Lab', *New Yorker* v31, 4/2

Baxter, L (1981) 'Les Baxter', *Soundtrack* n26, Summer

Behdad, A (1994) *Belated Travellers – Orientalism in the Age of Colonial Dissolution*, Durham and London: Duke University Press

Bell, C (1997) 'Sayonara Cruel World', *The Wire* 8/97

Bellman, J (1998) 'Indian Resonances in the British Invasion, 1965–68', in Bellman, J (ed) *The Exotic in Western Music*, Boston: Northeastern University Press

Bhaba, H (1994) *The Location of Culture*, London and New York: Routledge

Bongie, C (1991) *Exotic Memories, Literature, Colonialism and the Fin de Siècle*, Stanford: Stanford University Press

Bourdieu, P (1979) *Distinction – a social critique of the judgement of taste*, London: Routledge and Kegan Paul

Bowles, C (1954) 'The 'Brown Man's Burden' Analyzed', *New York Times Magazine* 5/10

Brainowski, A (1992) *The Yellow Lady – Australian Impressions of Asia*, Oxford-Auckland-New York: Oxford University Press

Breines, W (1992) *Young, White, and Miserable: Growing Up Female in the Fifties*, Boston: Beacon Press, 1992

———— (1994) 'The 'Other' Fifties: Beats and Bad Girls' in Meyerowitz, J (ed) *Not June Cleaver: Women and Gender in Postwar America, 1945–1960*, Philadelphia: Temple University Press

———— (1997) 'Postwar White Girls' Dark Others', in Foreman, J (ed) *The Other Fifties: Interrogating Midcentury American Icons*, Urbana and Chicago: University of Illinois Press

Brinton, C, Christopher, J.B, and Wolff, R.L (1955) *A History of Civilization* v1, *Prehistory to 1715*, New York: Prentice-Hall

Buck, E (1993) *Paradise Remade – The Politics of Culture and History in Hawai'i*, Philadelphia: Temple University Press

Burns, M and DiBonis, L (1988) *Fifties Homestyle: Popular Ornament of the USA*, New York: Harper & Row

Bush, R (1995) 'The Presence of the Past: Ethnographic Thinking/Literary Politics', in Barkan and Bush (eds)

Buxton, F and Owen, B (eds) (1977) *The Big Broadcast: 1920–1950* (Second edition), Lanham (U.S.A.) and London: Scarecrow Press

Chandrasekhar, S (1945) 'What does Iowa know of India and China?' *Asia and the Americas* v45

Chase, G (1987) *America's Music: From the Pilgrims to the Present* (Rev. 3rd ed.), Urbana: University of Illinois Press

Chocano, C (nd) 'The Lounge Generation', *Salon* [http://www.salon1999.com/weekly/lounge960826.html]

Clifford, J (1988) *The Predicament of Culture -Twentieth-Century Ethnography, Literature, and Art*, Cambridge and London: Harvard University Press

———— (1997) *Routes – Travel and Translation in the Late Twentieth Century*, Cambridge (U.S.A.): Harvard University Press

Colum, P (1937) *Legends of Hawaii*, New Haven (U.S.A.): Yale University Press

Cooke, M (1998) ' "The East in the West": Evocations of the Gamelan in Western Music', in Bellman, J (ed)

Cox, J (1990) 'The Town Crier of Weird', *Time* 22/1

Coyle, J and Coyle, R (1985) 'Aloha Australia – Hawaiian Music in Australia 1920–55', *Perfect Beat* v2n2, January

Dahlhaus, C (1989) *Nineteenth-Century Music*, Berkeley and Los Angeles: University of California Press

Dart, W (1996) 'Where Have All the Oranges Gone ?', *Rip It Up* (NZ) n221, January

De Mello, J (1962) 'The Magic of Island Music', *Paradise of the Pacific*, July/August

Debord, G (1977) *The Society of the Spectacle*, Detroit: Black and Red

Denny, M (1993) 'Martin Denny', in Juno and Vale (eds)

Ditchburn, J (1997) 'Lounging 'Round', *Rhythm Music* v6

Escal, F (1990) *Contrepoints – Musique et littérature*, Paris: Méridiens Klincksieck

Farquharson, M (1994) 'Over the Border' in *World Music: The Rough Guide*, London: Rough Guides

Farrell, G (1997) *Indian Music and the West*, Oxford: Clarendon Press

Feld, S (1994) 'From Schizophonia to Schismogenesis: On the Discourses and Commodification Processes of "World Music" and "World Beat"', in Keil, C and Feld, S *Music Grooves*, Chicago: University of Chicago Press

———— (1996) 'pygmy POP. A Genealogy of Schizophonic Mimesis', *1996 Yearbook for Traditional Music*, New York: International Council for Traditional Music

Flinn, C (1992) *Strains of Utopia: Gender, Nostalgia, and Hollywood Film Music*, Princeton (NJ): Princeton University Press

Foster, S (1982) 'The Exotic as a Symbolic System', *Dialectical Anthropology* v7

Gans, H.J (1967) *The Levittowners: Ways of Life and Politics in a new Suburban Community*, New York: Pantheon

Gerakiteys, T (1998) 'Yanni Dares to Dream', *Aerial Magazine* (Sydney: SBS Television) 9/6

Gibian, P (1984) 'Music Not to Be Listened to: Muzak and Beyond', *Tabloid* n8

Gibson, M (1988) *Accommodation without Assimilation: Sikh Immigrants in an American High School*, Ithaca and London: Cornell University Press

Ginsburg, L (1997) 'Hindsight 20/20: Tales and Tunes of The Residents' (booklet accompanying the Residents' compilation CD *Our Tired, Our Poor, Our Huddled Masses – Pluribus: History 1980–72*)

Godden, R (1952) 'Diwali Lights', *House and Garden* v101

Goodman, N (1978) *Ways of Worldmaking*, Cambridge (U.S.A.): Hackett

Gradenwitz, P (1977) *Musik zwischen Orient und Okzident. Eine Kulturgeschichte der Wechsel-beziehungen*, Wilhelmshaven-Hamburg: Heinrichshofer

Grenier, L (1989) 'From "Diversity" to "Difference". The Case of Socio-cultural Studies of Music', *New Formations* n9

Hagiwara, K (1983 – reprinted 1992), *Happii Endo Densetsu* (*The Legend of Happii Endo*), Tokyo: Shinko Music

Halberstam, D (1993) *The Fifties*, New York: Villard

Hall, S (1992) 'The West and the Rest: Discourse and Power' in Hall, S and Gieben, B (eds) *Formations of Modernity*, London: Polity Press

Harrison, C and Woods, P (eds) (1992) *Art in Theory*, Oxford: Blackwell

Hayward, P (1997) 'DANGER! RETR0-AFFECTIVITY! – The Cultural Career of the Theremin', *Convergence* v3n4, Winter

——— (1998) *Music at the Borders: Not Drowning, Waving and their engagement with Papua New Guinean Culture* (1986–96), Sydney: John Libbey & Co

——- (1999) 'Interplanetary Sound Clash – Music, Technology and Territorialisation in *Mars Attacks !*', *Convergence* v5 n1, Spring

Helweg, A, and Helweg, U (1990) *An Immigrant Success Story: East Indians in America*, Philadelphia: University of Pennsylvania Press

Hoffman, S (1991) (untitled) booklet notes for the 1991 compilation CD *Taboo- The Exotic Sound of the Arthur Lyman Group*

Holly, H (1951) 'Korla Pandit and Organ Attract Femmes to Video', *Down Beat* v18, 23/3

Hope, L (1968) *Selected Love Lyrics*, New York: Dodd and Mead

Hosokawa, S (1990), *Record no Bigaku* [*The Aesthetics of Recorded Sound*], Tokyo: Keisô Shobô

——— (1994a) 'East of Honolulu – Hawaiian Music in Japan from the 1920s to the 1940s', *Perfect Beat* v2 n1 July

——— (1994b) *Japanese Popular Music of the Past Twenty Years – Its Mainstream and Underground*, Tokyo: Japan Foundation

——— (1995) 'Pidgin-Japanisch – Zur Japano-Amerikanischen Sprachmischung in der Popmusik', in Guignard, S (ed) *Musik in Japan*, Munich: Iudicium Verlag

Hosono, H (1979 – reprinted 1985), *Chiheisen no Kaidan* [*Stairway on the Horizon*], Tokyo: Tokuma Shobô

——— (1984) *Ongakuô. Hosono Haruomi Monogatari* [*The King of Music. The Story of Haruomi Hosono*], Tokyo: Shinkô Music

——— (1992), *Endless Talking* (interview with Masakazu Kitanaka), Tokyo: Chikuma Shobô

Infusino, D (1989) 'Discovering Japan', *Pulse*, December

Ivy, M (1988), 'Tradition and Difference in the Japanese Mass Media', *Public Culture Bulletin* v1 n1

Iwabuchi, K (1994) 'Complicit Exoticism – Japan and its Other', *Continuum* v8 n2

194

Jackson, C.T (1994) *Vedanta for the West: The Ramakrishna Movement in the United States*, Bloomington and Indianapolis: Indiana University Press

Jackson, K.T (1985) *Crabgrass Frontier: The Suburbanization of the United States*, New York and Oxford: Oxford University Press

Jakle, J (1985) *The Tourist – Travel in Twentieth-Century North America*, Lincoln and London: University of Nebraska Press

Jensen, J (1988) *Passage from India*, New Haven: Yale University Press

Jezer, M (1982) *The Dark Ages: Life in the United States 1945–1970*, Boston: South End

Johnson, S (1988) *The Japanese through American Eyes*, Stanford: Stanford University Press

Jones, D (1997) *Ultra Lounge: The Lexicon of Easy Listening*, New York: Universe

Juno, A and Vale, V (eds) (1993) *Re/Search Incredibly Strange Music* San Francisco: Re/Search Publications

———— (eds) (1994) *Re/Search Incredibly Strange Music Volume Two*, San Francisco: Re/Search Publications

Kabbani, R (1986), *Europe's Myths of Orient*, Bloomington: Indiana University Press

Kaeppler, A (1988) *'Come Mek Me Hol' Yu Han'- The Impact of Tourism on Traditional Music*, Kingston: Jamaica Memory Bank

Kanahele, G (ed) (1979) *Hawaiian Music and Musicians – An Illustrated History*, Hawai'i: University Press of Hawai'i

Kanô, N (1985), *America no Kage* [*The Shadow of America*], Tokyo: Kawade Shobô Shinsha

Kaufman, L (1996) Liner notes to Karla Pundit, *Journey to the Ancient City*, (Dionysus)

Kelly, B.M (1993) *Expanding the American Dream: Building and Rebuilding Levittown*, Albany (U.S.A.): State University of New York Press

Kiell, N (1946) 'What GI's Learned in India', *Asia and the Americas* v46

Kisseloff, J (1995) *The Box: An Oral History of Television, 1920–1961*, New York and London: Penguin

Kitanaka, M (1989) '*Tokyo Rose*' (review) (in Japanese), *Music Magazine*, October

Lanza, J (1994) *Elevator Music: A Surreal History of Muzak, Easy-Listening, and Other Mood-song*, New York: Picador U.S.A.

Leydon, R (1997) ' "Ces nymphes, je les veux perpétuer": Pastoral Predicaments in Space-Age Bachelor-Pad Music', unpublished research paper.

Lipsitz, G (1990) 'The Meaning of Memory: Family, Class, and Ethnicity in Early Network Television', in Lipsitz, G *Time Passages: Collective Memory and American Popular Culture*, Minneapolis: University of Minnesota Press

MacCannell, D (1976) *The Tourist: A New Theory of the Leisure Class*, New York: Schocken

———— (1992) *Empty Meeting Grounds: The Tourist Papers*, London and New York: Routledge

Maeda, M and Hirahara, Y (1993), *Rokujû Nendai Fôku no Jidai* [*The Age of Folk Music in the 1960s*], Tokyo: Shinkô Music

Marchetti, G (1993), *Romance and the "Yellow Peril" – Race, Sex, and Discursive Strategies in Hollywood Fiction*, Berkeley – Los Angeles – London: University of California Press

May, E.T (1988) *Homeward Bound: American Families in the Cold War Era*, New York: Basic Books

McClary, S (1992) *Georges Bizet: Carmen*, Cambridge University Press (Cambridge Opera Handbook Series)

McDonough, J (1997) 'On Disk: The Original Cocktail Nation', *Wall Street Journal* 22/5

McGinn, R (1983), 'Stokowski and the Bell Laboratories: Collaboration in the Development of High-Fidelity Sound Reproduction', *Technology and Culture* v24 n1

McKenna, K (1988) 'Korla Pandit Still Spreading Metaphysical Message', *Los Angeles Times* 10/6

195

Meintjes, L (1990) 'Paul Simon's "Graceland", South Africa, and the Mediation of Musical Meaning', *Ethnomusicology* v34n1

Mertens, W (1983) *American Minimal Music*, London and New York: Kahn and Averill/Alexander Broude

Miller, R (1967) *The Japanese Language*, Chicago and London: University of Chicago Press

Minear, R (1980) 'Orientalism and the Study of Japan', *Journal of Asian Studies* v34 n3

Mitchell, L (1995) ''Catching Up with Korla': A Special Tribute', *Cult Movies* v16

Mitsui, T (1998) 'Domestic Exoticism – A recent trend in Japanese popular music', *Perfect Beat* v4n1, January

Miyazaki, K (1996) *Kakure Kirishitan no Shinkô Sekai*, Tokyo: Daigaku Shuppankai

Morley, D and Robins, K (1992) 'Techno-Orientalism – Futures, Foreigners and Phobias', *New Formations* v16

Morris, C (1995) 'Bachelor Pad Music from '50s, '60s is Swingin' Again', *Billboard* v107 9/9

Mühlhäusler, P (1986) *Pidgin and Creole Linguistics,* Oxford and New York: Basil Blackwell

Murakami, Y (1993) *Yellow Face*, Tokyo: Asahi Shinbun (in Japanese)

Neuenfeldt, K (1994) 'The Essentialistic, The Exotic, The Equivocal and the Absurd – The Cultural Production and Use of the Didjeridu in World Music', *Perfect Beat* v2 n1, July

Newcomb, H (1997) 'The Opening of America: Meaningful Difference in 1950s Television', in Foreman, R (ed), *The Other Fifties: Interrogating Midcentury Icons*, Urbana and Chicago: University of Illinois Press

North, M (1995) 'Modernism's African Mask: The Stein-Picasso Collaboration', in Barkan and Bush (eds)

Ogura, E (1989) *'Tokyo Rose'* ('Rock U.S.A.' summary review) (in Japanese) *Music Magazine*, October

Pandit, K (1966) untitled programme notes for organ recital series

—— (1994) 'Korla Pandit' (interview) in Juno and Vale (eds)

Parakilas, J (1998) 'How Spain Got a Soul' in Bellman, J (ed)

Parks, V.D (1996) 'Letter to the Editor', *Resonance* v4 n3

——— (1997) 'The Artwork used on the *Orange Crate Art* album', article on the Van Dyke Parks web site: www.brerwabbit.com/parks/vdparks.htm

Plant, S (1992) *The Most Radical Gesture – The Situationist International in a Postmodern Age*, London: Routledge

Powers, A (1998) 'Mining One Message in a Blur of World Influences', *New York Times* 16/6

Prunières, H (1926) 'Les Concerts – Trois Chansons Madécasses', *La Revue musicale* 7/7

Reck, D (1985) 'Beatles Orientalis: Influences from Asia in a Popular Song Tradition' *Asian Music* v27n1

Reich, S (1974) *Writings about Music*, Halifax: Press of the Nova Scotia College of Art and Design

Roberts, J.S (1979) *The Latin Tinge: The Impact of Latin American Music on the United States*, New York: Oxford University Press

Rosaldo, R (1989) 'Imperialist Nostalgia', *Representations* n26

Rothenberg, R (1997) 'The Swank Life', *Esquire* v127

Said, E (1978) *Orientalism*, New York: Pantheon

Sargeant, W (1950) 'Musical Events: The Lighter Side', *New Yorker* v25 7/1

Scott-Maxwell, A (1997) 'Oriental Exoticism in 1920s Australian Popular Music', *Perfect Beat* v3n3, July

Silverstone, R (ed) (1997) *Visions of Suburbia*, London and New York: Routledge

Smith, J (1996) Liner notes to *Mondo Exotica* (*Ultra-Lounge v1*) (Capitol)

Smith, R (1996) (Untitled) Interview with Les Baxter – in CD notes for *The Exotic Moods of Les Baxter* (1996) – Capitol Records

Sorrell, N (1990) *A Guide to the Gamelan*, London; Faber and Faber

Stanlaw, J (1992) 'For Beautiful Human Life: the Use of English in Japan', in Tobin, J (ed)

Starr, F (1995) *Bamboula! The Life and Time of Louis Moreau Gottschalk*, Oxford and New York: Oxford University Press

Starr, K (1985) *Inventing the Dream – California through the Progressive Era*, Oxford and New York: Oxford University Press

Stockfelt, O (1993) 'Adequate Modes of Listening', *Stanford Humanities Review* v3n2

Strauss, N (1995) 'Music Contrived to Ease the Angst', *New York Times* 7/8

Sugimoto, Y and Mauer, R (1986) *Images of Japanese Society*, London: Kegan Paul International

Sullivan, J (1997) 'Soothing, Melodious, Risk-Free Sounds from Yanni', *Boston Globe* 27/1

Sutherland, S (1997) 'Yanni *Tribute*', *Music Central Online* (http://seattle.sidewalk.com/detail/4117)

Tartar, E (1979) 'Introduction: What is Hawaiian Music', In Kanahele (ed)

——— (1987) *Strains of Change – The Impact of Tourism on Hawaiian Music*, Honolulu: Bernice P. Bishop Museum

Taylor, T (1997) *Global Pop: World Music, World Markets*, New York: Routledge

The Shorter Oxford English Dictionary (On Historical Principals) (1973), Oxford: Clarendon Press

Tiegel, E (1968) 'Entertainers strive for a contemporary image amid a hotbed of tourism and a centuries old culture', *Billboard*, 18/5

Tobin, J (ed) (1992) *Re-made in Japan – Everyday Life and Consumer Taste in a Changing Society*, New Haven and London: Yale University Press

Tomasulo, F (1996) 'A Road Less Travelled – Reflections on the Career of Van Dyke Parks', on the Van Dyke Parks' web site: www.brerwabbit.com/parks/vdparks.htm

Toop, D (1995) *Ocean of Sound – Aether talk, Ambient Sound and Imaginary Worlds*, London: Serpent's Tail

Turner, R (1941) *The Great Cultural Traditions: The Foundations of Civilization*, v1, *The Ancient Cities*, New York and London: McGraw-Hill

Ueda, M (1994) 'Datsu-Kindai, Datsuô Datsua, Datsu-Nihon' ['Escape from Modernity, Escape from Europe and Asia, Escape from Japan'], *Gendai Shisô* v22 n14

Unattributed (1933a) 'The Dance: Hindu Legends are Interpreted by Uday Shan-Kar [*sic*]', *News-Week* v2, 28/10

Unattributed (1933b) 'The West Sees the Real Hindu Dance', *Literary Digest* v115, 21/1

Unattributed (1937a) 'Brown Dancers', *Time* v29, 25/1

Unattributed (1937b) 'Dancing that Expresses the Soul of India', *Literary Digest* v115, 11/11

Unattributed (1937c) 'Here comes the Yogiman', *Time* v49, 17/3

Unattributed (1947) 'Yogi for the West' *Newsweek* v29, 10/3

Unattributed (1948) 'The Past for the Present', *Time* v52, 22/11

Unattributed (1950) 'Return of Shankar', *Newsweek* v35, 9/1

Unattributed (1951) 'Pandit Pasadena Gross Hits $3,000', *Billboard* v63, 22/9

Unattributed (1955) 'Musical Events: The Second Stage', *New Yorker* v31, 30/4

Unattributed (1995) 'Olivelandia', *Lounge* v2n1

Unattributed (1998) Virgin Records Promotional Materials for *Tribute* (Virgin Records, 338 N. Foothill Road, Beverly Hills, California 90210)

Unattributed (nd) 'The Lounge Fad', *Revolt in Style* [http://www.revoltinstyle.com/october/lounge/]

197

von Stroheim, O (1996) 'Boobam at the Moon', essay in CD booklet for CD re-issue of Arthur Lyman – *Hawaiian Sunset* (Rykodisc)

Wainwright, L (1998) 'Stones and Spice. And Bob', *New York Times* 16/1

Wallbank, T.W and Taylor, A.M (1954) *Civilization Past and Present*, Chicago: Scott, Foresman and Company

Whaples, M (1998) 'Early Exoticism Revisited', in Bellman, J (ed)

White, T (1998) 'The Importance of being Van Dyke Parks', on the Van Dyke Parks web site: www.brerwabbit.com/parks/vdparks.htm

Whiteoak, J (1995) 'Hawaiian Music and Jazzing', *Perfect Beat* v2 n3, July

Williamson, J (1986) 'Woman Is an Island. Femininity and Colonization', in Modleski, T (ed) *Studies in Entertainment*, Bloomington & Indianapolis: Indiana University Press

Worringer, W (1908 – English language translation 1963, by M. Bullock) *Abstraktion und Einfühling*, New York: Routledge and Kegan Paul

Yogananda, P (1921) *New Pilgrimages of the Spirit*, Boston: Beacon Press

———— (1946, reprinted 1981) *Autobiography of a Yogi*, Self-Realization Fellowship

Yoshie, A (1996) *Shinbutsu Shûgô* [*Shinto -Buddhist Syncretism*], Tokyo: Iwanami Shoten

Yoshimoto, M (1989) 'The Postmodern and Mass Images in Japan', *Public Culture* v1 n2

Young, R (1990) *White Mythologies: Writing History and the West*, London and New York: Routledge

Yutang, L (ed) (1942) *The Wisdom of China and India*, New York: Random House

Zemp, H (1996) 'The/An Ethnomusicologist and the Record Business', *1996 Yearbook for Traditional Music*, New York: International Council for Traditional Music

Zollo, P (1997) 'Songwriters on Songwriting – Van Dyke Parks' – interview on the Van Dyke Parks' web site: www.brerwabbit.com/parks/vdparks.htm

Index